WINNING LIBRARY REFERENDA CAMPAIGNS

A How-To-Do-It Manual

RICHARD B. HALL

*HOW-TO-DO-IT MANUALS
FOR LIBRARIANS*

Number 50

BIBLIOTHÈQUES
uOttawa
LIBRARIES

NEAL-SCHUMAN PUBLISHERS, INC.
New York, London

630485812

Published by Neal-Schuman Publishers Inc.
100 Varick Street
New York, NY 10013

Printed and bound in the United States of America.

Library of Congress Cataloging-in-Publication Data

Hall, Richard B.
    Winning library referenda campaigns : a how-to-do-it manual / Richard B. Hall
        p.   cm.   --   (How-to-do-it manuals for librarians : no. 50)
    Includes bibliographical references and index.
    ISBN 1-55570-224-4 (alk. paper)
        1. Public relations -- Libraries -- United States.   2. Public libraries -- United States -- Finance.   3. Public libraries -- Political aspects -- United States.   I. Title.   II. Series: How-to-do-it manuals for libraries : no. 50.
Z716.3.H26   1995
021.7--dc20   95-21726
                                                                                CIP

This book is dedicated to a carpenter who knew the value of an education and the wife who loved him.

CONTENTS

PHOTO AND ILLUSTRATION ACKNOWLEDGMENTS

Figure 4-1
"Grandfather and granddaughter, Tulsa City-County Library System,
Tulsa, Oklahoma." Provided courtesy of Tulsa City-County Library System.
Permission to publish granted by Tulsa City-County
Library System.

Figure 4-3
"A Library says a lot about a city, Denver Public Library,
Denver, Colorado." Provided courtesy of Denver Public Library.
Permission to publish granted by Rick J. Ashton, Library Director,
the Denver Public Library.

Figure 4-3
"When you're this stacked you need some support, Dallas (Texas) Public Library,
Dallas, Texas." Provided courtesy of Dallas (Texas) Public Library.
Permission to publish granted by Dallas (Texas) Public Library.

Figure 4-3
"Knowledge for the Ages, Rochester Hills Public Library,
Rochester Hills, Michigan." Provided courtesy of Rochester Hills Public Library
Permission to publish granted by Rochester Hills Public Library.

Figure 4-3
"Expanding our Horizons, Westerville Public Library,
Westerville, Ohio." Provided courtesy of Westerville Public Library
Permission to publish granted by Westerville Public Library.

Figure 4-4
"Photo of Volkswagen in front of the library, Grafton-Midview
Public Library, Grafton, Ohio." Provided courtesy of Grafton-Midview
 Public Library. Permission to publish granted by David E. Dial, Director,
Grafton-Midview Public Library.

Figure 4-5
"Proposed Columbiana Public Library, Columbiana Public Library,
Columbiana, Ohio." Provided courtesy of Columbiana Public Library.
Permission to publish granted by Susan E. Snyder, Library Director,
the Columbiana Public Library Board of Trustees.

Figure 10-4
"Community and Library: A Shared Future, Kings County Library
System, Seattle, Washington." Provided courtesy of King County Library.
Permission to publish granted by Jeanne Thorsen, Manager, Community Relations,
King County Library System.

Figure 10-5
"The New Wyandanch Public Library, Wyandanch Public Library,
Wyandanch, New York." Provided courtesy of Wyandanch Public
Library. Permission to publish granted by Wendell Cherry, Director,
Wyandanch Public Library.

Figure 10-6
"Welcome to the Brentwood Public Library, Brentwood Public Library,
Brentwood, New York." Provided courtesy of Brentwood Public Library.
Permission to publish granted by Doris Lewis Sargeant, Library Director,
Brentwood Public Library.

Figure 10-7
"DeKalb Public Library Facilities Development Proposal, DeKalb Public
Library, Decatur, Georgia." Provided courtesy of DeKalb County Public Library.
Permission granted by Donna C. Mancini, Library Director,
DeKalb County Public Library.

Figure 10-8
"Investment Portfolio brochure, City of Port Orange,
Florida." Provided courtesy of City of Port Orange.
Permission granted by Fred Hayes, City of Port Orange.

Figure 10-9
"It's Up To You Library Proposal #1, Pierce County Library District,
Tacoma, Washington." Provided courtesy of Pierce County Library
District. Permission granted by Neel Parikh, Library Director
Pierce County Library District.

Figure 10-10a
"One Year Only Library Levy, Fort Vancouver Regional Library,
Vancouver, Washington." Provided courtesy of Fort Vancouver Regional Library.
Permission granted by Sharon Hammer, Director,
Fort Vancouver Regional Library.

Figure 10-10b
"Bond Issue at a Glance, Spokane Public Library, Spokane,
Washington." Provided courtesy of Spokane Public Library.
Permission granted by Daniel L. Walters, Library Director,
Spokane Public Library.

Figure 10-11
"The Library Bond, Chesapeake Public Library, Chesapeake, Virginia."
Provided courtesy of Chesapeake Public Library. Permission granted by
Margaret P. Forehand, Director, Chesapeake Public Library.

Figure 10-11
"Yes, we use the libary!"
Provided courtesy of the Tulsa City County Library System,
Tulsa Oaklahoma.

Figure 10-12
"Overdue, Spokane Public Library, Spokane, Washington."
Provided courtesy of Spokane Public Library.
Permission granted by Daniel L. Walters, Library Director,
Spokane Public Library.

Figure 10-13
"Vote YES, Fairfield Public Library, Fairfield, Iowa." Provided courtesy
of Fairfield Public Library. Permission granted by Public Library, Fairfield, IA.

Figure 10-4
"Don't close the book on our children's future, Richland County Public Library,
Columbia, South Carolina." Provided courtesy of Richland County Public Library.
Permission granted by C. David Warren, Richland County Public Library.

Figure 10-15
"Measure L is for Library, Rockridge Library, Oakland, California."
Provided courtesy of Rockridge Branch Library. Permission granted by
Nancy Dutcher, Chair—Neighbors for a Rockridge Library.

Figure 10-16
"Say YES to Library Bonds, Kings County Library
System, Seattle, Washington." Provided courtesy of King County Library.
Permission to publish granted by Jeanne Thorsen, Mananger, Community Relations,
King County Library System.

Figure 10-17
"The Library Bond, Chesapeake Public Library, Chesapeake, Virginia."
Provided courtesy of Chesapeake Public Library. Permission granted by
Margaret P. Forehand, Director, Chesapeake Public Library.

Figure 10-18
"One Year Only Library Levy, Fort Vancouver Regional Library,
Vancouver, Washington." Provided courtesy of Fort Vancouver
Regional. Permission granted by Sharon Hammer, Director,
Fort Vancouver Regional Library.

Figure 10-19
"Don't close the book on our children's future, Richland County Public Library,
Columbia, South Carolina." Provided courtesy of Richland County Public Library.
Permission granted by C. David Warren, Richland County Public Library.

Figure 10-20
"Yes on Measure L, Rockridge Library, Oakland, California."
Provided courtesy of Rockridge Branch Library. Permission granted by
Nancy Dutcher, Chair—Neighbors for a Rockridge Library.

Figure 10-21
"Your library is Overdue, Willoughby-Eastlake Public Library,
Willoughby, Ohio." Provided courtesy of Willoughby-Eastlake
Public Library. Permission granted by Dolly D. Gunderson, Director,
Willoughby Public Library.

Figure 10-22
"YES, YES, YES Libraries, Kings County Library System,
Seattle, Washington." Provided courtesy of King County Library.
Permission to publish granted by King County Library System.

Figure 10-23
"Knock Softly . . ., Chesapeake Public Library, Chesapeake, Virginia."
Provided courtesy of Chesapeake Public Library. Permission granted by
Margaret P. Forehand, Director, Chesapeake Public Library.

Figure 10-23
"Save our Libraries! Vote Yes on Tuesday, Pasadena Public Library,
Pasadena, California." Provided courtesy of Pasadena Public Library.
Permission granted by Pasadena Public Library.

Figure 10-24
"The Library Bond button, Chesapeake Public Library, Chesapeake, Virginia."
Provided courtesy of Chesapeake Public Library. Permission granted by
Margaret P. Forehand, Director, Chesapeake Public Library.

Figure 10-24
"Vote Yes button, Las Vegas-Clark County Library District,
Las Vegas, Nevada." Provided courtesy of Las Vegas-Clark County
Library District. Permission to publish granted by Darrell Batson,
Las Vegas-Clark County Library District.

Figure 10-24
"The New Library: Make it fact or fiction button, Atlanta-Fulton Public
Library, Atlanta, Georgia." Provided courtesy of Friends of the Atlanta-Fulton

Public Library System. Permission to publish granted by Charlene P. Shucker, Director, Atlanta-Fulton Public Library.

Figure 10-24
"Vote YES Libraries button, Greensboro Public Library, Greensboro, North Carolina." Provided courtesy of Greensboro Public Library. Permission granted by George Viele, Library Director, Greensboro Public Library.

Figure 10-24
"Your library the best bargain around button, Upper Saddle River Public Library, Upper Saddle River, New Jersey." Provided courtesy of Upper Saddle River Public Library. Permission granted by Barbara Kruger, Upper Saddle River Public Library.

Figure 10-25
"Spokane Libraries Overdue button, Spokane Public Library, Spokane, Washington." Provided courtesy of Spokane Public Library. Permission granted by Daniel L. Walters, Library Director, Spokane Public Library.

Figure 10-25
"Stick with Libraries, Tulsa City-County Library System, Tulsa, Oklahoma." Provided courtesy of Tulsa City-County Library System. Permission to publish granted by Tulsa City-County Library System.

Figure 10-25
"Libraries 2001, Pierce County Library District, Tacoma, Washington." Provided courtesy of Pierce County Library District. Permission granted by Neel Parikh, Library Director Pierce County Library District.

Figure 10-25
Ask Me! Library Levy, Fort Vancouver Regional Library, Vancouver, Washington." Provided courtesy of Fort Vancouver Regional. Permission granted by Sharon Hammer, Director, Fort Vancouver Regional Library.

Figure 10-25
"Citizens for Montgomery County Libraries, Montgomery County Library, Conroe, Texas. " Provided courtesy of Montgomery County Libraries. Permission granted by Michael Baldwin, Library Director, Montgomery Public Library.

Figure 10-26
"Vote Yes, Livermore Public Library, Livermore, California."
Provided courtesy of Livermore Public Library. Permission granted
by Susan R. Gallinger, Livermore Public Library.

Figure 10-27
"Yes on Davis Library Expansion visor, Yolo County Library,
Woodland, California." Provided courtesy of Yes on Davis Library
Expansion, A Committee for Measure B. Permission granted by
Mary L. Stevens, County Librarian, Yolo County Library, Woodland, California.

Figure 10-28
"Photo of man holding a 'Great Cities Deserve Great Libraries' T-shirt,
Denver Public Library, Denver, Colorado." Provided courtesy of Denver Public Library.
Permission to publish granted by Rick J. Ashton, Library Director, the Denver Public Library.

Figure 10-29
"The Library Bond bumper sticker, Chesapeake Public Library, Chesapeake, Virginia."
Provided courtesy of Chesapeake Public Library. Permission granted by
Margaret P. Forehand, Director, Chesapeake Public Library.

Figure 10-29
"Yes, Libraries! bumper sticker, Tulsa City–County Library System, Tulsa, Oklahoma."
Provided Courtesy of Tulsa City–County Library System. Permission to publish granted
by Tulsa City–County Library.

Figure 10-29
"Support The Next Generation's Library Bond Proposal bumper sticker, The
Library of Hattiesburg, Petal, & Forrest County, Hattiesburg, Mississippi."
Provided courtesy of The Library of Hattiesburg, Petal, & Forrest County.
Permission granted by Pamela Pridgen, The Library of Hattiesburg, Petal,
& Forrest County.

Figure 10-29
"Vote Library January 15th, bumper sticker, Rapides Parish Library,
Louisiana." Provided courtesy of Steve Roggle, Library Director.
Permission granted by Rapides Parish Library.

Figure 10-30
"Our Library's Future portable display, Spokane Public Library, Spokane,
Washington." Provided courtesy of Spokane Public Library.
Permission granted by Daniel L. Walters, Library Director,
Spokane Public Library.

Figure 11-1
"I'm a Friend Won't You Be a Friend & Bring a Friend to the
Polls, Dekalb County Public Library, Decatur, Georgia."
Provided courtesy Dekalb County Public Library.
Permission to publish granted by Donna D. Mancini, Library Director,
Dekalb County Public Library.

Figure 13-1
"I Love Libraries poster, Tulsa City-County Library System,
Tulsa, Oklahoma." Provided courtesy of Tulsa City-County Library System.
Permission to publish granted by Tulsa City-County
Library System.

Figure 13-2
"Photo of "Overdue" yard signs, Spokane Public Library,
Spokane, Washington." Provided courtesy of Spokane Public Library.
Permission granted by Daniel L. Walters, Library Director,
 Spokane Public Library.

Figure 13-3
"Vote for your Library, Denver Public Library, Denver, Colorado."
Provided courtesy of Denver Public Library.
Permission to publish granted by Rick J. Ashton, Library Director,
the Denver Public Library

FOREWORD

Most public library administrators will have during their whole professional career, at most, one experience trying to win a referendum. Some few people will have two such experiences. Because for most librarians this "trial by ballot" is a one-time event, few administrators have any real preparation for it. Thus, it is all the more notable that this full-length and eminently helpful book is now available. This practical guide to a complex, important operation is full of good tips (of what to do and what not to do) drawn from recent public library referenda campaigns. I recommend that every public library director who is likely ever to participate in a bond issue referendum read this book at least five years in advance and again at least nine months before the election.

There are two main points in this book which I would emphasize. One is that the result of the vote on the referendum is often really a vote on the library's record for efficiency and for what Hall calls "confidence building" (p. 29). This applies to most other local institutions too, of course, but fortunately most public libraries have an enviable record in this regard as reflected in the high percentage of public library referenda that pass each year. The point is that how the library performs over the years is likely to be a major factor in its success or failure in passing a referendum. Simply put, always treat the public as though they were going to vote next week on a bond issue for the library.

The second point I consider especially important is that working for the success of a referendum is a thoroughly political activity. In the old days, librarians made a conscious effort to separate themselves from all political activity; that attitude is no longer realistic today. Organizing a referendum campaign for a public library building is the most politically challenging enterprise that a library director will face in his or her career. It is all the more gratifying that public library referenda have such a high percentage of success. The younger generation of librarians has learned to distinguish between partisan politics and activity in the political sphere; the latter is the essence of democracy.

I have known Richard Hall for almost twenty years. He has always had one main focus in his professional work, public library buildings. He has served with distinction in the Georgia State Library in charge of state grants for public library buildings, and now serves California in the same capacity. He writes frequently on this subject, including the recent book entitled *Financing Public Library Buildings* (Neal-Schuman, 1994). For the last several years he has conducted an annual survey of all U.S. state libraries on the results of public library referenda campaigns during the previous year; these results, printed annually in the June 15th issue of *Library Journal*, are the single most important source of data available on this subject. Richard Hall is now the library profession's leading authority on this topic.

Herbert Goldhor
University of Illinois
Urbana, Illinois

PREFACE

Several years ago, when I began writing my previous book, *Financing Public Library Buildings*, I intended to cover the techniques used in winning library referenda campaigns in one chapter. It is apparent though, from the length of this present book, that library campaigns provide more than sufficient fodder for a separate book. Thus, while *Financing Public Library Buildings* covers the whole spectrum of financing methods, this current book delves into the nitty-gritty details of the referendum—or ballot measure—process, which is by far the most important mechanism available to library supporters in their efforts to fund library expansion programs. Thus, these two books are essentially companion volumes.

Even though there are many new creative financing techniques being used to fund public library facilities, the single largest source of local funding has always been provided by debt instruments which require a referendum such as the general obligation bond. Going directly to the electorate has historically been, and remains to this day, one of the most sensible, democratic, and equitable means of providing public funds to build public libraries. Given this, the science of holding a referendum is extremely important to any agency endeavoring to finance and build a public library. This book is devoted entirely to the process of planning and running a campaign to obtain voter approval for a ballot question in support of a library facility improvement issue.

While the book is written specifically with capital campaigns in mind, many of the techniques discussed can be effectively used in campaigns for library operating levies as well. This book will be especially useful to those library planners and supporters who in the past have been afraid to attempt a referendum because of their fear that the campaign might fail. While there are no guarantees in the political arena, those utilizing the suggested planning methodologies and campaign techniques presented in this volume should gain the confidence and knowledge necessary to plan and run a successful grassroots campaign in their community.

Richard B. Hall
Library Consultant
California State Library

ACKNOWLEDGEMENTS

The author wishes to thank Barbara Loar, retired library director of the Dekalb Library System, Decatur, Georgia, Susan Gallinger, the library director of the Livermore Public Library, Livermore, California, Dr. Herbert Coldhor, retired director of the University of Illinois Graduate School of Library and Information Science, Urbana, Illinois, and Martin Gomez, the library director of the Oakland Public Library, Oakland, California for their willingness to read portions of the manuscript and provide me with comments and helpful suggestions. The author also wishes to thank John Berry of *Library Journal* for accepting my proposal to begin collecting and publishing data on library referenda. The author is indebted to *Library Journal* for its willingness to allow the reprinting of text and data from the June 15 (1988 to 1995) articles on public library referenda. All such information is copyrighted by Reed Publishing.

INTRODUCTION

OVERVIEW OF THE CAMPAIGN PLAN

Library supporters need to know that the size or wealth of a community does not necessarily impact their ability to run a successful campaign. Almost any community is capable of passing a referendum for a library building if they have an obvious need, are able to put together a campaign organization, plan an effective strategy, and exercise a reasonable degree of political muscle by working hard to move their inherent supporters to the polls.

This book has been written to be used by public libraries of all different levels of sophistication. There are methods discussed which will be appropriate for large metropolitan campaigns as well as alternative suggestions for small rural libraries. The reader should not be daunted by the amount of information in the book and the apparent complexity of campaigning. You don't have to do everything, nor do you need to do it in the exact way or order suggested in the book. This work is more of a smorgasbord from which to select and then organize a campaign which best fits your local situation.

Various campaign methods are presented in the book because they have been effective in one or more political campaigns and may be able to be adapted to the local conditions of future library campaigns. Campaign planners must evaluate the potential effectiveness of each method discussed, and then decide whether or not to utilize the method based on their own campaign strategy, as well as the availability of campaign resources. To win a referendum, the campaign leadership must effectively communicate a carefully crafted campaign message based upon local realities to a precisely targeted electorate in a way which will make them receptive to vote for the library issue, and then make sure those individuals go to the polls and vote on election day.

The best way to make sure that this happens in any campaign is to develop a comprehensive and well-documented campaign plan. There are a number of tools which help to document the overall campaign plan. In addition to defining the campaign's organizational structure with precise committee job descriptions, an opinion poll is one of the best methods of getting a hold on the major campaign issues and arguments as well as discovering the target groups which will be the campaign's high priority voter contact points. The campaign's main message, slogan, logo, and themes will come primarily out of the analysis of the poll results. Additional major components of a campaign plan are developing an overall campaign strategy, determining a campaign calendar, establishing a campaign budget, and creating a plan for fundraising and volunteer recruitment . Finally, the campaign plan should describe all of the specific campaign methods and techniques which will be used to execute the campaign such as direct mail, speakers bureaus, door-to-door and telephone canvassing, etc.

The plan should be developed through several drafts, expanded, and modified as time goes on through the preliminary planning stages of the campaign. Be sure to allocate enough time for planning the campaign. It is a lot better to put the planning time in prior to the campaign than to have to backtrack in the middle of a campaign because of a strategic blunder. Once a well-thought-out plan is established, there must be a strong commitment and almost fanatical attention to detail in carrying out the campaign plan. The steering committee should take nothing for granted. The campaign manager should always follow-up to ensure that things get done. If the campaign planning is done well, and there is a strong, well-informed grassroots organization in place with forceful campaign arguments, it is likely that the referendum will be successful.

The primary goal of any campaign plan is to communicate the most effective campaign message possible to the voters. Once the message has been determined, it must be targeted toward and *repeatedly* delivered to voters who are probable library supporters as well as undecided voters who are persuadable. Repetition is essential since most political and media communication experts feel that a message must be delivered at least seven to eight times before it takes effect. The campaign plan must be designed around increasing the number of repetitive voter contacts of the campaign message particularly close to election day. In short, if you get the right message to the electorate enough times, and move them to the polls to vote, you will greatly increase your chances of winning. With this in mind, the author offers the following book as a Neal-Schuman "How-To-Do-It" planning guide for *Winning Library Referenda Campaigns*.

1 LIBRARY JOURNAL SURVEY OF REFERENDA FOR PUBLIC LIBRARIES

The major funding source for public library buildings in the post-Carnegie era has been the local referendum or ballot measure. These referenda may be held to allocate funds from special assessments, sales taxes, special taxes, excise taxes, as well as other forms of taxation, but referenda are most commonly held to provide funds from property taxes. Over the years, there have been occasional and sporadic attempts to report on the passage of local library referenda. However, even though local referenda are the main source of funds for public library construction, the library profession has not until recently participated in a comprehensive effort to collect data on the subject.

DATA COLLECTION

In 1987, the author, with the cooperation of *Library Journal* and the 50 State Library agencies, began a data collection effort to fill this void in the library literature. Each year since 1987, survey forms have been distributed to local library jurisdictions through the State Library agencies which are used to collect basic information regarding referenda for public library buildings. The data reported in this book summarizes information in consecutive *Library Journal* articles from June 15, 1988 to June 15, 1995. The data collection and subsequent articles have provided basic statistical information regarding the referenda held as well as analysis of that data.

EIGHT YEAR COMPILATION OF REFERENDA FOR PUBLIC LIBRARY BUILDINGS

Table 1-1 shows all of the referenda reported for the eight years of data collection (1987–1994), listed by state, fiscal year and municipality. From this table, one can review the last eight years of local referenda for public library construction in the United States. While it is certain that some referenda have gone unreported, the 377 referenda that are listed here are in all likelihood a very reasonable representative sampling of the activity that is actually taking place nationwide.

TABLE 1-1   Referenda for Public Library Buildings 1987–1994****

Community	Library	% Vote For	Against	Amount of Referendum	Gen/Spec	Other Ballot Items
ALABAMA						
1994						
Valley	H. Grady Bradshaw Chambers Co. Lib.	51	49	$ 2,400,000	G	N
1993						
Birmingham	Birmingham Public Library	80	20	3,000,000	G	Y
1990						
Birmingham	Birmingham Public Library	73	27	3,000,000	G	Y
ALASKA						
1989						
Soldotna	Soldotna Public Library	75	25	1,100,000	G	N
ARIZONA						
1994						
Mesa	Mesa Public Library	63	37	4,000,000	G	Y
Tucson	Tucson-Pima Library	64	36	5,500,000	S	Y
1988						
Phoenix	Phoenix Public Library	58	42	55,000,000	S	Y
1987						
Glendale	Glendale Public Library	56	44	9,698,000	S	Y
ARKANSAS						
1994						
Cabot	Arlene Cherry Memorial Library	51	49	375,000	S	Y
Little Rock	Central Arkansas Library System	59	41	17,000,000	S	N
Maumelle	Central Arkansas Library System	79	21	1,000,000	S	N
1988						
Little Rock	Central Arkansas Library System	60	40	2,000,000	S	Y
CALIFORNIA**						
1994						
Mountain View*	Mountain View Public Library	64	36	15,500,000	G	N
1993						
Hemet*	Hemet Public Library	55	45	3,800,000	G	Y
Mission Viejo*	Orange County Public Library	57	43	5,000,000	G	N
Pacific Grove*	Pacific Grove Public Library	49	51	3,000,000	G	N
1991						
Los Altos	Santa Clara County Library	74	26	3,715,000	G	Y
Oakland	Oakland Public Library	81	19	1,500,000	G	Y
Rolling Hills Estates	Palos Verdes Library	70	30	16,000,000	G	N

TABLE 1-1   *Continued*

Community	Library	% Vote For	% Vote Against	Amount of Referendum	Gen/Spec	Other Ballot Items
1990						
Davis	Davis Branch Library	78	22	$ 4,100,000	G	Y
Menlo Park	Menlo Park Library	83	17	5,000,000	G	N
Salinas	Monterey County Free Library	51	49	7,558,000	G	Y
1989						
Livermore	Livermore Public Library	61	39	760,000	G	Y
Los Angeles*	Los Angeles Public Library	62	38	90,000,000	G	Y
Los Angeles	Los Angeles Public Library	68	32	53,400,000	G	Y
San Francisco	San Francisco Public Library	76	24	109,500,000	G	Y
Vacaville	Vacaville P.L./Solano County Lib.	52	48	2,900,000	G	Y
COLORADO						
1994						
Eagle	Eagle Valley Library District	66	34	6,000,000	G	Y
1992						
Longmont	Longmont Public Library	55	45	5,500,000	G	Y
1991						
Denver	Denver Public Library	75	25	91,600,000	G	Y
1987						
Steamboat Springs	Bud Werner Memorial Library	67	33	575,000	S	N
CONNECTICUT						
1994						
Cheshire	Cheshire Public Library	58	42	3,150,000	S	N
Groton	Groton Public Library	67	33	2,730,000	G	Y
Kent	Kent Memorial Library	100	0	20,000	S	N
Killingworth	Killingworth Library	66	34	200,000	S	N
Old Lyme	Old Lyme-Phoebe Griffin Noyes Lib.	61	39	1,500,000	S	N
1993						
Burlington	Burlington Public Library	99	1	1,126,133	G	N
Derby	Derby Public Library	67	33	2,920,000	S	Y
Thompson	Thompson Public Library	85	15	2,650,000	S	N
1992						
Seymour	Seymour Public Library	62	38	810,000	S	N
1988						
Ashford*	Babcock Library	43	57	1,420,000	S	N
Niantic	East Lyme Public Library	98	2	1,500,000	S	N

Continued

TABLE 1-1 *Continued*

Community	Library	% Vote For	Against	Amount of Referendum	Gen/Spec	Other Ballot Items
1987						
Anonymous	Anonymous	86	14	$ 350,000	S	N
Harwinton	T.A. Hungerford Memorial Library	51	49	855,000	S	Y
FLORIDA						
1993						
Gulf Breeze	West Florida Regional Library	78	22	247,500	S	N
Winter Park	Winter Park Public Library	68	32	1,000,000	G	Y
1991						
New Smyrna Beach*	New Smyrna Beach Brannon Library	31	69	3,400,000	S	N
Ocala*	Central Florida Regional Library	30	70	14,100,000	G	N
Port Orange*	Port Orange Regional Library	42	58	3,100,000	S	N
1987						
New Port Richey	Pasco County Library	52	48	10,000,000	G	Y
West Palm Beach	Palm Beach County Library	67	33	20,000,000	G	Y
GEORGIA						
1993						
Fayetteville	Fayette County Public Library	51	49	2,470,000	G	N
Marietta*	Cobb County Public Library	49	51	5,060,000	G	Y
Savannah	Chatham-Effingham-Liberty Reg. Lib.	66	34	5,000,000	S	Y
Waycross	Okefenokee Regional Library	73	27	1,500,000	S	Y
1991						
Quitman	Brooks County Library	57	43	336,442	G	Y
1990						
Valdosta	Valdosta-Lowndes County P.L.	88	12	500,000	S	Y
1989						
Villa Rica	Villa Rica Public Library	66	34	50,000	S	Y
1988						
Athens	Athens Regional Library	70	30	3,750,000	G	Y
1987						
Decatur	DeKalb County Public Library	67	33	29,000,000	G	Y
Marietta	Cobb County Public Library	71	29	7,160,000	G	Y
Sparta	Hancock County Public Library	99	1	735,000	S	N
IDAHO**						
1991						
Hayden	Kootenai County Libraries	83	17	2,400,000	S	N
Council Bluffs*	Free Public Library	46	54	4,900,000	S	N

TABLE 1-1   *Continued*

Community	Library	% Vote For	Against	Amount of Referendum	Gen/Spec	Other Ballot Items
1990						
Twin Falls	Twin Falls Public Library	71	29	$ 1,965,000	S	N
1988						
Pocatello*	Pocatello Public Library	46	54	1,500,000	S	N
ILLINOIS						
1994						
Bartlett	Bartlett Public Library District	70	30	3,200,000	G	Y
Bartonville	Alpha Park Public Library District	52	48	1,300,000	G	N
Crete	Crete Public Library District	55	45	2,975,000	G	N
Lemont*	Lemont Public Library District	42	58	1,900,000	G	N
Oswego*	Oswego Public Library District	42	58	4,600,000	G	N
Wheeling*	Indian Trails Public Library District	47	53	3,500,000	G	Y
Willowbrook	Indian Prairie Public Library District	56	44	4,950,000	G	N
1993						
Itasca	Itasca Community Library	54	46	2,000,000	G	N
Lemont*	Lemont Public Library District	49	51	1,900,000	G	N
O'Fallon	O'Fallon Public Library	58	42	1,500,000	G	Y
Park Ridge*	Park Ridge Public Library	47	53	8,700,000	G	N
1992						
Arlington Heights	Arlington Heights Memorial Library	60	40	8,900,000	G	N
Willowbrook*	Indian Prairie Public Lib. Dist.	46	54	5,350,000	G	Y
1990						
Barrington	Barrington Public Library District	60	40	5,325,000	G	Y
Coal City	Coal City Public Library District	61	39	1,850,000	G	N
Eldorado	Eldorado Memorial P.L. District	54	46	550,000	G	N
Lacon	Lacon Public Library District	80	20	68,151	G	N
Midlothian	Midlothian Public Library	78	22	1,700,000	G	N
Palatine	Palatine Public Library	52	48	15,500,000	G	N
Westmont	Westmont Public Library	59	41	3,900,000	G	N
1989						
Lake Zurich	Ela Area Public Library	66	34	3,550,000	G	N
Prospect Hts.	Prospect Heights Public Library	67	33	2,900,000	G	N
Richmond	Nippersink Public Library	54	46	695,000	G	N
1988						
Hinsdale	Hinsdale Public Library	64	36	3,200,000	G	Y
Homewood	Homewood Public Library	54	46	2,900,000	G	N
La Grange	La Grange Park Public Library	65	35	2,200,000	G	N
Riverdale	Riverdale Public Library District	71	29	900,000	G	Y

Continued

TABLE 1-1 *Continued*

Community	Library	% Vote For	% Vote Against	Amount of Referendum	Gen/Spec	Other Ballot Items
1987						
Palos Heights	Palos Heights Public Library	54	46	$ 639,000	G	Y
St. Charles	St. Charles Public Library	68	32	2,925,000	G	Y
Taylorville	Taylorville Public Library	55	45	300,000	G	Y
IOWA*						
1994						
Fairfield*	Fairfield Public Library	56	44	2,300,000	S	N
Fairfield	Fairfield Public Library	63	37	2,000,000	S	N
Manchester	Manchester Public Library	74	26	575,000	S	N
Marion	Marion Public Library	74	26	1,975,000	S	N
West Des Moines	West Des Moines Public Library	77	23	6,950,000	S	N
1991						
Boone	Ericson Public Library	71	29	2,700,000	S	Y
1990						
Anonymous	Anonymous	68	32	350,000	S	N
Newton	Newton Public Library	52	48	1,500,000	S	N
1989						
Cresco	Cresco Public Library	75	25	269,500	S	N
Nevada	Nevada Public Library	61	39	600,000	S	N
Slater*	Slater Public Library	42	58	230,000	S	N
KANSAS						
1993						
Overland Park	Johnson County Library	72	28	12,000,000	G	N
1992						
Meade	Meade Public Library	54	46	150,000	S	N
Wellington	Wellington Public Library	61	39	150,000	G	Y
1991						
Norton	Norton Public Library	77	23	650,000	G	N
1988						
Towanda	Towanda Public Library	89	11	60,000	S	N
KENTUCKY						
1992						
Louisville*	Louisville Free Public Library	48	52	16,500,000	G	N
LOUISIANA						
1994						
Minden	Webster Parish Library	73	27	3,000,000	G	N
Shreveport*	Shreve Memorial Library	46	5	22,000,000	S	N

TABLE 1-1 *Continued*

Community	Library	% Vote For	% Vote Against	Amount of Referendum	Gen/Spec	Other Ballot Items
1993						
Leesville	Vernon Parish Library	60	40	$2,500,000	S	Y
1991						
St. Martinville	St. Martin Parish Library	72	28	1,825,000	G	N
1988						
Shreveport*	Shreve Memorial Library	49	51	6,000,000	G	Y
1987						
Baton Rouge	East Baton Rouge Parish Library	67	33	12,000,000	G	Y
Natchitoches*	Natchitoches Parish Library	38	62	6,280,000	G	Y
New Orleans	New Orleans Public Library	68	32	1,600,000	S	Y
MARYLAND						
1991						
Hyattsville	Prince George's Co. Memorial Library	75	25	12,867,000	G	Y
Towson	Baltimore County Public Library	56	44	2,050,000	G	Y
1987						
Hyattsville	Prince George's Co. Memorial Library	82	18	3,600,000	G	Y
Towson	Baltimore County Public Library	71	29	500,000	G	Y
MASSACHUSETTS						
1994						
Ayer	Ayer Library	70	30	900,000	G	Y
Bedford	Bedford Free Public Library	52	48	3,973,000	S	Y
Dover	Dover Town Library	57	43	1,151,000	G	Y
Kingston	Frederic C. Adams Public Library	55	45	660,000	S	N
Winchester	Winchester Public Library	99	1	3,535,000	G	N
1993						
Bridgewater	Bridgewater Public Library	63	37	750,000	S	N
1992						
Ashfield	Belding Memorial Library	80	20	30,000	S	N
1991						
Halifax	Holmes Public Library	71	29	389,000	S	Y
Kingston	Frederic C. Adams Public Library	99	1	75,000	G	Y
Weston	Weston Public Library	100	0	3,700,000	G	Y
West Tisbury	West Tisbury Free Public Library	64	36	95,000	G	Y
1990						
Anonymous*	Anonymous	38	62	2,600,000	S	Y
Anonymous*	Anonymous	49	51	102,000	G	Y

Continued

TABLE 1-1   *Continued*

Community	Library	% Vote For	% Vote Against	Amount of Referendum	Gen/Spec	Other Ballot Items
MASSACHUSETTS, 1990 *(continued)*						
Marblehead	Abbot Public Library	92	8	$ 340,000	S	Y
Rockland	Rockland Memorial Library	100	0	771,943	S	N
1989						
Chelmsford*	Chelmsford Public Library	49	51	1,000,000	S	N
Anonymous*	Anonymous	46	54	1,592,000	G	N
Lynnfield	Lynnfield Public Library	62	38	500,000	G	Y
North Reading	Flint Memorial Library	56	44	2,970,148	S	N
Plymouth	Plymouth Public Library	51	49	8,525,000	S	N
Spencer	Richard Sugden Public Library	61	39	455,000	S	Y
West Tisbury*	West Tisbury Free Public Library	59	41	280,000	G	Y
Westminster*	Forbush Memorial Library	48	52	1,250,000	G	Y
Williamstown*	Williamstown Public Library	57	43	310,000	S	N
1988						
Amherst	Jones Library	100	0	1,000,000	G	Y
Anonymous*	Anonymous	39	61	2,000,000	G	Y
Bellingham	Bellingham Public Library	56	44	2,000,000	S	Y
Holden	Gale Free Library	96	4	1,218,852	G	Y
Littleton	Reuben Hoar Library	92	8	487,000	G	N
Pembroke	Pembroke Public Library	82	18	2,600,000	SS	N
Spencer	Richard Sugden Library	100	0	425,000	G	Y
Wareham*	Wareham Free Library	40	60	2,500,000	G	N
1987						
Eastham	Eastham Public Library	97	3	663,665	G	Y
Lincoln	Lincoln Public Library	95	5	2,250,000	S	Y
Littleton	Reuben Hoar Library	75	25	1,200,000	S	Y
Plymouth*	Plymouth Public Library	49	51	9,725,000	G	Y
Southborough	Southborough Library	62	38	1,300,000	S	N
Sterling	Conant Public Library	82	18	890,000	G	N
Wayland	Wayland Public Library	100	0	200,000	G	Y
West Bridgewater	West Bridgewater Public Library	81	19	1,600,000	G	Y
West Newbury	G.A.R. Memorial Library	93	7	850,000	G	Y
Westford	J.V. Fletcher Library	80	20	2,280,000	G	Y
MICHIGAN						
1994						
Northville	Northville District Library	60	40	4,500,000	S	N
Roseville*	Roseville Public Library	49	51	2,720,000	G	N
Sterling Heights*	Sterling Heights Public Library	47	53	8,900,000	G	N

TABLE 1-1 *Continued*

Community	Library	% Vote For	% Vote Against	Amount of Referendum	Gen/Spec	Other Ballot Items
1993						
Indian River	Indian River Area Library	67	33	$ 700,000	S	N
Portage	Portage Public Library	52	48	2,200,000	G	N
Waterford	Waterford Township Public Library	53	47	3,600,000	G	N
1991						
Marlette	Marlette District Library	75	25	120,000	G	N
1990						
Farmington Hills*	Farmington Community Library	49	51	14,500,000	G	N
Flushing*	Flushing Library	49	51	800,000	S	Y
Wixom	Wixom Public Library	51	49	1,500,000	S	Y
1989						
Howell	Howell Carnegie District Library	66	34	4,525,000	S	N
Rochester	Rochester Hills Public Library	56	44	10,200,000	G	N
Saginaw	Thomas Township Library	67	33	165,000	G	N
1988						
Grosse Pointe*	Grosse Pointe Public Library	41	59	8,625,000	G	Y
MINNESOTA						
1994						
Dawson*	Dawson Public Library	47	53	300,000	S	N
1992						
Aitkin*	Aitkin Public Library	42	58	250,000	S	N
Aitkin	Aitkin Public Library	61	39	100,000	S	N
1991						
Ada	Ada Public Library	58	42	250,000	S	N
Benson	Benson Public Library	54	46	250,000	S	N
Rochester	Rochester Public Library	59	41	14,000,000	G	Y
1988						
Detroit Lakes	Detroit Lakes Public Library	56	44	1,700,000	S	N
1987						
Forest Lake	Forest Lake Public Library	59	41	298,000	G	Y
MISSISSIPPI						
1992						
Hattiesburg	The Library of Hattiesburg, Petal & Forrest County	71	29	6,000,000	G	N
MISSOURI						
1994						
Columbia	Daniel Boone Regional Library	74	26	1,250,000	G	Y

Continued

TABLE 1-1 *Continued*

Community	Library	% Vote For	Against	Amount of Referendum	Gen/Spec	Other Ballot Items
1993						
Moberly	Randolph County Library Dist.	70	30	$2,500,000	G	N
MONTANA						
1992						
Helena	Lewis and Clark Library	53	47	100,000	G	Y
NEVADA						
1991						
Las Vegas	Las Vegas/Clark County Library	51	49	70,000,000	G	Y
NEW HAMPSHIRE**						
1994						
Conway*	Conway Public Library	49	51	1,500,000	G	N
Lincoln	Lincoln Public Library	100	0	40,000	G	Y
1993						
Hampstead	Hampstead Public Library	99	1	582,000	G	N
Raymond	Dudley-Tucker Library	69	31	286,000	G	Y
1992						
Warner*	Pillsbury Free Library	63	37	275,000	S	Y
1990						
Derry	Derry Public Library	71	29	2,345,000	S	N
Grantham*	Dunbar Free Library	49	51	275,000	G	Y
New London	Tracy Memorial Library	80	20	1,285,300	G	Y
Rye*	Rye Public Library	30	70	315,000	G	Y
Swanzey Ctr	Mt. Caesar Union Library	100	0	55,000	G	N
Temple	Mansfield Public Library	72	28	258,000	G	N
Webster	Webster Free Public Library	90	10	85,000	G	Y
1989						
Grantham*	Dunbar Free Library	49	51	350,000	G	Y
Hampstead*	Hampstead Public Library	65	35	825,000	G	Y
Hollis*	Hollis Social Library	55	45	600,000	G	Y
New Castle	New Castle Public Library	80	20	850,000	G	N
Rye	Rye Public Library	70	30	75,000	G	Y
1988						
Hampstead*	Hampstead Public Library	57	43	950,000	G	Y
Jaffrey*	Jaffrey Public Library	58	42	1,000,000	G	Y
Raymond*	Dudley-Tucker Library	55	45	600,000	G	N
NEW JERSEY						
1993						
Highland Park	Highland Park Public Library	65	35	1,880,000	S	N

TABLE 1-1   *Continued*

Community	Library	% Vote For	Against	Amount of Referendum	Gen/Spec	Other Ballot Items
NEW JERSEY, 1993 *(continued)*						
Long Valley*	Washington Township Library	47	53	$ 2,500,000	G	Y
River Edge	River Edge Public Library	60	40	1,250,000	G	N
Warren	Warren Township Library	51	49	1,500,000	S	N
1992						
Upper Saddle River	Upper Saddle River Public Library	56	44	500,000	G	Y
NEW MEXICO						
1989						
Clovis	Clovis-Carter Public Library	65	35	2,800,000	S	N
NEW YORK						
1994						
Baldwinsville	Balswinsville Public Library	69	31	3,700,000	S	N
Brightwaters	Bay Shore-Brightwaters Public Library	79	21	380,000	S	N
Johnstown*	Johnston Public Library	44	56	1,500,000	G	N
New Hartford*	New Hartford Public Library	49	51	600,000	S	N
1993						
Irvington	Irvington Public Library	57	43	1,500,000	G	N
Patchogue	Patchogue-Medford Library	55	45	350,000	G	N
Roslyn*	The Bryant Library	25	75	12,000,000	S	N
Shirley	Mastics-Moriches-Shirley Lib.	75	25	3,948,250	S	N
Waterford	Waterford Public Library	80	20	350,000	S	N
1992						
Saratoga Springs	Saratoga Springs Public Library	74	26	7,500,000	S	N
1991						
Farmingdale	Farmingdale Public Library	56	44	8,820,000	S	N
Hewlett	Hewlett-Woodmore Public Library	56	44	775,000	G	N
1988						
Babylon*	Babylon Public Library	29	71	2,500,000	G	Y
Bellmore	Bellmore Memorial Library	58	42	1,500,000	S	N
Cutchogue	Cutchogue Free Library	70	30	48,500	G	Y
Grand Island	Grand Island Memorial Library	64	36	1,686,250	S	N
Nanuet	Nanuet Public Library	68	32	2,500,000	S	N
1987						
Brentwood	Brentwood Public Library	76	24	7,980,000	S	N
Center Moriches	Center Moriches Free Public Library	54	46	1,800,000	S	N
Eden	Eden Free Library	100	0	250,000	G	N
Marlboro	Marlboro Free Library	80	20	249,000	S	N
Middle Island	Longwood Public Library	87	13	3,900,000	G	Y

Continued

TABLE 1-1   *Continued*

Community	Library	% Vote For	Against	Amount of Referendum	Gen/Spec	Other Ballot Items
NEW YORK, 1987 *(continued)*						
Montauk	Montauk Library	65	35	985,000	S	N
Spring Valley	Finkelstein Memorial Library	73	27	$ 3,000,000	S	N
Yorktown	John C. Hart Memorial Library	81	19	2,000,000	S	N
NORTH CAROLINA						
1993						
Asheboro	Randolph Public Library	75	25	1,500,000	S	Y
Fayetteville	Cumberland County Public Lib.	51	49	11,400,000	G	Y
1991						
Chapel Hill*	Chapel Hill Public Library	49	51	3,000,000	G	N
Greensboro	Greensboro Public Library	65	35	16,060,000	G	Y
1987						
Chapel Hill	Chapel Hill Public Library	77	23	4,000,000	G	Y
NORTH DAKOTA						
1987						
Bismarck	Bismarck Veterans Memorial P.L.	73	27	3,400,000	G	Y
OHIO						
1994						
Avon	Lorain Public Library System	56	44	1,100,000	G	Y
Lorain*	Lorian Public Library System	33	67	320,778	G	N
1993						
Centerville	Washington-Centerville Public Lib.	60	40	3,070,000	G	Y
North Ridgeville*	Lorain Public Library	34	66	2,850,000	G	N
Sunbury	Community Library on the Square	53	47	1,500,000	G	Y
Vermilion	Ritter Public Library	85	15	1,600,000	G	Y
Willard	Willard Memorial Library	62	38	750,000	S	Y
1992						
Cleveland	Cleveland Public Library	71	29	90,000,000	G	N
Elyria	Elyria Public Library	51	49	3,400,000	G	Y
Tipp City	Tipp City Public Library	67	33	300,000	G	N
Toledo*	Toledo-Lucas County Public Library	35	65	55,000,000	G	N
Westerville*	Westerville Public Library	49	51	8,500,000	G	Y
1991						
Garrettsville	Portage County District Library	54	46	910,000	G	Y
Tipp City	Tipp City Public Library	67	33	300,000	G	N
Twinsburg	Twinsburg Public Library	75	25	2,600,000	S	N
Willoughby	Willoughby-Eastlake Public Library	57	43	4,000,000	G	N

TABLE 1-1 *Continued*

Community	Library	% Vote For	% Vote Against	Amount of Referendum	Gen/Spec	Other Ballot Items
1990						
Columbiana	Columbiana Public Library	63	37	$ 500,000	G	N
Fairborn	Fairborn Public Library	56	44	1,750,000	G	N
Port Clinton	Port Clinton Public Library	70	30	1,200,000	G	N
1989						
Galion	Galion Public Library	67	33	900,000	G	N
Grafton	Grafton/Midview Public Library	55	45	650,000	S	N
Grove City*	Southwest Public Library	43	57	20,000,000	G	N
New Philadelphia	Tuscarawas City Library	60	40	1,500,000	G	Y
Oberlin	Oberlin Public Library	64	36	1,500,000	G	N
Shelby	Marvin Memorial Library	52	48	300,000	G	N
Zanesville	Muskingum County Public Library	51	49	5,000,000	G	Y
1988						
Brecksville	Cuyahoga County Public Library	58	42	2,500,000	G	N
Findlay*	Findlay-Hancock City Public Library	46	54	3,000,000	G	Y
Independence*	Cuyahoga County Public Library	48	52	2,500,000	G	N
London	London Public Library	58	42	650,000	G	Y
Mount Vernon	Public Library of Mt. Vernon	55	45	2,600,000	G	Y
North Ridgeville*	Lorain Public Library	42	58	1,300,000	G	Y
Orwell	Grand Valley Public Library	65	35	225,000	G	Y
1987						
Anonymous*	Anonymous	35	65	1,200,000	G	Y
Berea	Cuyahoga County Public Library	67	33	1,500,000	G	N
Columbus	Grandview Heights Public Library	66	34	4,460,000	G	Y
Columbus	P.L. of Columbus & Franklin Co.	53	47	45,000,000	G	Y
Fremont	Birchard Public Library/Sandusky Co.	56	44	3,600,000	G	N
Lebanon	Lebanon Public Library	65	35	1,350,000	G	N
Parma Heights	Cuyahoga County Public Library	57	43	1,000,000	G	N
Waynesville	Mary L. Cook Public Library	52	48	550,000	G	Y
OKLAHOMA						
1994						
Oklahoma City	Metropolitan Library System	54	46	15,900,000	S	Y
1991						
Stillwater	Stillwater Public Library	67	33	4,980,000	S	N
1989						
Checotah	Checotah Jim Lucas Library	77	23	300,000	S	Y
Tulsa	Tulsa City/County Library System	66	34	4,200,000	G	N

Continued

TABLE 1-1   *Continued*

Community	Library	% Vote For	% Vote Against	Amount of Referendum	Gen/Spec	Other Ballot Items
OREGON						
1994						
Eugene*	Eugene Public Library	49	51	$19,000,000	G	Y
Monmouth	Monmouth Public Library	59	41	1,400,000	G	N
1993						
Baker City	Baker County Public Library	55	45	124,100	S	N
Portland	Multnomah County Library	70	30	31,000,000	S	N
Salem*	Chemeketa Regional Library	38	62	1,615,000	G	Y
Scappoose	Scappoose Public Library Dist.	54	46	400,000	S	Y
1991						
Lincoln City	Driftwood Library/Lincoln City	63	37	600,000	G	N
1990						
Bend*	Deschutes County Library	47	53	8,448,000	G	Y
Corvallis	Corvallis-Benton Co. Public Library	69	31	6,850,000	G	N
Florence	Suislaw Public Library District	70	30	1,150,000	S	N
1989						
Dallas	Dallas Public Library	62	38	650,000	G	Y
Eugene*	Eugene Public Library	42	58	12,000,000	S	N
Stayton	Stayton Public Library	60	40	150,000	G	Y
1988						
Roseburg*	Douglas County Library System	46	54	2,285,000	S	N
Sisters	Deschutes County Library	73	27	25,000	S	N
Stayton*	Stayton Public Library	46	54	275,000	S	Y
1987						
North Bend	North Bend Public Library	67	33	1,650,000	G	Y
Portland	Multnomah County Library	60	40	5,890,000	G	Y
West Linn	West Linn Public Library	64	36	1,200,000	G	Y
Wilsonville	Wilsonville Public Library	56	44	2,250,000	S	Y
PENNSYLVANIA						
1991						
Dresher*	Upper Dublin Public Library	45	55	3,500,000	G	Y
1990						
Huntingdon Valley	Huntingdon Valley Library	70	30	1,785,000	S	N
RHODE ISLAND						
1988						
South Kingstown	South Kingstown Public Library	75	25	100,000	S	Y

TABLE 1-1   *Continued*

Community	Library	% Vote For	Against	Amount of Referendum	Gen/Spec	Other Ballot Items
1987						
South Kingstown	South Kingstown Public Library	73	27	$ 750,000	G	Y
SOUTH CAROLINA						
1993						
Spartanburg	Spartanburg County Public Lib.	64	36	11,000,000	G	N
1991						
Conway	Horry County Public Library	100	0	4,000,000	S	Y
1989						
Columbia	Richland County Public Library	72	28	27,000,000	S	N
1987						
Charleston	Charleston County Library	76	24	15,465,234	G	N
TENNESSEE						
1991						
Kingston	Kingston City Library	61	39	564,000	G	N
TEXAS						
1994						
El Paso*	El Paso Public Library	49	51	35,000,000	S	Y
Laredo	Laredo Public Library	73	27	7,000,000	G	Y
1993						
Anonomous*	Anonomous	30	70	7,200,000	G	Y
Alvin	Brazoria County Library System	57	43	1,600,000	S	Y
Lubbock	Lubbock City-County Library	52	48	1,784,000	G	Y
Richardson	Richardson Public Library	75	25	3,137,000	S	Y
1992						
Conroe	Montgomery County Library	63	37	8,750,000	G	N
Houston	Houston Public Library	62	38	9,000,000	G	Y
1991						
Baytown	Sterling Municipal	64	36	1,870,700	S	Y
Grand Prairie	Grand Prairie Memorial Library	54	46	2,700,000	S	Y
Plano	Plano Public Library	51	49	6,600,000	S	Y
San Marcos	San Marcos Public Library	53	47	2,135,000	G	Y
1990						
Angleton	Brazoria County Library System	79	21	1,020,000	S	Y
Conroe*	Montgomery County Library	46	54	17,650,000	G	Y
Coppell	William T. Cozby Public Library	64	36	2,600,000	S	Y
DeSoto	DeSoto Public Library	64	36	2,754,000	S	Y
Duncanville	Duncanville Public Library	67	33	500,000	S	Y

Continued

TABLE 1-1 *Continued*

Community	Library	% Vote For	% Vote Against	Amount of Referendum	Gen/Spec	Other Ballot Items
TEXAS, 1990 *(continued)*						
Pasadena	Pasadena Public Library	65	35	$ 1,200,000	S	Y
Richmond	Fort Bend County Library	69	31	10,900,000	G	N
Weatherford	Weatherford Public Library	57	43	600,000	S	Y
1989						
Freeport	Brazoria County Library System	64	36	750,000	G	N
1988						
Anonymous*	Anonymous	41	59	600,000	G	Y
Houston	Harris City Public Library	60	40	3,500,000	G	Y
1987						
Universal City*	Universal City Library	29	71	750,000	S	N
VERMONT						
1993						
Anonomous*	Anonomous	33	67	275,000	G	N
1988						
Middlebury	Ilsley Public Library	58	42	680,000	S	N
VIRGINIA						
1994						
Blacksburg	Montgomery-Floyd Regional Library	62	38	1,885,000	G	Y
Williamsburg	Williamsburg Regional Library	78	22	5,200,000	S	N
1993						
Orange	Orange County Library	61	39	500,000	G	Y
Roanoke	Roanoke County Public Library	77	23	1,500,000	G	Y
1991						
Christiansburg*	Montgomery-Floyd Regional Library	46	54	1,400,000	G	Y
Fredericksburg	Central Rappahannock Library	56	44	1,350,000	G	Y
1990						
Fairfax	Fairfax County Public Library	62	38	39,100,000	G	Y
Fredericksburg*	Central Rappahannock Library	45	55	3,000,000	S	Y
1989						
Chesapeake	Chesapeake Public Library	58	42	10,600,000	G	N
Richmond	County of Henrico Public Library	67	33	3,000,000	S	Y
WASHINGTON*						
1993						
Arlington*	Arlington Library	58	42	900,000	G	N
Arlington*	Arlington Library	58	42	900,000	G	N

TABLE 1-1   *Continued*

Community	Library	% Vote For	% Vote Against	Amount of Referendum	Gen/Spec	Other Ballot Items
1991						
Ferndale	Ferndale Library	63	37	$ 1,250,000	G	Y
Spokane	Spokane Public Library	65	35	28,883,000	G	N
Vancouver	Fort Vancouver Regional Library	64	36	2,100,000	S	Y
1990						
Auburn*	Auburn Public Library	56	44	2,000,000	G	Y
Enumclaw	Enumclaw Public Library	63	37	1,250,000	G	N
Port Hadlock	Jefferson Co. Rural Library District	73	27	400,000	S	N
1989						
Enumclaw	Enumclaw Public Library	72	28	1,250,000	S	N
Kennewick*	Mid-Columbia Library	52	48	183,000	G	N
1988						
Spokane	Spokane County Library District	64	36	4,465,000	S	Y
1987						
Cheney	Cheney Community Library	79	21	275,000	G	Y
WEST VIRGINIA						
1992						
Morgantown	Morgantown Public Library	80	20	600,000	S	Y
1989						
Morgantown	Morgantown Public Library	71	29	600,000	S	Y
WISCONSIN						
1994						
Hartland	Hartland Public Library	70	30	1,375,000	S	Y
1989						
Stoughton	Stoughton Public Library	65	35	1,000,000	G	N
TOTALS	**377 Projects**	63	37	**$1,964,268,446**	G – 62% S – 38%	Y – 50% N – 50%

*Referenda that failed

**Required two-thirds approval for passage

***Required 60% approval for passage

****Copyright © 1988 –1995 Reed Publishing

MAJOR LIBRARY REFERENDA CAMPAIGNS

Table 1-2 shows a selection of the 42 library referenda campaigns for more than $10 million each listed by the amount of funds requested. These major campaigns account for almost 1.25 billion dollars which is approximately 63 percent of all funds reported to have been placed before the voters during the same eight year period. This means that a little over 11 percent of the campaigns held during that time accounted for almost two-thirds of all of the dollars placed on local ballots nationwide. Further, a half dozen (less than two percent of all campaigns) referenda accounted for approximately one third of all funds requested.

This is not to diminish the importance of smaller campaigns in smaller communities, but it does provide some perspective on the funding patterns of library referenda in this country. It is interesting to note that the success rate of 69 percent for these major campaigns is lower than that of all referenda (77 percent). This means that campaigns under $10 million may have a slightly higher chance for success than the ones over $10 million; however the percentage of the amount of funds approved by the electorate was nearly identical when the major campaigns were compared to all referenda.

TABLE 1-2   Major Referenda Campaigns for Public Libraries**

LOCATION	AMOUNT (IN MILLIONS)	YEAR
San Francisco, CA	$109.5	1989
Denver, CO	91.6	1991
Cleveland, OH	90	1992
Los Angeles, CA *	90	1989
Las Vegas, NV	70	1991
Toledo, OH *	55	1992
Phoenix, AZ	55	1988
Los Angeles, CA	53.4	1989
Columbus, OH	45	1987
Fairfax, VA	39.1	1990
El Paso, TX *	35	1994
Portland, OR	31	1993
Decatur, GA	29	1987
Spokane, WA	28.9	1991
Columbia, SC	27	1989

Continued

TABLE 1-2   *Continued*

LOCATION	AMOUNT (IN MILLIONS)	YEAR
Shreveport, LA *	22	1994
West Palm Beach, FL	20	1987
Grove City, OH *	20	1989
Eugene, OR *	19	1994
Conroe, TX *	17.6	1990
Little Rock, AR	17	1994
Louisville, KY *	16.5	1992
Greensboro, NC	16	1991
Rolling Hills Estates, CA	16	1991
Oklahoma City, OK	15.9	1994
Mountain View, CA *	15.5	1994
Palatine, IL	15.5	1990
Charleston, SC	15.5	1987
Farmington Hills, MI *	14.5	1990
Ocala, FL *	14.1	1991
Rochester, MN	14	1991
Hyattsville, MY	12.9	1991
Overland Park, KS	12	1993
Roslyn, NY *	12	1993
Baton Rouge, LA	12	1987
Eugene, OR *	12	1989
Fayetteville, NC	11.4	1993
Spartanburg, SC	11	1993
Richmond, TX	10.9	1990
Chesapeake, VA	10.6	1989
Rochester, MI	10.2	1989
New Port Richey, FL	10	1987
TOTAL:	**$1,243,200,000**	

* Referenda that failed

** © 1988–1995 Reed Publishing

EIGHT YEAR SUMMARY OF REFERENDA FUNDS

Table 1-3 shows a summary, by year, of the amount of funding requested along with the amount of funds that were approved and the amount of funds that were not approved. On average, approximately $246 million per year has been requested, with $180 million being approved and $66 million being rejected by the voters. Of the $1,964,268,446 attempted, approximately 73 percent was approved and only 27 percent was turned down by the voters. It should be encouraging to library supporters that almost three-quarters of all funding attempted for public library construction by referenda in this nation is approved by the public.

TABLE 1-3   Eight Year Summary of Referenda Funds**

FY	Total Amount Requested	Amount Approved	Amount Not Approved
1994	$ 244,389,778	$ 124,749,000	$119,640,778
1993	$ 185,874,983	$ 130,174,983	$ 55,700,000
1992	$ 227,665,000	$ 141,790,000	$ 85,875,000
1991	$ 348,420,142	$ 315,020,142	$ 33,400,000
1990	$ 182,755,394	$ 133,065,394	$ 49,690,000
1989	$ 394,759,648*	$ 266,139,648	$128,620,000
1988	$ 138,475,602	$ 101,420,602	$ 37,055,000
1987	$ 241,927,899	$ 223,972,899	$ 17,955,000
TOTAL	**$1,964,268,446**	**$1,436,332,668**	**$527,935,778**
AVE	$ 245,533,556	$ 179,541,584	$ 65,991,972
		73%	27%

* Included $75 million of public library construction funds approved in a California state-wide referendum.
** © 1988–1995 Reed Publishing

EIGHT YEAR SUMMARY OF REFERENDA DATA

Table 1-4 summarizes by each year the critical information in Table 1-1. The table shows the number of referenda held each year, the percentage to pass and fail, the total amount of funds requested, the percentage of the vote "for" and "against," the percentage of referenda that were held during general elections and special elections, and finally the percentage of referenda that had competition from other ballot items ("Yes") and those without competition ("No").

TABLE 1-4			Eight Year Summary of Referenda for Public Library Buildings*								
					VOTE		**ELECTION**		**OTHER BALLOT ITEMS**		
YEAR	**#**	**PERCENTAGE PASS/FAIL**		**AMOUNT**	**PRO**	**CON**	**GEN**	**SPEC**	**YES**	**NO**
1994	53	72%	28%	$ 244,389,778	61%	39%	53%	47%	36%	64%
1993	56	75%	25%	185,874,983	61%	39%	64%	36%	45%	55%
1992	23	74%	26%	227,665,000	59%	41%	65%	35%	43%	57%
1991	46	85%	15%	348,420,142	63%	37%	65%	35%	54%	46%
1990	49	80%	20%	182,755,394	65%	35%	59%	41%	51%	49%
1989	51	75%	25%	394,759,648	61%	39%	65%	35%	41%	59%
1988	45	64%	36%	138,475,602	61%	39%	60%	40%	58%	42%
1987	54	93%	7%	241,927,899	69%	31%	69%	31%	67%	33%
ALL	**377**			**1,964,268,446**						
AVE	47	77%	23%	$ 245,533,556	63%	37%	62%	38%	50%	50%

PASS/FAIL RATE FOR REFERENDA FOR PUBLIC LIBRARY BUILDINGS

The good news provided by this on-going data collection effort, is that for referenda held to finance capital improvements for public libraries for the eight years between July 1, 1986 and June 30, 1994, approximately 77 percent of those reported passed. While the reporting system is entirely voluntary, and there certainly are some campaigns that are missed by the survey method, it is encouraging to note that based on the referenda reported, the chances of success for public library referenda campaigns is better than 3 to 1! It is obvious that this figure may be somewhat on the high side of what is actually the case, assuming that those whose referenda fail are less likely to report their loss than those who succeed. Nevertheless, the actual success rate is probably still significantly higher than the rate of failure.

VOTER APPROVAL RATE

As can be seen from Table 1-4, when the percentages of votes for and against all of the referenda are averaged, the national success rate of voter approval is 63 percent. The range in the approval rate has consistently remained between 59 and 69 percent. This enviable approval rate for public library capital campaigns is just short of a two-third's approval rate. This fact is significant since a number of states require a super majority approval rate for a referendum to pass. States such as Washington, Mississippi, West Virginia, North Dakota, and Iowa require a 60% approval rate and the states of California, Idaho, Missouri, and New Hampshire require a two-thirds percent approval rate. Referenda in these states are a real challenge, but one which has been met in many cases.

SPECIAL VERSUS GENERAL ELECTIONS

For the eight year period, 62 percent of the referenda were held during general elections and 38 percent were held during special elections. For the purposes of the survey, a general election is defined as a "regularly scheduled election" such as the November general elections or any primary election. Special elections are those which are set up in addition to those elections which are normally scheduled in any given year. In comparing the success rates of referenda held during special elections (84 percent), and those held during general elections (74 percent), it appears that special elections have a significant although obviously not large edge overall for the eight year period.

ELECTIONS BY SEASON

When an election is held has an impact on the success rate as well as whether the election was a special or general election. It is interesting to look at the data by seasonal success rates. For example, Table 1-5 shows a very high success rate for special elections held in either the Summer (85 percent), Fall (85 percent), or Winter (91 percent). The success rate for library referenda held during Spring special elections drops to 77 percent. Although this rate is the lowest of all seasons for special elections, it still is higher than the average success rate of 74 percent for all general elections.

The Spring is the season with the lowest success rate for library referenda held during general elections as well with an approval rate of only 67 percent. The next lowest success rate for general elections is the Fall when most general elections are held. The approval rate during the

TABLE 1-5   Capital Outlay Referenda Pass/Fail Ratio By Season*

| | ELECTION | | | | | |
| | SPECIAL | | GENERAL | | ALL | |
SEASON	Pass	Fail	Pass	Fail	Pass	Fail
Spring	77%	23%	67%	33%	71%	29%
Summer	85%	15%	86%	14%	86%	14%
Fall	85%	15%	75%	25%	78%	22%
Winter	91%	9%	100%	0%	92%	8%
AVE	84%	16%	74%	26%	77%	23%

* © 1988–1995 Reed Publishing

Fall is 75 percent, which while low compared to the Summer (86 percent) and the Winter (100 percent), is still not all that bad being just below the average success rate of all referenda (77 percent). Clearly, there are implications in this data about the advisability of Spring elections for library referenda, and in particular, Spring general elections.

BALLOT COMPETITION

For the eight year period, 50 percent of the library referenda held had some form of competition from another capital ballot measure and 50 percent did not. These figures show that there are as many library issues decided with ballot competition as without it. The eight years of data also show that 78 percent of the referenda with competition passed, while 77 percent of the referenda without competition passed. Looking back over the years, it does not appear that merely having competition on the ballot (or the lack thereof) is particularly significant in predicting the success or failure of a library referendum. As will be discussed in-depth in Chapter 5, a more important consideration is the type of competition and the perception of the electorate toward the competing ballot items.

AGENCY AUTHORIZING REFERENDA

There are many kinds of local agencies which can authorize referenda for public libraries. The most frequent authorizing agency is the local municipality or city. In some localities, however, counties, school and library districts, New England towns, parishes, and even special authorities may hold referenda. Table 1-6 shows the allocation of the referenda by the authorizing agency. For the eight year period, municipalities lead with 40 percent. When combined with New England towns, the figure increases to 57 percent. Counties, school and library districts account for another 37 percent, with the remaining six percent spread out over various miscellaneous authorities.

TYPES OF REFERENDA

Most referenda for public library capital improvement projects result in the issuance of general obligation bonds. However, other funding mechanisms used to raise capital through a referendum include sales taxes, excise taxes, special taxes, as well as property tax millage increases, but these methods vary tremendously from state to state and are in the minority of preferred methods. General obligation bond issues continue to be the most popular method of financing public library buildings. Over 80 percent of the referenda held during the eight year period resulted in the issuance of bonds. Almost all of these bonds were general obligation bonds, whereby the full taxing authority of the funding agency stands behind the debt instrument. In the cases where bonds were not issued, the most typical form of financing was either a limited property tax millage or increased revenues from a sales tax increase for a specific period of time. Both approaches usually provided an adequate revenue stream to complete a small project without having to resort to selling bonds.

TABLE 1-6   Authorizing Agencies for Library Referenda*

AGENCY	PERCENTAGE
Municipality	40%
New England Town	17%
County	16%
Library District	11%
School District	10%
Parish	2%
City / County	1%
Township	1%
Village	1%
Special Authorities	.5%
Borough	.5%

* © 1988–1995 Reed Publishing

LIBRARY REFERENDA FOR OPERATING FUNDS

While there is eight years worth of data for library referenda for library buildings, 1994 is the first year that data was collected on a national basis for library referenda campaigns for the purpose of securing operating funds. While Table 1-7 represents only one year of data collection, it is the most current and comprehensive information available to the library community at this time. The information will become more meaningful in the future as more data is collected, but for 1994 it is remarkable to note that 50 of the 54 referenda passed, representing an incredibly high 93 percent success rate.

THE NATIONAL DATA'S RELATION TO INDIVIDUAL REFERENDA

The preceding data analysis of the national data is important in understanding the overall national trends for public library referenda. This information is useful to the reader to help place an individual local referendum which is under consideration into a relative context with other previously held library referenda, however, *it is essential to view each and every local referendum as a unique political action set in its own political environment*. The national data can be used as a guide to help understand the best way to proceed with a local referendum, but it should not unduly influence local decisions based upon specific local circumstances. In other words, it is important to keep an eye cast towards the results of the national data during the formation of a campaign plan, but the most important information is at the local community level. There is one thing, however, that is common to almost all successful referenda, and that is an effective campaign organization, which is the topic of Chapter 2.

TABLE 1-7   Referenda for Public Library Operations Funds 1994

Community	Library	% Vote For	% Vote Against	Amount of Referendum $/Year	# YRS	Gen/Spec	Other Ballot Items
ALABAMA							
Huntsville*	Huntsville-Madison County P. L.	47%	53%	$2,400,000	8	G	Y
Robertsdale*	Baldwin County Library System	32%	68%	850,000	Ind	S	N
ARKANSAS							
Fort Smith	Fort Smith Public Library	56%	44%	500,000	10	S	N
Little Rock	Central Arkansas Library System	62%	38%	1,266,300	Ind	S	Y
Little Rock	Central Arkansas Library System	54%	46%	415,800	Ind	S	Y
CALIFORNIA**							
Albany	Albany Library	77%	23%	275,000	Ind	G	Y
Altadena	Altadena Library	85%	15%	430,000	5	G	Y
Cameron Park****	El Dorado County Library	54%	46%	190,000	Ind	G	Y
Corte Madera	Marin County Free Library	75%	25%	131,148	4	S	Y
Fairfax/West Marin	Marin County Free Library	68%	32%	364,284	4	G	Y
Oakland	Oakland Public Library	74%	26%	3,756,333	15	G	Y
Palm Springs****	Palm Springs Public Library	55%	45%	300,000	3	G	Y
San Rafael (Zone 2)	Marin County Free Library	68%	32%	1,432,944	4	S	Y
Santa Paula	Santa Paula Union High School/P. L.	70%	30%	210,000	Ind	G	Y
South Pasadena	South Pasadena Public Library	69%	31%	220,000	5	G	Y
ILLINOIS							
Gurnee	Warren-Newport Public Library	67%	33%	500,000	Ind	G	Y
Wheeling*	Indian Trails Public Library District	47%	53%	71,000	Ind	G	Y
IOWA***							
Cedar Rapids	Cedar Rapids Public Library	75%	25%	121,000	10	G	Y
LOUISIANA							
Alexandria	Rapides Parish Library	59%	41%	1,500,000	10	G	Y
Crowley	Acadia Parish Library	74%	26%	425,000	10	S	Y
Shreveport	Shreve Memorial Library	61%	39%	2,914,007	10	S	Y
MICHIGAN							
Battle Creek	Willard Library	75%	25%	2,200,000	1	G	Y
East Jordan	Jordan Valley District Library	61%	39%	136,641	Ind	S	N
Grand Rapids	Grand Rapids Public Library	66%	34%	5,905,644	Ind	G	Y
Northville	Northville District library	57%	43%	757,000	Ind	S	Y
Wyandotte	Bacon Memorial District Library	76%	24%	555,000	Ind	G	Y
MISSOURI							
Center	Ralls County Library	80%	20%	86,000	Ind	S	N
Eldon	Eldon Public Library	60%	40%	50,000	Ind	G	Y
St. Peters	St. Charles City-Co. Library District	52%	48%	1,375,000	Ind	G	Y

TABLE 1-7 *Continued*

Community	Library	% Vote For	% Vote Against	Amount of Referendum $/Year	# YRS	Gen/Spec	Other Ballot Items
NEW YORK							
Baldwinsville	Baldwinsville Public Library	80%	20%	524,500	1	S	Y
Corfu	Corfu Public Library	68%	32%	6,500	1	G	Y
Fairport	Fairport Public Library	63%	37%	1,015,152	1	G	Y
Glens Falls	Crandall Public Library	55%	45%	627,497	1	G	Y
Holley	Community Free Library	60%	40%	40,750	1	G	Y
Medina	Lee-Whedon Memorial Library	63%	37%	256,029	1	G	Y
New City	New City Library	62%	38%	2,759,200	1	S	N
Pearl River	Pearl River Public Library	64%	36%	1,015,291	1	S	Y
Rockville Centre	Rockville Centre Public Library	64%	36%	1,465,250	1	G	Y
Spring Valley	Finkelstein Memorial Library	68%	32%	3,200,000	1	G	Y
OHIO							
Archbold	McLaughlin Memorial Library	81%	19%	60,000	5	G	Y
Columbia Township*	Lorain Public Library System	33%	67%	114,000	10	G	N
Mentor	Mentor Public Library	60%	40%	489,000	5	G	Y
Wooster	Wayne County Public Library	55%	45%	1,000,000	5	G	Y
OREGON							
Corvallis	Corvallis-Benton County Public Library	59%	41%	1,300,000	Ind	G	Y
Florence	Siuslaw Public Library	55%	45%	480,000	3	S	N
Oak Grove	Lib. Info. Network of Clackamas Co.	60%	40%	5,600,000	3	G	Y
Prineville	Crook County Public Library	51%	49%	235,889	3	S	Y
Sherwood	Sherwood Public Library	70%	30%	111,054	3	G	Y
Sweet Home	Sweet Home Public Library	56%	44%	83,600	3	S	Y
Tillamook	Tillamook County Library	58%	42%	750,000	3	S	Y
Veneta	Fern Ridge Library	71%	29%	150,000	Ind	G	Y
PENNSYLVANIA							
Somerset	Mary S. Biesecker Public Library	57%	43%	27,650	Ind	G	Y
VERMONT							
Essex Junction	Brownell Library	59%	41%	15,000	1.5	G	Y
WASHINGTON							
Friday Harbor	San Juan Island Library District	59%	41%	120,000	Ind	G	Y
TOTALS	**54 Referenda** **4 Failed / 50 Passed**	63%	37%	$50,784,463	—	G 67% S 33%	Y 87% N 13%

Ind = Indefinite

*Referenda that failed

**Required two-thirds approval for passage

***Required 60% approval for passage

****Advisory (non-binding)

2 CAMPAIGN ORGANIZATION

FORMATION OF THE CAMPAIGN ORGANIZATION

Two of the most important aspects of any library referendum campaign are the organization and commitment of the campaign leadership. All successful referendum efforts have an organization of individuals who are supportive of the ballot issue. Many campaigns are won or lost based on how effectively these campaign volunteers are organized to get out the campaign message. One of the hard realities of politics is that it doesn't matter how worthy a library issue is if the supporters don't have the organizational skills to direct and manage a campaign organization. Regardless of how large or small a campaign is, there must be a workable organizational structure. It is usually best for all concerned to establish this structure early in the campaign so that duties are clearly defined, lines of communication are open, and levels of authority are determined and agreed to by those who will be most active in the campaign.

At the center of any campaign organization will be a core of highly committed and motivated people who are willing to work hard for the issue over a sustained period of time. As the campaign progresses, these people will surround themselves with consultants who will perform necessary campaign services such as polling, public relations, etc. They will also recruit volunteers who will provide the essential grassroots legwork necessary for door-to-door canvassing, mailings, or telephone banks. These latter people will be transient and will only come to the campaign based on the efforts of those at the heart of the campaign organization. The quality and commitment of these "core campaigners" is essential to success.

COMMITMENT TO THE CAMPAIGN

One of the first steps in any campaign is to make certain that the necessary commitment to the project and campaign is present. The decision to begin a referendum campaign is not one that should be taken lightly. Library planners must be unanimous, if possible, in supporting the campaign and quickly obtain consensus on how the campaign will be run. From the outset, the library management and supporters should be in the game to win and should plan accordingly. The library may gain many other benefits from the campaign, but passing the measure is the supreme test of success with the public and the politicians. In order to win, the library director and all other library supporters will have to make a very significant commitment of time and energy. A referendum campaign is one of the most focused and intensive activities that library supporters will face, and it will demand a good deal of personal time from each individual including the library director. There will be many late evening and weekend meetings particularly during the final weeks of the campaign when the all out effort to reach the voters is in high gear.

If commitment and consensus cannot be accomplished early, the campaign should not be started at all, or at least not until those involved can make a strong commitment to the campaign. In short, if support and commitment are lacking now, it is better to wait to build consensus, because without the strong support of its organizers, the campaign is likely to fail. One thing that is common to all campaigns is unending work on the part of the team members. Without the commitment necessary to support this, the campaign will be crippled from the outset. While half-hearted attempts occasionally do succeed, those who have an effective campaign strategy and a hard-working core team of campaigners significantly improve their chances of success. Library referenda frequently fail not only because of voter apathy but because of neglect and lack of commitment on the part of campaign workers.

There must be enough volunteers to do the work, they must be well organized, and they must have a high degree of enthusiasm for the issue. It is exceedingly important to infuse emotional involvement into the campaign players and turn them into "true believers." While campaign enthusiasm is contagious, it must start somewhere. This enthusiasm must emanate from the center of the campaign leadership. Given this, it is essential to pick the right people for the campaign steering committee.

PICKING "MOVERS & SHAKERS"

The first step in any successful campaign is to organize a core of committed, influential individuals who will form the steering committee for the campaign. Great care must be taken to select the most politically savvy and influential individuals possible, who are not only committed to the campaign issue, but who can produce the desired results. These individuals must be "movers and shakers" in the community. It can't be emphasized enough how critical this step is to the success of the campaign, because the campaign will be placed in the hands of these people. Having the right people on the steering committee can mean a smooth running, effective, well thought out, and successful campaign. The wrong selection of even one committee member can mean disaster or at the very least greatly hamper campaign efforts.

People who are already community leaders in one form or another usually make good campaign committee members because they enhance the campaign' visibility. Heads of community service organizations, corporate CEOs, and political activists may be excellent possibilities. It is particularly important to look for people who have had previous fund raising and political campaign experience. In many communities, a small group of acknowledged "campaigners" are selected time and again to run successful community campaigns. It is important to try to identify these individuals from the outset. It will frequently be surprising who these people are in a community. Sometimes it is obvious, but occasionally they turn out to be "sweet little quiet tigers [who have] been working in the political arena some 65 years."[1] It is worth the time to find out who in the community has run successful campaigns relatively recently and tap into their political expertise.

What if these experienced political workhorses aren't available for the campaign, or worse, they just refuse to become involved for whatever reason? Accessing their political knowledge, or the knowledge of any elected official, can sometimes be as helpful as their actual involvement in the campaign. When asking if they would be willing to advise the steering committee as the campaign progresses, ask them for their recommendations for the steering committee members. While they may not be able to run the campaign, they may know of some young, politically savvy newcomer who could do the job. If library supporters can't recruit the most experienced "old pros" for the campaign, they may be able to find out which individuals in a community have good political instincts even if they don't yet have a track record to prove it. Sometimes these individuals aspire to higher political goals and are willing to work very hard for the library campaign to prove their effectiveness to the community and its political insiders.

Individuals who participated in the planning process for the library project are another good source of steering committee members. Candidates who have a clear understanding of the needs assessment, facilities master plan, and the building program are excellent choices since they have a strong vested interest in the project as well as a good working knowledge of the specifics of the project. This knowledge will serve the campaign well if questions arise over why one building approach is being considered over an alternative. Further, since these individuals have participated in the planning process, they have effectively "bought-into" the project and will usually defend it vigorously. Political campaigns have demonstrated time and again, that those who have helped plan a project turn out to be the best public supporters of the project.

COMMUNITY REPRESENTATION

Good selection of steering committee members assists in building coalitions with many community groups and organizations. For example, if the campaign will need the support of the business community, it will be critical to have a respected member from this sector of the community on the steering committee. This member will be expected to go to the business community and deliver the necessary fundraising support and votes to help carry the library issue. For any critical group, direct personal involvement by "one of their own" has been demonstrated to be the most successful method of gaining support and involvement for a political issue. This is true for all community sectors from the educational community to various ethnic groups.

Along with making sure that the committee members are recognized leaders in the community, planners should also ensure that they are representative of the community as a whole. It is particularly important that the steering committee be representative of the community, especially if significant numbers of minorities form part of the community. Any political campaign is an effort to arrive at political consensus between a large number of individuals and groups in the community. If any significant portion of a community is ignored or untapped, the chances of success are diminished. The steering committee can include library trustees, members of the Friends group, business representatives or members of the community at large; the more diverse the committee is, the better its chances for success. Campaigns usually gain credibility if the public perceives that there is cooperation among interest groups that don't typically support one another.

CREDIBILITY

When looking for steering committee members, and particularly the campaign manager, it is essential to consider how credible the individuals are in the community. Credibility means visibility and stature. Building credibility with the electorate is essential in referenda campaigns. The campaign steering committee and the library's management must be perceived as worthy of handling hard-earned tax dollars. Credibility is rarely built overnight. Public approval of a referendum may well be the culmination of many years of groundwork by the library management. Years of frugal spending and confidence building creates credibility so that the public will trust and believe in the library's issue. No amount of slick public relations and campaign organization can make up for good, solid public representation and administration. Informing voters of the need for a new or improved facility or increased operational funds takes years, not weeks. Richard L. Waters stated this well at an ALA conference program in the early-80s: "Though the campaign may be short, winning bond issues is essentially a long-term proposition, based on how the people have experienced and feel about the library over the years."[2]

Citizen involvement in all phases of the process is essential in developing credibility. Throughout the needs assessment process, the project budget development, and the campaign itself, credibility must be maintained at all costs. In the taxpayers' eyes, it should not be a question of what library supporters are saying about spending tax money; instead, taxpayers should view the campaign as a community effort to allocate the funds from a shared community chest to an obviously worthwhile project which will benefit everyone. If this approach is effectively implemented, a successful outcome is usually a foregone conclusion when the issue finally comes before the voters.

This approach taps into the true meaning of the word "community," which is a sense of common ownership and participation. The steering committee members and in particular the campaign manager must be perceived by the electorate as leaders who have the best interest of all of the people in mind. They must be individuals who have the respect of citizens and who can convince them not only to vote for the issue because it's in their best interest, but also to participate in the campaign to influence others because it is in the best interest of all members of the community. In short, the steering committee members must be able to convince people to buy into the library issue and make it their own. Of all of the individuals on the steering committee, it is most important to find a campaign manager who has these abilities and whose credibility is firmly established.

THE CAMPAIGN STEERING COMMITTEE

CAMPAIGN MANAGER

The campaign manager is the head of the steering committee. Whether called a campaign manager, chairperson, or coordinator, it is usually best to place the campaign primarily in the hands of one person. While input from the steering committee is essential, the best campaigns are not run by committee. "The best campaigns are benevolent dictatorships run by a campaign manager who is a strong leader, a compelling motivator and a good communicator."[3] Preferably, this person should be a well-recognized community leader who has previously had this kind of campaign experience, who is well known by the local press, and who will be a good spokesperson for the campaign. Frequently, the busiest people make the best campaign managers. While the campaign manager may be a figurehead, it is usually preferable that he or she also actively participates in running the campaign. Campaign managers are responsible for the "big picture," but they are also usually involved in coordinating the daily activities of other campaign leaders. That is, the campaign manager should be orchestrating the campaign as a whole and all the while coordinating the committee work of the various steering committee members.

Along with credibility and good political judgement, campaign managers should have sound organizational skills. In short, they should be good managers. They must be able to communicate effectively and they must be able to plan, delegate duties, and set realistic deadlines. Most of all, they should have the time and patience to followup with steering committee members to make sure that the work is being done and on time. While it's not necessary for the campaign managers to be intimately familiar with the operation of the library, i.e., they do not have to be or have been a former library trustee or Friend, it is important that they are at least minimally familiar with the library organization and they must be well informed on the major campaign issues. While it is important to have the campaign manager know about the library, it is far more important that he or she be knowledgeable about local politics and community groups. Finally, although time is always at a premium with community leaders, the campaign manager must be able to commit an adequate amount of time to effectively run the campaign. A good leader who doesn't make the time to do the job won't do the campaign effort much good.

Sometimes campaign planners select honorary or figurehead campaign chairpersons. This is usually done to obtain the visibility that comes with name recognition. In the recent Los Angeles bond campaign, "The board obtained three outstanding library devotees—Ray Bradbury, Charlton Heston, Irving Wallace—as committee chairs."[4] Generally, these figureheads do not attend to the day-to-day campaign activities, because they are primarily lending their names to the campaign. In these cases, a lower visibility campaign manager will have to be named to see that the overall campaign strategy is implemented by coordinating the work of all campaign committee chairpersons, precinct captains, and campaign workers.

CAMPAIGN COMMITTEES

It is impossible for one individual to run all aspects of a campaign. In most campaigns, there should be several committee chairpersons, as well as the campaign manager, to tie together the day-to-day details of running the campaign. The committee chairpersons will be primarily responsible for the routine duties of their individual committees. Each of the committee chairpersons should represent their committee and sit on the overall steering committee. The advantage to this type of campaign structure is that it provides a built in communications system for the campaign organization as a whole. The campaign manager communicates directly with the steering committee members and these committee chairpersons then communicate with their individual committee members, who then can pass necessary information along to precinct captains and ultimately the support troops who are working on the front lines.

This method of communication is invaluable because it not only allows for communications to be effectively made from the "top down," but also provides a built-in mechanism for communication from the "bottom up." This can be particularly important when a campaign is underway and, for example, door-to-door canvassers are continually bombarded with a specific negative issue. These workers can communicate this issue to their committee members and the committee chairperson can then bring the issue to the attention of the campaign manager and the steering committee as a whole for discussion. In this way, all campaign workers will provide an invaluable service by gathering information from the community.

This will be especially vital if adjustments in the campaign strategy are necessary because of an unforeseen problem which arises during the campaign. Without this ability to modify and fine tune the campaign effectively and quickly, a minor issue can become life-threatening to a campaign. It is essential that everyone on the steering committee understands the major campaign issues and has quick and easy access to new information affecting the campaign as it comes up. For this reason, it is important to have frequent steering committee meetings during

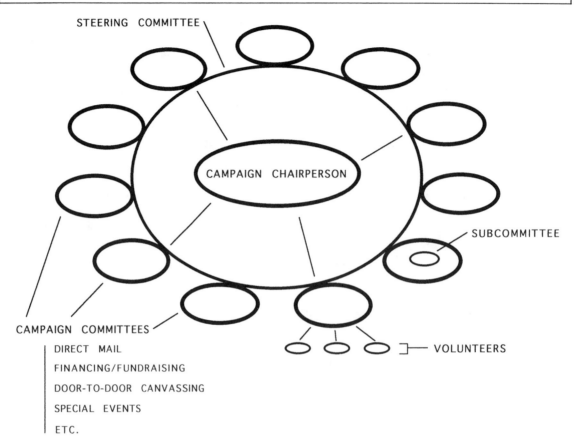

FIGURE 2-1   Campaign Organization Chart

STEERING COMMITTEE

CAMPAIGN CHAIRPERSON

SUBCOMMITTEE

CAMPAIGN COMMITTEES

DIRECT MAIL

FINANCING/FUNDRAISING

DOOR-TO-DOOR CANVASSING

SPECIAL EVENTS

ETC.

VOLUNTEERS

the campaign, especially during the last few weeks of the campaign. Monthly planning meetings may suffice at the very beginning of the campaign, but the frequency will need to increase to twice a month, weekly, or even more frequently if necessary, toward the end of the campaign.

It is essential that campaign committee members and the campaign manager be able to communicate with one another when emergencies arise. This frequently happens at the end of the campaign, and usually tends to come up at the most inconvenient time, like weekends and late evenings. All members of the steering committee should exchange telephone numbers and information on how to reach one another *at any time* during the campaign. Further, it is wise to set up a crisis management team made up of a few unflappable individuals who can act for the campaign when the rest of the steering committee can't be reached.

All of the campaign committees will distribute campaign information in some form, establish and detail the duties of their membership, develop individual committee campaign calendars, and disseminate telephone numbers of campaign workers within their own committees. They must also effectively keep supporters informed of the campaign structure and strategy. In order to avoid conflicts of activities between committees, it is important to document the activities of each committee as part of the campaign plan. Writing down the specific duties of each committee in as much detail as possible leaves nothing to chance. In large committees, it may be wise to even document the duties of individual committee members, especially if subcommittees are formed with committee members becoming the head of various subcommittees. A good campaign manager will assist committee chairpersons in writing their planned committee activities and then make sure that they dovetail with the overall campaign strategy.

Campaign committees can make or break a campaign. The question often comes up: *How many committees should there be and what duties should be assigned to them?* The campaign's strategic plan will answer this question. It is best to start with a relatively small group of committed campaigners on the steering committee and then expand as needed. A steering committee start-up size of five to seven members is ideal. This size group allows everyone to be heard and provides an odd number for decision making if votes are necessary to decide issues. In large campaigns, the number of committee members may have to increase as the campaign unfolds. While not all campaigns will have the same number and type of committees, there are some activities which are fairly standard to all campaigns. While the size of the steering committee, and therefore the number of campaign committees, can vary depending upon the campaign plan as well as the size of the campaign, most campaigns start off with at least some of the following committees:

Financing/Fundraising
Volunteers
Public Relations
Campaign Literature
Direct Mail
Door-to-Door Canvassing
Posters & Yard Signs
Speaker's Bureau
Special Events
Telephone Bank
Endorsements
Voter Registration

The steering committee and various campaign committee planning forms which follow can be used to help organize the preliminary committee assignments. These committees can be limited or expanded as necessary depending upon workload. Subcommittees within each committee can be formed for specific activities which are of short duration. If a subcommittee is formed early in the campaign and it looks like it will be needed throughout the campaign for significant activities, then it probably should be elevated to full committee status with representation on the steering committee.

Assigning the right people to head up the various committees is a challenge in itself. It is generally best to allow people to chair or at least work on committees that they are most interested in since they will tend to do their best work in these positions, but it should be up to the campaign manager to make the committee assignments. The actual size of the individual committees can vary tremendously depending upon the nature of the committee and the amount of work to be done. In some cases, a committee of just a few people will suffice, in

---

FIGURE 2-2   Steering Committee Planning Form

Steering Committee Planning Form

STEERING COMMITTEE:

    Chairperson (Campaign Manager):   _____

    Vice-Chairperson (Finance):   _____

    Member: (Volunteers)   _____

    Member: (Public Relations)   _____

    Member: (Campaign Literature)   _____

    Member: (Direct Mail)   _____

    Member: (Door-to-door Canvassing) _____

    Member: (Posters & Yard Signs)   _____

    Member: (Speaker's Bureau)   _____

    Member: (Special Events)   _____

    Member: (Telephone Bank)   _____

    Member: (Endorsements)   _____

    Member: (Voter Registration)   _____

    Member: (   )   _____

    Member: (   )   _____

    Member: (   )   _____

    Member: (   )   _____

---

other cases the necessity for many contacts in the community (such as the volunteer coordination committee) may dictate a very large committee membership.

The size of the committees also depends upon the size of the campaign. In small campaigns, a committee may literally be run by one person. In larger campaigns, which have to reach many people over a large geographical area, campaign committees may be very large and may even have geographical representation. This geographical approach can be very important where there are multiple and distinct geographical segments of the community. In this case, it may be wise to make sure that each area has representation on each of the major committees.

Finally, it is important to recognize that while the campaign organization is important to any campaign, it is also important not to allow the structure of the organization to get in the way of the effort. In other words, there does need to be some flexibility to make sure the job gets done. If that means that one committee must "borrow" workers from another committee during a crunch period, then that should be able to happen quickly and without dissension or acrimony. Whatever the campaign's structure, the individuals involved must be able to communicate and work together harmoniously in a manner which furthers the library issue.

FIGURE 2-3   Campaign Committee Planning Form

Finance/Fundraising Committee Planning Form

FINANCE/FUNDRAISING:

       Chairperson (Treasurer):   _____

       Vice-Chairperson: _____

       Member: _____

       Member: _____

       Member: _____

       Member: _____

       Member: _____

       Member: _____

       Member: _____

       Member: _____

       Member: _____

FIGURE 2-4   Campaign Committee Planning Form

Volunteers Committee Planning Form

VOLUNTEERS:

       Chairperson: _____

       Vice-Chairperson: _____

       Member: _____

       Member: _____

       Member: _____

       Member: _____

       Member: _____

       Member: _____

       Member: _____

       Member: _____

       Member: _____

FIGURE 2-5   Campaign Committee Planning Form

Public Relations Committee Planning Form

PUBLIC RELATIONS:

Chairperson: _____

Vice-Chairperson: _____

Member: _____

Member: _____

Member: _____

Member: _____

Member: _____

Member: _____

Member: _____

Member: _____

Member: _____

FIGURE 2-6   Campaign Committee Planning Form

Campaign Literature Committee Planning Form

CAMPAIGN LITERATURE:

Chairperson: _____

Vice-Chairperson: _____

Member: _____

Member: _____

Member: _____

Member: _____

Member: _____

Member: _____

Member: _____

Member: _____

Member: _____

FIGURE 2-7   Campaign Committee Planning Form

Direct Mail Committee Planning Form

DIRECT MAIL:

    Chairperson: _____

    Vice-Chairperson: _____

    Member: _____

    Member: _____

    Member: _____

    Member: _____

    Member: _____

    Member: _____

    Member: _____

    Member: _____

    Member: _____

FIGURE 2-8   Campaign Committee Planning Form

Door-to-Door Canvassing Committee Planning Form

DOOR-TO-DOOR CANVASSING:

    Chairperson: _____

    Vice-Chairperson: _____

    Member: _____

    Member: _____

    Member: _____

    Member: _____

    Member: _____

    Member: _____

    Member: _____

    Member: _____

    Member: _____

FIGURE 2-9   Campaign Committee Planning Form

Posters & Yard Signs Committee Planning Form

POSTERS & YARD SIGNS:

    Chairperson: _____

    Vice-Chairperson: _____

    Member: _____

    Member: _____

    Member: _____

    Member: _____

    Member: _____

    Member: _____

    Member: _____

    Member: _____

    Member: _____

FIGURE 2-10   Campaign Committee Planning Form

Speaker's Bureau Committee Planning Form

SPEAKER'S BUREAU:

    Chairperson: _____

    Vice-Chairperson: _____

    Member: _____

    Member: _____

    Member: _____

    Member: _____

    Member: _____

    Member: _____

    Member: _____

    Member: _____

    Member: _____

FIGURE 2-11   Campaign Committee Planning Form

Special Events Committee Planning Form

SPECIAL EVENTS:

Chairperson: _____

Vice-Chairperson: _____

Member: _____

Member: _____

Member: _____

Member: _____

Member: _____

Member: _____

Member: _____

Member: _____

Member: _____

Member: _____

FIGURE 2-12   Campaign Committee Planning Form

Telephone Bank Committee Planning Form

TELEPHONE BANK:

Chairperson: _____

Vice-Chairperson: _____

Member: _____

Member: _____

Member: _____

Member: _____

Member: _____

Member: _____

Member: _____

Member: _____

Member: _____

Member: _____

FIGURE 2-13   Campaign Committee Planning Form

Endorsements Committee Planning Form

ENDORSEMENTS:

Chairperson: _____

Vice-Chairperson: _____

Member: _____

Member: _____

Member: _____

Member: _____

Member: _____

Member: _____

Member: _____

Member: _____

Member: _____

FIGURE 2-14   Campaign Committee Planning Form

Voter Registration Committee Planning Form

VOTER REGISTRATION:

Chairperson: _____

Vice-Chairperson: _____

Member: _____

Member: _____

Member: _____

Member: _____

Member: _____

Member: _____

Member: _____

Member: _____

Member: _____

FIGURE 2-15   Campaign Committee Planning Form

Committee Name Committee Planning Form

COMMITTEE NAME: _____

    Chairperson: _____

    Vice-Chairperson: _____

    Member: _____

    Member: _____

    Member: _____

    Member: _____

    Member: _____

    Member: _____

    Member: _____

    Member: _____

    Member: _____

---

acrimony. Whatever the campaign's structure, the individuals involved must be able to communicate and work together harmoniously in a manner which furthers the library issue.

DEALING WITH CONFLICT WITHIN THE CAMPAIGN

Regardless of how effectively any campaign is managed, there will undoubtedly arise instances where there will be disagreements on how the campaign is to proceed. These disagreements may come from differences in philosophy, campaign strategy or with the campaign methods and techniques being utilized. What is important is that these differences are judiciously brought before the steering committee and discussed with all points of view fully explored. When the steering committee makes a decision, the reasons behind the decision should be communicated to campaign workers and the situation should be monitored for possible future developments.

Sometimes serious internal conflicts occur which threaten to split the campaign workers in such a way that the campaign can no longer be effective. These issues often require a great deal of time and attention on the part of the steering committee and campaign manager. They cannot be ignored. There may be several approaches to resolving these conflicts. It may be possible for the campaign manager to intercede on a personal one-on-one basis and resolve the problem. In other cases, it may be necessary to hold a meeting of all of the steering committee members as well as all applicable committee members and any campaign workers who feel strongly about the issue.

What needs to be accomplished at this kind of meeting is that all points of view are aired and that hopefully for the good of the campaign some form of compromise and consensus can be achieved. If this does not happen, it is entirely possible that the campaign effort will break down and become ineffective. Further, the dissension can even become a negative campaign issue in itself. There is nothing like a rift in the campaign organization to encourage opposition groups and destroy credibility with the electorate. Effective resolution of conflict in the campaign organization is essential if the campaign is to be successful. Frequently conflicts can be avoided altogether, if the responsibilities of all major campaign staff are clearly defined from the very beginning of the campaign through the use of job descriptions and the development of a written campaign plan so that there is no room for misinterpretation.

In order to assist with the development of the campaign plan and strategy, the next step in most campaigns is to hire professionals such as political consultants or pollsters. This should be done as soon as possible after the campaign leadership and organization has formed. It won't matter how well organized a campaign is if it doesn't have some form of research upon which to base a campaign strategy.

REFERENCES

1. Parsons, John W. A. "Landslide Referendum Victories are made in the Streets." *Illinois Libraries* 63:5 (May 1981) p. 383.
2. Waters, Richard L. "Local Sources" in *Facilities Funding Finesse: Financing and Promotion of Public Library Facilities*, Chicago: American Library Association, LAMA, 1982, p. 6.
3. Jean Drodshaug Dugan et. al. *Campaigning to Win: A Workbook for Women in Politics.* Washington, D.C.: National Women's Political Caucus, 1993, p. V-3.
4. Reagan, Robert. "A Tale of Two Bond Campaigns: The Los Angeles Public Library." *Library Journal* 115:11 (June 15, 1992) p. 45.

3 CAMPAIGN CONSULTANTS, MARKET RESEARCH & POLLING

Some of the first questions that face campaign committees are *"Should we hire a political consultant?" "Should we do a poll?"* and *"Do we need professional help with the poll?"* In most cases, the answer to all three questions is definitely "Yes!" unless the campaign is so small or strapped for cash that none of the above is feasible. There are so many important questions that demand answers at the beginning of a library referendum campaign, that it is wise to obtain the best political advice possible, as well as a clear and unbiased view of what the electorate is thinking about the library issue.

In almost all cases, the use of scientific polling techniques as well as seasoned political advisors will significantly improve the chances of success for a ballot measure. Any money spent for either of the two will likely return cost savings in other aspects of the campaign. Further, regardless of how much money is spent on the campaign, having the results of a scientific poll will mean that the funds will be allocated to the most cost-effective methods of reaching the electorate with the most persuasive campaign message. Campaign consultants come in many forms; the most common of these are political consultants, public relations consultants, political pollsters, and market research firms.

POLITICAL CONSULTANTS

Political consultants tend to be the generalists in the field and frequently have knowledge in all aspects of campaigning. In the areas where they are less strong, they sometimes have an on-going relationship with a specialist such as a political pollster. Library campaigners should look for a political consultant who has lots of experience, especially someone who has experience in running ballot issue elections in addition to candidate campaigns. Library planners should try to get the very best possible professional political advice and assistance for their campaign just as they have hopefully gotten the best professional advice from architects and engineers in the design of the library building.

Political consultants should be hired early in the campaign so that they can assist with the political poll as well as the early brainstorming sessions that lay the ground work for the campaign's overall strategy. In order to help ensure success, campaign planners should retain a political consultant or public relations firm to help plan the campaign strategy as well as advise throughout the campaign. While hiring such professional help is most important for larger campaigns or when the political environment is particularly hostile, it can benefit to any campaign. Political consultants generally have a wealth of practical campaign information, tried and true methods of working with the media, as well as political savvy regarding the electorate and important target groups that may not be resident in local campaign planners.

Because a major part of any campaign is communicating with the electorate through the media, public relations firms are occasionally hired to help run a library campaign. These firms understand marketing and they may be of great assistance to a campaign through manipulating the media as well as developing campaign literature. However, unless they specialize in political campaigning, they usually do not have the experience that full service political consulting firms bring to a campaign.

Political consultants command substantial fees (frequently as high as $750 to $1,000 per day), but some are occasionally willing to provide discounts because of the public service aspect of a library campaign. When evaluating either a public relations or political consultant, campaign planners should try to determine what marketing and political skills they are most in need of for the campaign at hand. Although it has been practiced in one form or another for many years, political consulting is not a precise profession. The field has grown in recent years, and practitioner's skills vary tremendously. Generally, those consultants that stay in the business for any period of time develop many skills, take care of their clients, and develop a credible success rate for the campaigns they work on. Therefore, it is smart to talk to some recent clients of any consultant under consideration.

Political consultants are frequently hired using the RFP (Request for Proposal) process. One thing that is important to keep in mind during the selection process, along with experience and track record, is the number of campaigns the consulting firm will be actively working on when the library campaign is in full swing. Firms which take on too large of a work load often can't allocate the time needed by each client, or frequently limit the time of the principals severely so that junior partners or analysts perform most of the work on the library's campaign. Another important consideration is how available the consultants will be in times of emergency—for example, can they be reached on short notice and respond effectively when critical information is needed immediately? Along with their availablity, it cannot be stressed enough that political consultants must have a good grasp on all aspects of campaigning.

To be effective, political consultants have to understand the psyche of the electorate as well as their client. They need to have good media skills, be able to interpret the hidden meaning of poll results, understand the basics of political law, know how to target specific subgroups in the community, and understand how to reach those target groups through telephone and door-to-door canvassing or by designing direct mailing campaigns through the use of computerized databases. Further, they need to be able to assist in planning events and tasks like political dinners, receptions, press conferences, circulate petitions, and organize voter registration drives, as well as understand and counteract any potential opposition. If the consultant can't do all of these things, they should be able to provide campaign planners with contacts of individuals or firms that can provide the needed expertise when necessary.

A political and media consultant was employed with excellent results during a referendum campaign in Chesapeake, Virginia.[1] The campaign strategy developed in part by the political consultant, was successful in overcoming almost insurmountable odds by utilizing relatively inexpensive techniques which were appropriate to the individual community and campaign. The use of a political consultant does not, however, guarantee success. In a recent library referendum in Mountain View, California, the use of a political consultant was not enough to garner the two-third's super majority required in California. Although the library issue received 64 percent of the vote, it was still defeated. While many campaigns do without either public relations firms or political consultants, research shows that both can be very helpful in many situations. In addition to political consultants, many library planners use market research survey and political polling firms.

MARKET RESEARCH SURVEYS

Frequently as a precursor to hiring a political consultant or performing a political poll, library planners will commission a study—loosely termed a "market research survey"—as part of the preliminary planning or needs assessment for the building project. Market research surveys can be general and exploratory in nature or very specific by zeroing in on precise issues and questions of concern to library planners. Along with helping assess the needs for the library project, market research surveys can be used to find the potentially "hot issues" regarding the project that can later be confirmed by polling. To some extent a market research survey can form a bridge between the preliminary planning for the project and the political strategizing for the referendum campaign.

In order to design the survey tool, it is useful for the library management and planning committee to sit down with the market survey group and brainstorm issues and concerns. Frequently, focus groups are used to ensure that important issues regarding the project are not overlooked or underemphasized. Usually as a double check, survey marketing firms perform a pilot survey on a small group of patrons or a representative sample of members of the community to fine tune the survey instrument before it is distributed on a mass basis. Campaign organizers should be aware that this type of study is usually based on the public at large—for example, the community to be served by the library and not exclusively registered voters. Demographic differences (such as educational attainment and income) may exist between these two populations.

Obtaining research surveys can be expensive because they are usually performed by highly trained specialists. However, some market research firms can be convinced to provide an in-kind donation of staff and materials to produce surveys. Further, many large corporations, universities, and other local groups have the staff with the expertise to perform these kinds of surveys, and will do so as a community service project if asked by library planners. All possible avenues for obtaining survey information should be explored.

Because market research is usually performed fairly early in the facility planning stage, it will have an impact on the library management's plan for services and programs as well as in the evaluation of the facility development alternatives. For example, if the library is currently in an old and decrepit Carnegie building, it may not be possible to expand and renovate this facility to suit the library program, but it may be discovered with a research survey, that abandoning the building is political suicide. Many library building campaigns have failed or have been greatly hampered by this very issue. It is best to identify this problem early, if it is present, and address it rather than let it fester and potentially stop the campaign for a new building cold. If the existing Carnegie cannot be cost effectively used as a library, and the reasons are well documented, an alternative use for the facility may need to be part of the overall proposal and campaign.

Market research surveys (and to some extent, political polls) raise awareness of the library issue in the community. Surveying the community is an excellent pre-campaign technique to generate interest in the library issue and lay some ground work for the campaign. Sometimes these surveys can even stimulate the support for the project that they are attempting to analyze. Further, surveying is a democratic process that places the importance of citizen involvement where it should be: at the forefront.

Both market research surveys and political polls gather information about the community, but market surveys are usually paid for by the library jurisdiction or its parent funding agency, while political polls are generally paid for by a separate library campaign committee. There is a very important reason for this distinction. Because the market research report is usually paid for with public funds, it is publicly accessible to all and should consequently be widely disseminated early in the planning process. This document, or an executive summary, often provides the library's public relations department with a valuable pre-campaign tool for getting the library issue before the eye of the electorate, as well as elected officials, without actually "lobbying" politically for a ballot measure.

On the other hand, since the political poll is paid for by a campaign committee—presumably with private political contributions—the results of the poll do not have to be released to the public, media, or anyone outside of the immediate campaign committee. This is particularly important if the poll indicates that the chances of the ballot measure's success are less than outstanding. The ability to withhold the poll results is important in a campaign where there is opposition to the library issue and the campaign planners don't want to give the opposition any more information than absolutely necessary. In other words, there is no reason to share the poll results paid for by campaign funds with the opposition if it will benefit them.

In some cases though, it is wise to disseminate some poll results if doing so will further the purposes of the campaign's objectives. For example, if the poll shows overwhelming support for exactly what the ballot measure would accomplish—for example, building a new branch, remodeling the main library, or adding Sunday hours—it is usually advantageous to release these results at the proper time. Local newspapers are often willing to work with the campaign planners and publish this information in an article, and radio and television stations may even be interested in reporting the poll results and developing a special report on the library issue. This kind of positive "advertising" for the campaign and its chances of success can be extremely valuable in the early stages of a campaign because it sets the stage for the bandwagon which will roll the ballot measure into the victory circle on election day.

POLLS AND POLLSTERS

POLITICAL POLLSTERS

While market research firms and political pollsters both use modern scientific methods of survey research, there is a difference in these two types of firms. It is natural to consider giving the political polling commission to the same market research firm that recently completed an excellent survey research report for the library, but think twice about doing so unless the firm also specializes in political polling. Political polling is a specialty field which requires expertise beyond that available in many market research firms.

Hiring a political pollster is similar to hiring a political consultant. It is better to get one that has considerable experience, particularly in ballot issues when possible, and make certain that the principals in the firm have the time to effectively monitor the library campaign from beginning to end. A good pollster will work with the campaign steering committee to establish the survey questions, perform the survey, analyze the results, and provide written recommendations regarding target groups and the specific campaign message that should be delivered to each of these priority segments of the electorate. In short, the pollster should become an integral part of the campaign's strategic planning committee and, if funds permit, remain so to the end of the campaign by monitoring campaign activities and performing tracking polls just to make sure the campaign stays on course all the way to election day.

Professionally performed political polls are expensive, but they are extremely valuable. The following information provides a guide for budgeting for a poll:

> "Most campaigns budget about five percent to ten percent of the overall campaign budget for research. The costs of a research program are based on the size and scope of the campaign, and there are two key variables—the length of the questionnaire and the number of people interviewed (sample size). A typical benchmark poll contains about 75 response items, and usually takes about 20 minutes to complete.

> "For a high-quality, professional public opinion survey, expect to pay anywhere from $12,000 to $17,000 for a sample size of 400. Shorter, follow-up polls, taken midway through a campaign, are less expensive. Overnight tracking polls taken for fine-tuning near the conclusion of a campaign cost even less."[2]

Although polling costs a significant amount of money, when done correctly, it may be the single most important step in formulating a successful campaign strategy.

When funds are not available to finance a poll, it may be possible for campaign planners to perform their own poll, but this is difficult and time consuming. *If a professional pollster cannot be hired, it is generally not recommended that campaign planners spend any time or money on a "do-it-yourself" effort.* Polling is a scientific discipline and if it's not done properly, the results could be flawed, biased, and downright harmful to the campaign particularly if they are inaccurate or misinterpreted. Having made this disclaimer, the author recognizes that there are library organizations in communities that simply cannot afford the cost of a professionally conducted poll, but would like to have some information about the electorate before beginning a referendum campaign. Frequently, campaign planners can get help from the faculty of political science or survey research departments in local colleges and universities. If these individuals can't construct the survey for campaign planners, they may be willing to at least review the survey questions to make certain that the results will be worth the effort. They may also be available to assist with processing and interpreting the data. This can probably be done at a nominal cost, and may save a great deal of trouble in the long run. The book *"Public Opinion Polling"*[3] is a useful guide to survey research for those who can't afford a pollster.

INFORMAL POLLS

In addition to formal polling, campaigns can perform informal polls while doing telephone and door-to-door canvassing. These activities can provide campaign planners with a "feel" for what is going on with the campaign, but the results are often biased by campaign workers who hear and report only what is positive and not negative. This information should be used with caution for a number of reasons. For example, homeowners may give a canvasser a positive response because they know that is the quickest way to get rid of them. The same can be true of telephone bank calls. Although this information may be useful to some extent in gauging the progress of the campaign, don't allow campaign efforts to be diminished because of it, particularly if the formal polls show that the election is too close to call.

In any campaign, it is always important to listen to what people are saying "on the street." Comments made at shopping malls, in coffee shops, banks, and even beauty salons can provide invaluable information about how the public really perceives the campaign. Listening carefully to the people that one comes into contact with through daily activities is important as an early warning device to detect mood swings in the voters. However, it is also important to test the validity of this information through a representative sampling of the voters. Otherwise campaign planners will fall into the trap of believing only those individuals who happen to fall into their immediate circle of contact.

"Failing to understand that the people with whom you are in touch are often not representative of the district at large can seriously jeopardize a campaign. A poll is conducted with a random sample of likely voters, not just those activists or those with whom you are in contact."[4] Remember, the library issue will be decided upon by all of the voters in a community, and not a small vocal group of individuals. Although many campaigns cannot afford to go beyond informal or "do-it-yourself" polling, others are able to procure in-depth opinion polls to assist them in planning their campaign. Those that can afford a poll have a very definite advantage.

POLITICAL OPINION POLLS

One of the main reasons for library campaign planners to perform a poll is to understand what the position of the electorate is in respect to the library issue. Often this can be accomplished by piggybacking a single question with another poll that is already being performed in the community. Regardless of how it is performed, the intent is to get a preliminary indication if the electorate will support the library ballot measure, and if so, at what level. This type of feasibility poll can be a cost-effective method to "test the waters" before committing to the expense of a full-fledged campaign. The results help the steering committee gauge the chances of success and degree of effort that must be expended in order to be successful.

There are a number of ways to refine the response of those polled in addition to asking a straight "Yes"/"No" question. Frequently, it is important to ascertain how firm the support (or opposition) is for the library question. One can do this by asking the respondents to categorize their support by stating if they are "Definitely supportive" or "Leaning toward supporting" the library issue. The same can be done for those opposed, and even those who indicate that they are undecided can be asked if they are "Leaning for" or "Leaning against" the ballot issue. Another trick to ascertain how firm the support is for an issue is to ask the respondent how he or she thinks their neighbors would vote for the library issue. A large disparity between how respondents say they would respond and how they think their neighbors would respond is an indication that support for the issue may not be all that firm with the electorate. The general approach to understanding the degree of support or opposition can be very helpful, particularly if the election is close and the steering committee needs to know where its support is strongest and where it is marginal.

Performing a preliminary poll to gauge public opinion was used effectively in a Marietta, Georgia, campaign in the 1980s where a voter survey was instrumental in building confidence with local officials regarding the chance of success of the library issue. The preliminary poll showed that the referendum had a very good chance of passing. The decision was made early to run a limited campaign, and the result was an overwhelming (71 percent) victory for the library bond question. A similar strategy was used in the early 1990s in a campaign for the Denver central library and several branches. Based upon preliminary polling information, it was decided to use a "low-key informational effort targeting the most likely voters who were also library users."[5] Since the library issue was already well positioned with the electorate, there was no point in running a high profile media campaign which could create opposition that otherwise would never have formed. Again, this approach worked because the Denver campaign went on to garner a 75 percent approval rate on election day.

Performing a preliminary campaign feasibility poll is frequently important in the effort to convince local officials to place the library issue on the ballot. In communities where funding agencies or even library boards need a push to get the library issue on the ballot, the use of a preliminary poll may prove invaluable. There is nothing like a little political "reality check" to push fence sitters in the desired direction, particularly if the poll shows that the voters are overwhelmingly in favor of the library issue. This is often the case since, as discussed in Chapter 1, library referenda issues pass on average with 63 percent of the vote. Another reason to perform a poll early in a campaign is to use the results to help raise money for the campaign. Campaign fundraisers who can demonstrate a significant chance of success to potential donors are usually well-rewarded because most people are willing to give to a winning cause.

It is possible for a poll to have the reverse effect, however. For example, an early poll may show that the library issue doesn't have a chance of passing no matter how well organized the campaign is. When this occurs, it is frequently wise to assess the reasons for this sentiment and take any corrective steps prior to launching a referendum campaign. There are many reasons that the electorate may not support a library issue. These may include a lack of credibility on the part of the library's management, that the need is not clearly perceived by the public, the economy may be in difficulty, or it may simply be that the electorate feels the amount of increased taxation is higher than they are willing to support.

TAX THRESHOLDS

The issue of taxation is a very important one in most communities, and it is often on the shoals of this issue that many library ballot measures founder. A very important aspect of a political poll is to assess the amount of funding or level of taxation which is likely to be approved by the voters for the library issue. It may be that the referendum amount needs to be adjusted up or down based upon polling results. For example, if a library project will cost $5 million, but the polls indicate that anything over $4 million will not pass, library planners know that they will have to find an alternative way of raising the additional $1 million or face the likely defeat of the measure. Another effective way of asking this question is to specify the actual taxation levels such as $30, $40, or $50 per parcel or the dollar level per $1,000 of property value. Based upon the reported willingness to accept various levels of taxes, campaign planners can determine the maximum tax threshold above which the ballot measure would not be successful.

An example of this approach was performed in the 1994 Voter Survey for the Alameda County (CA) Library:

"With respect to specific tax thresholds, 72% of the respondents indicated support for the tax measure at a $27 per year tax threshold (24% opposed), while 65% of the respondents supported a $38 per year tax threshold (32% opposed). More than half of the respondents were opposed to any tax threshold tested that was greater than $38 per year. An opposition level of 33% will result in defeat of a library tax measure. It is advisable, should the Alameda County Library decide to pursue the measure, for the tax liability to be set at a rate not to exceed $27 per year thereby increasing the level of support and decreasing the level of opposition."[6]

WHEN TO POLL

Obviously poll results need to be known early so that the financing of the ballot measure and the project can be worked out in advance of the campaign. For this reason, the political poll should be held early. It is also important to hold the poll early before the campaign's strategy has been constructed. "A poll should be conducted early, before the campaign begins in earnest, so that the message, the announcement speech, and early walking brochures are all guided by the poll results. It is better to have the message designed right the first time than to spend the rest of the campaign correcting it."[7] The campaign strategy should be based upon these early poll results, but it must be remembered that polls are only good for that point in time in which they are taken.

For this reason and as stated earlier, it is also useful to periodically poll throughout the campaign right up to the last few weeks of the campaign in order to monitor the the campaign's effects and shifts in public perception (especially regarding negative campaign issues such as a poor economy, anti-tax sentiment, etc., since these concerns have the potential to prove disastrous to the campaign's outcome). The ability of campaign planners to recognize shifting trends in voter opinion regarding the campaign issues is facilitated by continuous polling and is often critical to responding to opposition if it develops.

POLL ONLY REGISTERED VOTERS WHO ARE LIKELY TO VOTE

Regardless of when and how often polls should be taken, one of the most critical questions about polling is who to poll. Many political novices attempt to poll everybody. While it is important to get the input from the entire community when planning library services so that the needs of everyone in the service area are met, a political poll should be limited only to *registered voters likely to vote in the upcoming election*. Campaign planners need to know the opinions of those who are likely to vote in the election, not the general public. Frankly, at this point, the opinions of someone who is not registered to vote or who won't make the effort to vote don't really matter to the campaign leadership. This may seem harsh and almost elitist, but when one becomes serious about entering the political arena and campaigning for a ballot measure, it is essential to focus on those who will decide the issue and forget about those who are essentially "cheerleaders on the sidelines."

The key to targeting those who will be deciding the library issue at the next election is to poll registered voters who voted in a similar recent election. The idea is to simulate the upcoming election as much as possible. In other words, if the library issue will be decided at a special election, then it would be wise to poll registered voters who voted in a recent special election, particularly one which decided an educational or cultural issue like a school bond issue or a tax measure to finance a civic center. The closer the match, the more confidence one can have in the results of the poll. Given this, the campaign steering committee needs to acquire a list of registered voters and zero in on those who are likely to vote on the library issue based upon their previous voting behavior. This can be accomplished with the assistance of the pollster and the local elections board or clerk's office.

This approach is valid whether a professional pollster is used or if the effort is an amateur one. For example, if funds are very limited and even volunteers are scarce for polling, it may be possible to perform a crude although reasonably valid poll through the use of a survey published in a local newspaper which is an easy way to get the survey distributed. Unfortunately, results of this type are questionable because of the method of distribution. For example, the opinions of registered voters who cannot read will probably not be accounted for. Even so, this may still be a viable and inexpensive method of discovering the opinions of the targeted registered voters if a simple "screening question" is asked at the beginning of the survey.

For example, the opinions of the targeted registered voters can be separated from those of the public as a whole by asking, "Are you registered to vote, and did you vote in the last school bond special election?" When this is done, the results of the poll can then be tabulated for only those who responded affirmatively to the screening question and the remaining respondents can be discarded or analyzed separately. Not only does this approach provide information from the targeted electorate, but it also cuts down on the processing time for the analysis. The next question that needs to be answered is "How many voters must be sampled?"

SAMPLE SIZE

When surveying or polling, it is necessary to determine an adequate sample size to ensure that there is a reasonable degree of confidence in the results. Because most people don't understand sampling and the mechanics of probability theory, determination of the sample size is best based on the expertise and recommendation of a professional pollster. The determination of the sample size is a case-by-case consideration based on a variety of factors such as the degree of confidence and the margin of error acceptable, the diversity of the population and the variability of opinions in the community, the importance and the size of sub-groups in the population, as well as the type of questions (open-ended versus close-ended) being asked.

Oddly enough, the size of the sample is not highly dependent upon the size of the total population being studied. While the size of the sample does have some impact on the degree of confidence in the results and the margin of error, there is a point of diminishing return where increasing the sample size improves the accuracy of the results only in very small increments. Further, since increasing the sample size adds considerably to the cost of the survey or poll, it is usually best to keep the sample size as low as possible and retain a reasonable degree of confidence in the results.

Pollsters, social scientists, and the public at large consider a 95 percent confidence level with a margin of error no greater than 5 percent to be acceptable. This means that if an issue's approval rate is 60 percent, chances are 95 in 100 that the total population's approval rate will actually fall somewhere between 55 and 65 percent (plus or minus 5 percent on either side of 60 percent). From a practical standpoint, the question still remains: "Approximately what sample size in most communities will provide a 95 percent confidence level with a margin of error of no more than 5 percent?" The answer is not clear-cut. However, the following statement is a reasonable guide for those who don't have access to professional assistance: "It is not the most efficient way to choose a sample size, but 400 residents responding by mail or phone will provide results with a margin of error of plus or minus 5 percentage points, even if opinions are evenly divided."[8]

So for many surveys and polls, a sample size of 400 will be adequate. However, if there is high interest in cross tabulations by sub-groups, particularly multiple cross tabulations—for example: by attitude, by age, by education etc.—and the subgroup populations are relatively small, a larger sample size will be necessary to obtain a reasonable degree of confidence in the subgroup results. As will be discussed later, understanding the opinions of subgroups is very important in political polls and this is why "Most sample size decisions do not focus on estimates for the total population. Rather they are concentrated on the minimum sample sizes that can be tolerated for the smallest subgroups of importance."[9] Ultimately, pollsters consultating with campaign officials must decide how crucial it is for the campaign strategy to increase the size of the sample for more extensive subgroup analysis, and whether the results are worth the increased rates.

A REPRESENTATIVE SAMPLE

One of the most important aspects of any poll, in addition to making sure the sample size is adequate, is ensuring that the sample is representative of the target population so the poll will provide unbiased results. Generally, the key is to randomly select those on the list to be polled. If campaign planners are performing their own poll, this can be accomplished by using a book of random numbers. The goal is to get the opinions of a representative sample of the people who will be voting in the election. Any sample which skews the actual results one way or the other creates problems for campaign strategists. For example, randomly selecting individuals from a registered voter list results in less bias than having campaign volunteers call only those people on the list they already know. Again, the point is to obtain a clear picture of what is in the minds of those who will be voting on the library issue.

SURVEY DATA COLLECTION METHODS

Once the names of individuals to be polled has been determined the next question is how to contact them? There are numerous methods of data collection such as telephone interviews, mailing written surveys, or obtaining information from questionnaires administered individually during face-to-face interviews. A written survey questionnaire can be handed out over the library desk for patron surveys, but this method is difficult to use with targeted political polls. The written questionnaire can be mailed out directly to a representative sample of the targeted registered voters, but the return rate is usually poor. Survey researchers can physically go to the addresses of randomly selected registered voters, but doing so is both time-consuming and expensive. Telephone interviewing is probably the most prevalent method of data collection.

While it is true that local campaign volunteers can be used to perform telephone interviews, this approach should be avoided unless there is absolutely no other alternative. The reasons for this are many, but the most important is that campaign volunteers tend to be biased. Not only will this skew the results of the poll, but campaign volunteers often can't resist trying to convince the individual being interviewed to vote for the ballot issue. This inherent lack of objectivity is one reason why campaign volunteers can't be trusted to deliver unbiased, dependable poll results. Further, volunteers are often significantly slower at performing telephone interviews than trained interviewers. This tends to drag out the time needed to conduct the poll as well as resulting in a higher incidence of incomplete interviews because the interviewee disengages due to the amount of time the interview is taking. A final reason to avoid amateur polls performed by campaign volunteers is that their credibility is often questioned by elected officials and potential campaign donors.

SURVEY QUESTIONS

Determining what questions to ask and asking them in the right way is critical. Careful design of the survey questions is one of the most important aspects of the polling process and is an area where political polling expertise is particularly helpful, because unsophisticated polling efforts tend to bias the questions as well as the answers in order to obtain the desired response. This outcome is counterproductive to both understanding voters' real concerns and helping the steering committee position the campaign to respond correctly to those areas where the library issue may be most vulnerable or to emphasize its strongest areas. In short, if the survey results are nothing more than a reflection of what the campaign planners want to hear, they won't be of much use and a strategy based upon such information will be inherently unreliable.

A meeting between the pollster and the campaign steering committee to determine survey questions is usually the first step towards designing a poll. Obviously, the questions which will be asked are very important. Campaign planners must define exactly what they want to know. It is helpful to brainstorm and ask one another how the information being gathered will be used. Above all, keep the survey simple. Don't bother to ask for information that is not needed, on the other hand, don't be afraid to ask for information if it will be helpful. The key is to design a concise yet inclusive questionnaire structured to facilitate the survey process. For example, the order in which the questions are asked can be important. Sensitive questions (like the income level or age of the respondent) should be placed at the end of a survey since people will usually tend to be more willing to reply if a rapport has been established between them and the interviewer instead of refusing to answer the question or continue with the survey if they had been asked such personal questions "cold" early in the survey.

Regardless of which questions are asked, the survey instrument should be pretested before it is used. This provides a method to determine if there are any confusing questions or other problems which would invalidate the results or make them difficult to interpret. Again, this is where a professional pollster will be of great assistance. Further, the background and experience of a pollster will assist with the crafting of the questions so that the survey will uncover the critical issues that will impact the campaign.

MAJOR CAMPAIGN ISSUES AND ARGUMENTS

Next to understanding the electorate's overall position on the library issue, *the most important reasons to poll are to identify sympathetic target groups and to uncover the campaign messages that will most effectively influence those target groups to support the ballot measure.* Without this kind of information, campaign planners are at a distinct disadvantage. The main strategic advantage of polls is that they help the campaign planning team better understand the areas of strength or weakness in the library issue. One of the main advantages of a properly performed political opinion poll is that it forces the campaign steering committee to take off the rose colored glasses and look at the hard cold facts regarding how the electorate perceives the library issue.

Once the steering committee knows what the electorate believes about the library issue, it can begin to define a campaign strategy which will address the major issues and emphasize the winning arguments. The key is to find out what is important to the voters and then find out how to communicate with them most effectively given the campaign's limited resources. The poll should be designed to uncover the major issues which will affect the campaign so that the steering committee can plan in advance how to best argue the library issue before the electorate. Essentially, a major aspect of any poll is to uncover the "magic bullet" arguments which can both stimulate support for the library issue and diminish opposition.

By polling, the steering committee can find out who will be the main supporters of the issue as well as those groups who will likely become the opposition. Different methods of presenting the library's case to these groups can be tested during a poll. There is no reason that in advance of the campaign different strategies or arguments can't be pretested for effectiveness to see which approach will put the library issue in the best light with the voters. Every community will have both supporters and opponents of the library issue. By testing the various possible arguments in advance, the steering committee will be in the best possible position to control the direction and tenor of the campaign once it starts in earnest. In political campaigns, as with most things in life, it is certainly better to be in control than to be controlled by one's opponents.

As well as identifying opposition groups, polling can also, hopefully, uncover the vulnerable points of the opposition's arguments. The key to doing this is to understand the basis of the opposition. Those who indicate that they are not in favor of the ballot measure during the poll can also be asked: "If opposed to the library issue, what is the reason?" There may be many responses to this question, but usually at least a couple of areas will stand out like "Taxes are already too high" or "I don't like the library site that's been chosen." A frequent citing of any one such reason bears investigating. It may be that a change in the project will be necessary in order for the referendum to pass, an educational effort may be needed, or it may simply be that the library leadership needs to prepare the necessary arguments to fight the opposition.

The steering committee can use arguments which counteract the opposition early in the campaign to disarm the opposition and diminish it from forming or actively organizing. While such a "preemptive strike" approach can be very effective, it can also occasionally backfire and stimulate a more organized opposition than would have otherwise developed. A second strategy is to hold the counter arguments in reserve, ready to be used as a quick response to any last minute attack by the opposition. How information about the opposition will be used in the campaign should be based upon the overall strategy. Frequently, the best campaign strategy is not to respond to the opposition at all, but instead to keep pouring out positive messages that encourage library supporters to get out and vote while ignoring the opposition altogether.

In any case, it is essential to know who the supporters of the library issue are, identify major issues which concern them, and determine which campaign messages will best persuade them to vote in support of the library. It can be very encouraging to campaign planners to find out early that, if they can get the word out about the library issue, the chances of success are good. It can also assist campaign planners to determine if the electorate will respond positively to the planned arguments for the issue. To get an accurate picture of the electorate's perception of the library issue, it is wise to present both the positive as well as the negative arguments for and against the issue. In the 1988 San Francisco campaign, voters were asked if they would support a bond issue for a new central building package and it was found that there was only a 50 percent approval rate. However, other voters who were given the arguments in support of the new building, and then asked if they would support the issue, responded favorably two-thirds of the time. This is a significant increase and particularly important in California where a two-thirds super majority is required to pass a referendum.

In this case, the campaign planners knew that if they could communicate their message to the voters, they would be successful, but if they did not effectively present their arguments for the new building to the electorate, they would probably fail. Obviously, the key in any referendum campaign is uncovering the critical arguments and getting the message out. Identifying "hot buttons" for the library issue is one of the major challenges at the beginning of the campaign. There are a few major positive themes which seem effective in almost all library campaigns.

CHILDREN

The electorate's perception that public libraries are a positive influence for children and young adults is fairly consistent across the nation. In the 1994 statewide California Voter Opinion Poll,[10] 95% of those polled agreed with the statement that libraries play an essential role in the education of children. This is the one argument that most libraries (other than those serving retirement communities) can feel fairly secure using even if they can't afford a poll. However, it is always wise to poll to confirm the validity of this argument in each campaign, as well as fine tune the specifics of how to deliver the message. Obviously, given the usefulness of this argument, library planners should be interested in knowing the percentage and location of households with school-aged children, since parents of school-aged children generally tend to supportive of library issues at the polls. The message about children and the library must be delivered repeatedly to these target households.

YOUNG ADULTS & CRIME

In 1994, 63% of Californians polled felt that well-funded libraries could reduce the crime rate. Since crime is a major issue, this perception may form the basis for a very effective library campaign. Many urban and suburban communities want to provide young people with good, solid alternatives to gang related activities during the after school hours. As an example, a Mountain View, California, poll showed that the single most important argument for a new library project was that there currently was not an adequate amount of space in the existing library for kids during after school hours. New spaces or services addressing this concern, like a supervised "homework center," will frequently be received well by the electorate. One such successful program is the Tobie Grant Homework Library in the Dekalb County Public Library in Decatur, Georgia. In areas where youthful crime is a concern, the beneficial effect of libraries on young lives should be a major campaign message.

LITERACY

Another increasingly popular argument which can be used to the benefit of libraries is the rising awareness and concern regarding literacy. This is particularly effective in regions with a high percentage of individuals who cannot read at a functional level. Most voters care about literacy and want librarians to offer literacy tutoring programs. Librarians can turn this knowledge into votes by developing a solid literacy program. The recently completed South Chula Vista Branch Library, Chula Vista, California, and the Malcolm X Library and Performing Arts Center in San Diego, California, are examples of library buildings that have literacy space specifically designed which will serve as models for many years to come.

NEW ELECTRONIC TECHNOLOGIES

Growing public awareness of the various methods of electronic delivery of information such as CD-ROM and the Internet has increased support for libraries using new technologies in many communities. However, this issue can be a double-edged sword since some people perceive rapidly developing technologies as negating the need for libraries in the future. It is wise to poll to see how the electorate perceives this issue and attempt to find effective arguments ahead of time because in this day and age the issue will likely come up during the campaign. For example, in the 1994 statewide California poll, 63% of the respondents disagreed with the statement that "Due to computers, libraries should not spend more on buildings." Obviously, voters' perceptions in the Silicon Valley may be very different than those in other parts of the country. However, without a poll, campaign planners cannot tell where the electorate stands on the issue and may inadvertently design a campaign message which is exactly the opposite of what should be used to persuade voters to support the library issue.

There are many other local community issues which can be turned into effective campaign arguments for the library issue, but unless a poll is performed they may not be discovered, or at least their effectiveness may not be able to be measured. Polls are not a foolproof method of winning a campaign, but they are a powerful weapon in the arsenal of campaign planners. Campaign planners are simply "shooting in the dark" if they attempt to run a campaign without understanding where the support for the library issue resides and knowing which issues need to form the basis of a cogent campaign message. Often the most compelling campaign messages must be delivered very precisely to specific targeted subgroups in the community. Only through polling can this information be discovered with any degree of confidence.

DETERMINATION OF TARGET GROUPS BY CROSS TABULATION

In order to identify specific target groups, most polls will ask a series of questions which facilitate "cross tabulating" the data to show how various subclasses of the entire sample are likely to respond to the other questions asked in the poll. This process can be extremely helpful in determining how specific groups will vote on election day, as well as how likely they are to respond to various arguments. Utilizing cross tabulation can be very complex and time consuming unless the results are analyzed by computer. While this is yet another reason to use professional pollsters, there are campaign software programs that facilitate cross tabulation. One campaign professional advises clients that "the best buy is campaign software that has polling features along with budgeting, targeting, scheduling, direct-mailing, and word-processing functions."[11]

AGE & SENIOR CITIZENS

Some examples of the usefulness of cross tabulation may be helpful. In order to determine what people of different ages are thinking, it is necessary to ask respondents to provide their age. This is usually done by the interviewer providing a range of ages like "between 35 and 54" or "over 65." Following this approach, the responses to various questions can be sorted by age brackets to reveal not only how strongly the library question is supported by people in various age groups, but also how well these different age groups respond to different arguments supporting the library issue. If the steering committee wants to know how individuals over the age of 65 are planning on voting on the library issue, a database can be queried to select the responses to the appropriate question for only those individuals who responded that they were over 65 years of age. If the sample size is large enough, multiple cross tabulations can be performed in order to obtain even more precise information. For example, the steering committee may want to know how strongly senior citizens responded to a tax levy for automation versus one for increased hours.

It will come as no surprise to many library administrators that national polls[12] consistently show that the older an individual is the less they tend to use the library. Since there is a very strong correlation between use of the library and political support at the polls, this also means that older citizens tend not to support library issues as strongly as younger members of the electorate. This is somewhat of a problem for public libraries since senior citizens tend to vote more consistently than younger ones. Clearly then, it's important that the campaign address senior citizens particularly if there is a significant number of them living in the community. Where there is a high percentage of seniors, as in retirement communities, the library needs to identify issues which are important to seniors and address them positively. Do senior citizens want more large print books, more books on tape, or a better local history collection? Do they want a quiet room they can use without interruption from young adults? Is there a way the library can provide them with meaningful volunteer activities such as literacy tutoring or participating in the "Grandparents and Books" program?[13]

Campaign planners also need to identify the campaign messages which will motivate seniors to vote for the library issue. Finding out that a large percentage of the seniors are very interested in the library's genealogy collection clearly implies a campaign message. Other issues important to seniors may be less obvious. For example, a branch library site on a heavily traveled thoroughfare may seem ideal with respect to visibility to library planners, but it can be a major stumbling block for a ballot measure if the major users are senior citizens who hate to travel on that particular street because of heavy traffic. Finding this out early can literally save a campaign that would otherwise be defeated at the polls.

ETHNIC HERITAGE

Cross tabulation can be performed on any number of questions and levels. Along with the age of individuals, knowledge of their ethnic background can be helpful. If the poll shows that one particular ethnic heritage is strongly favorable toward the library issue, it would be wise to target this group and make sure that these individuals get positive reinforcement and get out and vote on election day. This can be accomplished with a campaign message matched to this group and delivered through campaign literature or other methods. In multicultural communities, it may be wise to deliver the message in the native language of the major support group. In addition to showing that campaign planners are culturally sensitive, this approach may actually have more impact because it may reach more individuals, especially if a high percentage of the voters in this group have a low literacy level in English.

When reviewing poll data regarding the ethnic background of the electorate and planning a campaign strategy, it is important to keep in mind the voter registration and voter propensity rates of the various ethnic categories. For example, in a 1994 statewide California poll, 53% of those polled indicated that they would support a statewide $100 million bond issue for public library construction. Closer inspection of the results revealed that 77% of the Latinos surveyed supported the issue! This appeared to clearly show a demographic subgroup which should be targeted in any statewide campaign. However, further investigation revealed some interesting facts. The survey sample for the poll was composed of voters who had voted in the previous November general election. When the ethnic breakdown of the voter sample was analyzed, it showed that only 8% of the people who voted in the previous general election were Latino. The implications were clear. Even though Latinos would support the library issue strongly, they have not been voting at a high enough rate to produce the raw number of votes needed to warrant a concentrated targeting effort, i.e., 77% of only 8% of the likely voters would not produce enough actual votes to justify a high expenditure of campaign funds in targeting this subgroup.

EDUCATIONAL LEVELS

The educational level of the electorate can be a very significant factor in a campaign. A recent Harris poll demonstrates the high degree of correlation between library use and the educational level:[14]

Education Level	% Who Have Used Library In The Last Year
Less than High School	48%
High school graduate	61%
Some college	81%
College graduate	83%
Postgraduate	90%

It is certainly understandable why this correlation between library use and education exists, and in most cases it will probably generalize to most local library campaigns and be a realistic indicator of voter support. However, local library planners need to verify the correlation by polling on the library issue in their own community since there may be other issues at play in any given locale.

INCOME LEVELS

Once again, polls show that public library use increases as household annual income level increases, although the difference between the top and the bottom of the scale is not as dramatic as with the level of education. While higher income level neighborhoods usually strongly support library issues, lower income level neighborhoods have on occasion been known to turn out strongly in favor of library issues as well. In a recent campaign in Pasadena, California, the precinct with the lowest income levels most strongly supported the library issue.

While there is a high degree of correlation between library use and voter support, the income factor can occasionally throw library planners a curve in another way. This usually happens at the extreme upper end of the scale with households of over $75,000 per year. In some communities, households in this upper income bracket tend to be fairly conservative in political ideology, and this combination frequently results in somewhat of a downturn of voter support.

POLITICAL IDEOLOGY & PARTY

Generally, Liberals and Democrats tend to support library issues at the polls more than Conservatives and Republicans. As one might expect, moderates and independents fall in the middle of the two extremes of the political spectrum. However, libraries are frequently able to transcend partisan politics and these categorizations may not be as meaningful as some others when planning a library strategy based on polling data.

HOME OWNERSHIP

Home ownership can be a very important factor, especially if the ballot measure will raise property taxes. Increased taxation is one of the major hurdles that any ballot measure must overcome. Because of this, it is frequently wise to poll homeowners to see if there is an alternative financing method which is more acceptable. It may be, for example, that homeowners are more supportive of a library ballot measure based upon a parcel tax and assessed at a flat and fixed level for all homeowners instead of an *ad valorem* property tax which increases with the value of the property. If this information is uncovered early enough through polling, it may be possible to structure the ballot measure to accommodate homeowners. Clearly, if this is done, the main campaign message which should be emphasized to homeowners is self-evident. Sometimes a library ballot measure can be sold to homeowners on the premise that the new library facility will actually put money in their pockets in the long run. If the construction of a new library is seen by homeowners as a good way to maintain or even increase the property values of homes in their area, campaign planners may have discovered the best possible message that could be delivered to homeowners.

VOTER PRECINCTS

The views of the electorate by geographical location has long been considered important to campaign planners. Most polls are performed from registered voters lists and the precinct number of the voter has already been identified. If not, the question can be included in the questionnaire. Knowing the predisposition of voters by precinct can be extremely helpful when, for example, door-to-door canvassing is performed in various neighborhoods. Again, the campaign message can be specifically tailored by precinct. This is not to suggest that library campaigners should be saying one thing in one neighborhood and the exact opposite in another, but that different aspects of the library issue should be emphasized or deemphasized depending upon the territory that the campaign's volunteers are working.

GENDER

While there are variables from community to community and library to library, nationally there is a statistically significant difference between the amount of use of the public library by men and women. Women tend to use the library 5–10% more often than men. Many local opinion polls have also shown that women tend to support library issues at a somewhat higher rate than men and they tend to be swayed by supportive arguments more than men. Clearly, it may be helpful for local library campaigns to target women for the voting booth.

MEDIA SOURCES

In addition to their physical location, understanding the predominant ways that voters receive information and entertainment can be useful in a campaign. Knowing which forms of media will have the greatest impact on potentially supportive voters can be very important, particularly when campaign resources are limited. For example, if campaign planners are trying to decide how to best allocate their projected advertising budget, it may be helpful to ask which radio stations the voter listens to or which cable television channels they watch most frequently. This information will help campaign planners to buy media time in a manner which will most effectively reach the targeted electorate. The same is true if there are competing newspapers in an area or various neighborhood supplements or "readers" which have lower advertising rates.

GENERAL QUESTIONS

Along with a series of specific questions, campaign planners may want to ask a few general questions like "Are things in the community going in the right direction?" "Generally, is the library management on the right track?" or "How would you rank the quality of services provided by city government?" This is helpful to determine if there is a general credibility problem with the library's or the city's administration. The problem may be directly related to the library project, or it may simply be that the electorate is mad at "City Hall" and the situation will change in a few months. Clearly, it's not to the library's advantage to have the electorate vent their anger at City officials on the library ballot.

OPEN ENDED QUESTIONS

It is often helpful to have an open-ended question at the end of all surveys and polls that allows individuals to bring up concerns or issues which campaign planners have not thought about. In this way, the survey or poll can provide important factual information to the campaign planners that would otherwise never be considered. This information can then be evaluated and included in more precise form in later surveys or polls in order to develop a larger opinion base. Sometimes polls can uncover completely unexpected issues which campaign planners were unaware of and which might have been devastating to the campaign if they had not been identified and addressed early in the campaign strategy. This reason alone can be one of the most important aspects of conducting a poll, particularly if campaign planners aren't seasoned political activists in the community.

REFERENCES

1. Hall, Richard B. "Winning a Bond Issue for a New Library; The Chesapeake, Virginia, Campaign" *The Bottom Line* 3:2 (1989), pp. 22–27
2. Meadow, Robert G. and Heidi von Szeliski. "10 Myths About Political Polling" *Campaigns & Elections* 14:3 (August 1993), p. 50.
3. Lake, Celinda C. I. with Pat Callbeck Harper. *Public Opinion Polling: A Handbook for Public Interest and Citizen Advocacy Groups.* Washington, D.C.: Island Press, 1987.
4. Meadow and Szeliski, p. 49.
5. Floyd Ciruli. "Library 1990 Campaign Press Coverage." Denver, Colorado: Ciruli Associates, September, 1990.

6. Kent Price. "Alameda County Library 1994 Voter Survey." San Ramon, California: Price Research, 1994, p. 51.
7. Meadow, and Szeliski, p. 50.
8. Miller and Miller, p. 39.
9. Floyd J. Fowler. *Survey Research Methods*. Newbury Park, California: Sage Publications, 1988, p. 42–3
10. Binder, David, *California Voter Opinion Poll*. Sacramento, CA, California Library Association, 1994.
11. Duquin, Lorene Hanely. "The Pluses and Minuses of Do-It-Yourself Polling." *Campaigns & Elections* 5:3 (Fall 1984), p. 20.
12. Westin, Alan F. and Anne L. Finger, *Using the Public Library in the Computer Age*. Chicago: American Library Association, 1991, pp. 26–27.
13. Wade, Maureen and Susan Patron, *Grandparents and Books Trainer's Manual*. Los Angeles, California: Los Angeles Public Library, 1991.
14. Westin and Finger, pp. 15–17.

4 CAMPAIGN STRATEGY

OVERVIEW OF THE CAMPAIGN STRATEGY

The most important aspect of any campaign plan is the determination of an all encompassing campaign strategy. Such a strategy is not just an assortment of campaign tactics, but a cohesive way of viewing and taking into account all aspects of the community, its voters, the library's project, the campaign environment, and the current political climate. The strategy must not be some esoteric ideal of how the campaign "should" be run, but a very practical "nuts and bolts" tool for planning and implementing the campaign. The goal of any campaign strategy is to convince a majority of voters to vote for the library issue. As a result, the campaign strategy must answer the question, *"What does the campaign have to do in order to get the necessary majority of voters to approve the ballot measure?"*

Voters are often predisposed to vote against issues that will affect their pocketbooks unless given a very good reason not to, and so the challenge of any campaign strategy is to give the electorate a good reason to vote "Yes" for the library issue. While it is important to do this with as many voters as possible, campaign resources are always limited. There is never enough time, money, or volunteers to do what is often desired to support a library issue, so planners must design a strategy which utilizes the resources that are available to the best extent possible. Developing a campaign strategy requires planners to make decisions about how to run the campaign in the early planning stages. However, the advantage to making these choices through strategic planning is that they will be made based on a process of logically weighing competing alternatives, and not on the arbitrary basis of simply running out of time, money, or volunteers late in the campaign.

Establishing a campaign strategy requires information, political savvy, flexibility, and discipline. Campaign planners should force themselves early on to develop a campaign strategy, and then write it down as the beginning of a campaign plan. The strategy should include both a broad general strategic approach and specific tactics and activities. While major strategic directions are essential, detailed specifics about the campaign techniques that will be used and when, are also important. The more specific campaign planners can get, the better. For example, will the campaign run ten radio spots twenty times each during the last week of the campaign or will it mail out flyers to 20,000 targeted voters on the east side of town four days before the election? The right answer to this question can mean the difference between victory and failure in a close campaign.

Without a strategy, it is far too easy to squander limited resources and find that campaign volunteers are wasting their time working on ineffective activities, or that precious campaign funds have been expended for purposes that provide few votes. An effective strategic plan brings campaign workers together in the knowledge that they are working in the most effective way possible to reach their common goal. This knowledge usually promotes a greater willingness to work long hours for the campaign when it becomes necessary. The degree of commitment and effort on the part of campaign workers is not only related to the belief in the cause, but also to their confidence in the approach to the campaign.

STRATEGIC QUESTIONS

Through the use of effectively applied strategic questions invaluable information can be ascertained for running a successful campaign.

- What do we have to do to convince a majority of the voters in our community that they want to tax themselves for a new library building or expanded library services?
- Who are the voters that will most likely vote for the library issue?
- What kind of campaign techniques will we need to use to win a referendum in our community?
- When should we use specific campaign tools?
- How much money will it take to run an effective campaign?
- Will the campaign be a "grassroots" one relying heavily on volunteers?
- How long should the campaign run?
- Will the campaign be a hard fought, highly charged emotional one; or will it be a low key, low profile one?
- Will there be any opposition, and if so, who are they and what is going to be the main argument they use against the library issue?
- What is the ballot competition?
- Are there other highly divisive issues about to be placed before the voters?
- Can we establish mutually beneficial coalitions with other groups in the community?
- Should the referendum be held during a general or special election?
- What does the current and future economic climate look like?
- What are the critical win/fail issues?
- What should the main campaign message be?
- Which people in the community should be targeted?
- In which precincts should we campaign the hardest?

A strategic plan will need to address all of the above questions and more, but it cannot be borrowed from a previous campaign. The strategy should be specific to the individual campaign and will have to be based on the local situation. A campaign strategy that works well in one library referendum may fail miserably in another; therefore, each campaign must be tailored to the specific community and its own political zeitgeist.

THE START OF A STRATEGIC PLAN

The first draft of the campaign strategy should be developed shortly after the steering committee forms. A second, and more realistic draft, usually comes right after the results of any initial poll or market survey have been made available to campaign planners. The strategic plan should focus on this information, any available demographic information about the community, as well as previous voting records. The campaign strategy will also have its roots in the needs assessment and any other preliminary planning for the project. The strategic plan should outline in as much detail as possible the general tone and major issues of the campaign. Both the major strengths and weaknesses of the library issue should be identified.

Formulating a successful campaign strategy is the art, as well as the science, of political assessment. In the beginning, planners should begin by brainstorming, and then discussing numerous possible scenarios for the campaign without judgmental comments. After all possibilities and variations have been thoroughly explored, the steering committee should attempt to synthesize the best possible strategy or strategies for the campaign. Political consultants can greatly enhance and expedite this process because their background and experience enables them to get to the heart of the matter quickly and disregard relatively unimportant information.

It may be important to develop alternative options in case there is a turn of events which would significantly alter the campaign environment and necessitate change in the campaign. In any event, one primary plan should be developed which best meets the current circumstances known at the beginning of the campaign effort even though it may be refined as the campaign proceeds. Coming to consensus on this plan may take considerable effort in some cases, but it is essential to come up with a workable plan that makes sense to most all of the campaign planners.

As stated earlier, developing a strategic plan early in the campaign is critical. It is not uncommon to begin planning six months or more prior to the election. It is also important to start early to begin the process of raising awareness of the problem in the community the referendum addresses. These two processes can go hand in hand. As the steering committee starts to form and the strategic plan is developed, press releases can be issued indicating that a citizens' group is forming to assist the library with its "problem."

"What problem?" some may ask. This question provides the opportunity to start the long process of explaining the library issue. These early inquires allow the steering committee the opportunity to explore various options and test different arguments as well as begin to hone their own persuasive skills. Some leaders may find that they are not as informed about the issue as they thought when they can't effectively explain the situation to others. It is best to discover this and correct it early in the campaign rather than later.

At this preliminary stage, steering committee members need to do lots of low key talking, but more importantly, they need to do a lot of listening. They should seek campaign advice from elected officials and other community leaders. This approach both informs these individuals about the issue and helps planners gauge their support (or lack thereof). It also is a good way to begin to recruit campaign supporters and volunteers. Most importantly, this preliminary information provides a basis for discussion in the steering committee and begins to position the campaign strategically, by identifying sensitive emotional areas that may become major campaign issues and to develop effective arguments.

ADJUSTMENTS IN THE CAMPAIGN STRATEGY

When the final draft of the campaign strategy has been completed, it should be shared with the full steering committee. This will make certain that there are no misconceptions and will help to ensure a smoothly run campaign organization. Remember, the campaign strategy doesn't have to be lengthy, but it should be comprehensive and detailed enough to be useful. It should also be updated throughout the campaign as necessary. The campaign strategy should not become a rigid doctrine that cannot be modified, but should be fluid and adjusted as the campaign proceeds and circumstances warrant.

This is not to say that the campaign strategy should whipsaw wildly throughout the campaign by desperately trying to respond to attacks from the opposition. Changing strategy in midstream numerous times in response to the opposition only allows one's opponents to define the campaign issue. While it is usually better to find the best strategy early and stick with it, planners must monitor the strategy's effectiveness throughout the campaign and be aware of the opposition, the political atmosphere, and new information gained through polling. If the strategy needs to be modified to respond to an important issue, it should be done so *only* after thoughtful consideration on the part of the entire steering committee.

Dealing with the Unexpected

Because campaigners must be prepared to deal with the unexpected, their strategy must be flexible. This is particularly important if an unexpected issue comes up. If, for example, the economy suddenly goes south, or property owners find out their assessments are being increased dramatically right before the election, the impact on the campaign may be devastating unless campaign planners can respond effectively and recover. It pays to be vigilant because there are many potential ways that library campaigners can get blind sided just before the election. There could be an outcry from the public over local officials getting large salary raises or a controversy over the construction of some other public facility that has no relation to the library.

Sometimes last minute developments are not always bad. Occasionally events happen that actually help a library referendum. For example, shortly before the referendum for the Statesboro (Georgia) Public Library, a fire devastated the existing library. Voters turned out and passed the library issue, in part, due to a "sympathy vote." Anything can happen, like the earthquake that hit just before the referendum in Menlo Park, California. If the steering committee is prepared, these kinds of unfortunate events can be capitalized on and turned into opportunity. The rewards for the campaign planners "being on their toes" may be substantial, especially in a close campaign.

However, even though the campaign should be able to respond quickly and effectively to a sudden turn of events, it is important to do so with careful consideration and caution especially if the event is negative. Library supporters should attempt to run a proactive campaign rather than a reactive one. When the library campaign only reacts to the opposition, library supporters are in effect letting the opposition define the issues for the campaign. For example, it is not in the best interest of a campaign to allow itself to be placed on the defensive and be constantly responding to negative questions from an opposition group particularly in the last few days of the campaign. In these cases, it is very important to "stay on course" with the strategic approach already mapped out and to not panic because of the last minute smear tactics. Be forewarned that one commonly used technique for opposition groups is to attack an issue very late in the campaign and provide inaccurate and damaging information which gets headlines and attracts the attention of voters just before going to the polls. This occurred in the Loudoun County, Virginia, campaign when the opposition took out a full-page ad in the local newspaper in the waning days of the campaign and referred to the "sheer extravagance"[1] of the library project.

This kind of last minute propaganda can be detrimental if the steering committee does not have time to respond appropriately. One approach to combat this problem is for the steering committee to plan a last minute offensive maneuver of its own. Since the last few days of the campaign are so crucial, the steering committee may want to plan a special feature article in the Sunday paper before election day or reserve funds for a last minute advertisement to rebut any false claims from the opposition

THE DECISION TO ACTIVELY CAMPAIGN OR NOT

When strong opposition to a library issue is possible, sometimes the most important strategic decision is not to campaign at all. There are occasions when the best campaign is a low profile or even invisible one (however, make sure this approach is not being selected just because there's less effort involved than running an active campaign). If there is potential opposition from a very strong anti-tax group, for example, it may be best to try to blend into the political landscape and not put the issue strongly into the public eye through the media. Martha Schaer, Director of the Newton, Iowa, Public Library stated this quite well when she remarked, "Our goal was to identify "Yes" voters and get those people out to vote. We deliberately avoided conducting a media campaign under the assumption that publicity would generate as many "No" votes as "Yes" votes. We were working against tremendous odds, and we determined that our goal was to win, not to educate!"[2]

Sometimes, a campaign may be won before it has begun, and the only thing that an active campaign may do is bring out the opposition that might not have otherwise formed. Further, if the outcome of the ballot question is a foregone conclusion, it may simply be a waste of time and effort to formally campaign. While a limited or "non-campaign" can occasionally be the best tact, this is the exception and not the rule. If the decision is made to actively campaign, it behooves the campaign workers to *never take the outcome of a referendum for granted*. It is always best to never let up, but keep working hard right up until the polls close on election day. Regardless if the campaign will be low key or an all out effort, or if there is opposition or not, emphasizing certain aspects of the public library can help any campaign.

THE POLITICAL ADVANTAGE OF THE PUBLIC LIBRARY

During the development of the strategic plan, the campaign leadership should always keep in mind that the public library has a tremendous political advantage from the outset in that it is generally highly regarded by the public. For the most part, public libraries are like "Mom, apple pie, and the American way." It is wise to make effective use of this intrinsically positive image, and, like all good bandwagons, ride it as far as it will go. Politicians would pay big bucks for this kind of advantage, which libraries have from the start. The following public perceptions should be considered when planning campaign tactics.

EDUCATION

Most people feel the library is an important part of the educational system. In fact, public libraries have become an integral part of the American educational ideal of life-long learning beyond traditional secondary school and university course work. Libraries are essential in fostering an informed electorate, and they help prevent illiteracy. Finally, don't forget that people love books! Use the power inherent in this affinity for learning and knowledge to the campaign's advantage.

QUALITY OF LIFE

Libraries are considered to be an important quality of life issue in most communities and an integral part of the civic fabric. The availability of books and media are essential to support recreational reading as well as serious research. Further, the public library is becoming the basis for the "electronic libraries" of the future which will foster greater access to knowledge through the "information superhighway." The public library can be relatively easily sold as an "on ramp" to the information superhighway especially in communities where the purchase of a home computer is not economically feasible for most people.

ECONOMIC DEVELOPMENT

Libraries are generally recognized as beneficial to attracting new business or industry. Increased business investments in a community creates jobs and economic growth and frequently results in increased residential property values. Libraries foster economic opportunities and increased productivity for those who use them. By providing access to information, libraries allow citizens to become more competitive in the world marketplace. One of the major causes of small business failure is the lack of management information which public libraries can provide.[3] It should also not be overlooked that the new library project will create construction jobs in the community which will also provide an economic stimulus. This aspect can be particularly important during recessionary periods.

SERVICE TO ALL SECTORS OF SOCIETY

It is usually recognized that libraries serve all sectors of society: children, young adults, adults, senior citizens, wealthy, middle-class, poor, the well-educated and those seeking literacy skills. All individuals, regardless of their ethnic or cultural background, benefit from public library services. Libraries promote the well being of the community in general and therefore have a connection with all individuals in the community.

QUALITY OF LIBRARY SERVICE IN THE PAST

Research shows that library administrators feel that the past quality of library service provided by the library is the second most important determinant of referenda success.[4] This demonstrates that working hard to satisfy consumers may well be rewarded by a public mandate for improved physical facilities, and provides an incentive to library staff and management to do as good as possible regardless of existing conditions and funding.

It is relatively easy to perform a survey to determine the general satisfaction level of the public with existing library service. If such a survey reveals the satisfaction level is low, a second one can focus on the reasons for dissatisfaction. In many cases, the existing condition of the present library or limited operating hours may be listed as one of the primary reasons for dissatisfaction. If this is the case, the steering committee has a tangible argument. All that is needed is to effectively promote awareness of this shortcoming, and the resulting need.

AWARENESS RAISING

"In many ways, the library issue sells itself. But a product, no matter how wonderful it is, will remain unpurchased unless people know about it."[5] Raising awareness regarding the library and the placement of the library question on the ballot is often critical to the success of any referendum. To a large extent, this is what a library campaign is all about—informing the public of the issue. Campaign planners should keep in mind that the success rate of library referenda is very high with approximately 77 percent of all referenda reported in the last eight years having passed. While library campaigns are generally not as well financed as other types, libraries can promote themselves by informing the electorate; after all, libraries *are* in the information business. How well and how frequently the library's case is presented to the voters may be the most important aspect of any library campaign.

A low-key approach can simply raise awareness without looking like a political campaign. For starters, simply promote the library services and programs already offered by the library more strenuously than in the past. The library staff can hold readathons or AV festivals and generally step up both its adult and children's programming during the year before the election. Bring in special speakers and authors who attract a crowd and who are willing to explain the benefits of the library and talk a little about how it helped them in their youth. The Friends group can be especially helpful in this realm by hosting receptions, dinners, and luncheons. Holding library card registration drives at local shopping centers or government buildings can be a particularly effective technique as well.

PUBLIC SERVICE ANNOUNCEMENTS (PSAs)

Public Service Announcements (PSA) can be an effective way to "soft-sell" the library to the electorate. PSAs can inform, but they cannot be used to explicitly promote a "Yes" vote. PSAs can cover any number of topics and can be run in newspapers as well as on television and radio stations. PSAs can start early and be run right up to the election date. They are probably most effective when they look like endorsements by influential community leaders and politicians. The Dekalb County Library System utilized this approach effectively by running PSAs throughout the campaign, and most frequently in the two weeks immediately preceding the election. They featured several local dignitaries including the chairman of the County Commission, several prominent local authors, as well as a respected state legislator and library board member who was also a member of the community's predominant minority group.

While none of these PSAs ever mentioned voting "Yes" for the library issue, most people make the connection of a positive image at election time with the library ballot question. This approach is a very cost-effective way to advertise the library and should not be overlooked.

THE NEED FOR A NEW OR IMPROVED LIBRARY FACILITY

If the referendum would finance a new facility, it goes without saying that there should be a demonstrable need for a new or improved library building to justify putting the issue on the ballot. The question is, has a thorough community-based needs assessment been performed? If the needs assessment has been completed, then the step of defining the need is done; if not, it is wise to postpone the campaign until this process is completed. The best way to win support for the library project is at the grass-roots level. It is always best if local citizens have been actively involved in the needs assessment process. Citizens representative of the community should oversee not only the needs assessment, but also the development of the master plan for facilities and even the writing of the building program. A grass-roots understanding of the beginning phase of the plan provides invaluable, broad-based support as well as potential volunteers for the campaign organization.

Again, research has shown that library administrators believe that the need for the new or improved library building was the single most important factor in those campaigns that passed, but it was one of the least important factors in those campaigns that failed.[6] Are we then to assume that libraries with referenda that failed really did not need the new or improved building? Even though this is unlikely, it can still be the public's perception. Further, the need may have been there, but not adequately communicated to the public. This further points out the importance of having credible community leaders on the planning team who can effectively sell the library issue to the electorate.

It may also be necessary to persuade the electorate by marketing or "selling" the need for a new or improved facility. As with selling any product, the campaign steering committee must convince the public that they can't live without the good library service which can only be provided by a new or improved building. The approach of playing on local community pride is often effective in accomplishing this goal. If a nearby community has recently built a new public library building, it may be possible to compare this "wonderful, new library" with the "existing, dilapidated, worn-out, poor excuse for a public facility" which currently exists at home. However, what is obvious to the library administration may not always be so self-evident to the public. The story must be effectively communicated.

In order to do this, it is essential for the steering committee to obtain all of the pertinent "facts and figures" regarding the need and the recommended solution. If the steering committee members are uninformed on the issue, they can not hope to inform the public. Further, the steering committee must not only be informed, but must be intimately acquainted with this information so that they can be conversant on a moments notice at a public gathering or during an impromptu interview. As will be discussed more fully in later chapters, there is much to learn about how the library's need can be effectively communicated through campaign literature such as fact sheets, flyers, brochures, "glossies," and the like. It is possible to get the attention of voters by packaging important points in campaign literature which define the need for the library in a manner that appeals to them both rationally and emotionally.

EMOTIONAL ISSUES

Sometimes no amount of detailed study, facts, figures, or statistics will convince the public of the need if they are not aware of what good library service is or do not understand why or how their community's library is substandard compared to others. It is necessary to humanize the issue as much as possible. This is where public relation techniques become important. While it is important to have the necessary reports and statistics in hand, it is also important to present that information in a way that "grabs" people emotionally. Using a public relations firm or someone in the campaign with some marketing experience and a good graphics artist can help sell the library issue with effectively designed campaign literature and media advertising that appeals in a positive way to voters' emotions. The facts must be presented in a straight forward manner, but it is important to add an emotional "hook" to produce sympathy and ultimately

FIGURE 4-1   Grandfather and Granddaughter, Tulsa, Oklahoma. Provided Courtesy of Tulsa City–County Library System, Tulsa, OK.

support at the polls. Campaign planners simply need to discover what will work in each local community to convince taxpayers that they want to invest in good library service.

Knowing which emotional issues motivate voters is essential. A dry and logical campaign that does not touch the voter in some way will often fall flat, and one that plays on the heartstrings will frequently rally its constituency. Most people vote based upon their emotions as much as their logic. There are many potential emotional issues which can be effective. In some suburban communities, promoting the education of children is one of the best. In other communities, providing services to senior citizens is more appropriate. These areas are the basis for a visual campaign which shows children or seniors in a positive way. Photos of children with books can be an inspiring visual tool for the campaign. The San Francisco and the Atlanta-Fulton County campaigns both utilized this approach effectively by producing various campaign ads and brochures which featured emotional appeals regarding the children in the community. An emotional appeal regarding both seniors and children was successfully used in the Tulsa, Oklahoma campaign as can be seen in the photo in Figure 4-1 of a grandfather and granddaughter reading.

VISITS TO RECENTLY BUILT LIBRARY FACILITIES

Community pride is a very powerful emotional issue that library campaigns can exploit. Sometimes it is helpful to organize visits to nearby recently constructed facilities for local officials and influential community leaders as well as library planners. This kind of trip can be ideal especially if a bus or van can be borrowed or rented for the participants because library promoters then have a captive audience for the entire trip to and from the nearby facilities. All during this trip, library promoters can explain the shortcomings of the existing library and do a little "arm twisting" to gain support and potentially even commitments from those whose support is necessary to get the issue on the ballot or help have it approved by the electorate. These trips usually work because very well-built, attractive new public libraries tend to sell themselves. It is not uncommon to have participants come back from these trips all charged up and ready to campaign to get the same kind of educational opportunity for their own community.

RESEARCH

Regardless of the campaign, the steering committee must find the pertinent social and emotional issues which will motivate the electorate and provide sufficient impetus to vote for the library issue. Is it that our young adults don't have anything do to in the community, and they are all getting into trouble and into drugs? Or is it that the SAT scores for our college bound students have fallen dramatically in the last few years? Sometimes it takes a considerable amount of research to find the important issues around which the campaign should be positioned. Once campaign planners identify these, they can effectively plan a campaign strategy. Campaign planners must be as sure of the issues as possible since most of the campaign literature and advertising will be based upon this research.

Where does one go to identify the critical issues in a community? As discussed in Chapter 3, a political poll is an excellent way of determining the critical campaign issues. However, if funds are not available for a poll, scan community newspapers in the library's collection for just this purpose for the last year or two. Attend City Council, County Commission, Parent Teacher Association (PTA) meetings, etc. Talk with political leaders and community leaders. Don't forget the library staff, particularly the circulation and reference staff, who are on the "front lines" and who meet and talk with potential voters every day. It is surprising how many good campaign issues can come from canvassing the public service staff of the library. The staff knows a lot about the community because they know what they ask for when they call or come into the library. Sometimes it is helpful to hold focus groups at the library on community affairs and issues. This will undoubtedly give campaign planners an inside track on any emerging community concerns.

Look for trends in issues. Don't focus on an issue which has recently been solved and is, in effect, "old news." Look for what is on the horizon or is currently heavily discussed at dinner parties and other social events. Is the library's low number of books per capita a major point of discussion at these activities? Not likely. It's not that these kinds of issues aren't important, it's just difficult to get very excited about statistics. However, if an emotional issue can be created around the small size of the library compared to libraries in nearby communities or the relatively limited supply of books, then such an issue should be fully developed. The object is to create an emotional connection between the library and the voter; it doesn't really matter how it's done. Political campaigning can, in part, be defined as the process of affecting change by manipulating the electorate. If this sounds a little too Machiavellian, keep in mind that the library is a positive force for good in any community. Library managers often quickly learn that political campaigning can be a hardball game. If they are not willing to play the game by the rules necessary to win, it's usually better not to play at all.

It is important to identify both positive and negative issues which carry a high degree of emotional content. What is the local sentiment towards new taxes? What does the general state of the economy look like? Are there organized opposition groups waiting to pounce on any new bond offering? If the answer is yes to any of these questions, it may be wise to delay the referendum until the situation improves. If this is not feasible, or if the opposition is likely to remain for a significant time to come, it may be necessary to proceed regardless, but it will be essential to take these factors into account in planning the campaign strategy. The steering committee must identify the campaign issues that will have an impact on the largest number of voters and concentrate on these issues. While it is important to address all of the important issues, it is essential to concentrate on the issues critical to the success of the campaign and keep hammering on them throughout the campaign. The key is getting out a simple, straightforward, and easy to understand message.

THE CAMPAIGN MESSAGE

After considering all of the major issues, discussing all of the options for the campaign, and brainstorming on how to make emotional connections, it will be necessary to condense all of this into a simple and effective campaign message. The campaign message must distill the major issues and campaign themes into one central statement. A pyramid is a useful symbol for understanding the process. The message is the apex of the pyramid, but it must be based in the grass roots of the community. The process is one of narrowing down from major issues, to specific themes, to one overall main campaign message. Campaign literature, community presentations, endorsements, and paid advertisements should all be tied together by this message. Although the campaign may have several themes, there should always be an attempt to relate these themes directly back to the main campaign message. Once the message has been articulated, the challenge is to communicate this message to the electorate through every practical means available to the steering committee. In order to win, the campaign message must be dramatic and convincing enough to get a majority of voters to pull the "Yes" lever in the voting booth.

FIGURE 4-2   Campaign Planning Pyramid

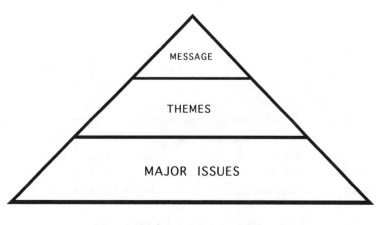

GRASSROOTS COMMUNITY

Trying to communicate the campaign's message during an election, particularly general elections where there is a lot of competition, is difficult to say the least. The trick is to compose a campaign message that not only communicates the main point of the library issue, but stands out from all of the other campaign "noise" created by commercials for candidates, the opposition or other ballot items. The goal is a well-designed, catchy, and relevant campaign message that is emotionally charged and visually appealing. Getting it—and then communicating it in a persuasive manner—takes time, research, patience, creativity, political insight, and sometimes money. Once developed, however, it can be the ticket to success.

THEMES

Along with one main campaign message, each campaign may identify several themes which need special attention. For example, support for the education of youth may be the major message of a campaign that includes several supporting themes such as support for early intervention at the elementary level with supplementary reading material to help prevent illiteracy, specialized assistance for targeted "at risk" groups such as potential dropouts, or providing a wholesome after school alternative to youth violence, drugs, and gangs. To be effective, themes must be "sold" through use of emotionally oriented "advertising" which makes a positive connection with the electorate. Most importantly, the campaign themes should be firmly rooted in the community, generated from voter research, and clearly related to the need for the project to be funded by the referendum. Such themes may include rapid population growth, the need to provide bilingual materials and literacy training, being behind in national SAT scores, or simply the desire to have an attractive new building to foster community pride and demonstrate economic vitality. Campaign planners can also promote the general economic improvement that results from most new library facilities. For example, good libraries help to strengthen minds, strong minds foster increased economic growth, which means residents will be able to get better jobs, which in turn generally improves their chances for having a better quality of life.

SLOGANS & LOGOS

The campaign message may be communicated in many ways. One of the most effective methods is to embody the campaign message in a campaign slogan or logo. Slogans and logos elevate the library's name and symbol recognition. They can be reproduced on all campaign literature, paraphernalia, and letterhead. The more exposure, the better, to drum in the message and increase the visibility of the library issue. This helps the library's campaign stand out from other ballot issues. The more effectively the slogan and logo grabs voters' attention, the better. They should be distinctive, easily recognizable, and quickly identified with the library issue. One word of caution with respect to the design of slogans and logos. While it is important to get the attention of the voter, the slogan and logo—and all other campaign materials—should always be in good taste and not offensive in any manner.

Most campaigns use one short, snappy, effective slogan. The slogan must be pertinent, catchy, and memorable. It is best if the slogan is short and sweet so that it will be easier to remember and fits on all campaign literature and paraphernalia. The following are some examples of slogans used in recent library campaigns:

"GROWING BY LEAPS AND BONDS"
— Dekalb County, GA

"VOTE YES – GOOD FOR YOU. GOOD FOR PHOENIX."
— Phoenix, AZ

"YOUR VOTE MEANS VOLUMES"
— Winter Park, FL

"COME GROW WITH US"
— River Edge, NJ

"OUR LIBRARY, IT'S WORTH IT"
— Highland Park, NJ

"CHECK IT OUT — THE PALATINE PUBLIC LIBRARY"
— Palatine, IL

"WHEN YOU'RE THIS STACKED, YOU NEED SOME SUPPORT"
— Dallas, TX

"BUILD A BRIGHTER TOMORROW"
— Bartlesville, OK

"VOTE LIBRARY"
— Coppell, TX

"THE SPOKANE LIBRARY . . . OVERDUE" and
"OVERDUE: VOTE YES FOR SPOKANE LIBRARIES"
— Spokane, WA

"LIBRARIES JUST DON'T GROW ON TREES. PEOPLE BUILD THEM"
— Fort Lauderdale, FL

"HELP KEEP THE LIBRARIES FROM FAILING OUR CHILDREN"
— Atlanta-Fulton County, GA

"STEVENS LIBRARY: LONG OVERDUE"
— North Andover, MA

"DON'T CLOSE THE BOOK ON OUR CHILDREN'S FUTURE"
— Richland County, SC

"BUILD FOR EXCELLENCE"
— Hinsdale, IL

"RENEW THE LIBRARY"
— Los Altos, CA

"WE'VE MADE THE LIBRARY LEVY AN OPEN BOOK"
— Multnomah County Library, Portland, OR

"A NEW LEAF FOR THE . . . LIBRARY"
— Port Clinton, OH

"MAKE YOUR VOTE ONE FOR THE BOOKS"
— Lake Jackson and Conroe, TX

"MORE BOOKS, FEWER CROOKS"
— Bend, OR

"THE LIBRARY BOND: MAKE BOOKS A PRIORITY IN YOUR LIFE"
— Chesapeake, VA

"INVEST IN THE FUTURE"
— Council Bluffs, IA

"A LIBRARY SAYS A LOT ABOUT A CITY"
— Denver, CO

Logos are essentially slogans only in a graphic format. They should attempt to define the issue and raise awareness of the library through the use of form and color. A good logo communicates a message in an easily recognizable form. The simpler the better is the rule for logos. Logos should make a strong impression and catch the eye quickly. Colors are important in accomplishing this goal, particularly contrasting colors like blue and yellow. Too many colors and too much detail clutter up the logo and make it difficult to reproduce, as well as increase printing costs. As with the slogan, the logo should be placed on all campaign literature and paraphernalia. Frequently logos and slogans are combined for added impact. In a pinch, the ALA Library Logo (the reader symbol in a circle) can always be used in a campaign along with a local slogan.

A GIMMICK

Just as in show business, it's good for a campaign to have a gimmick. A gimmick is simply an attention getter, and usually the more outrageous the better. Maybe you could have all of the speakers for the campaign wear plaid skirts and pants or polka dot blouses and shirts, or maybe campaign planners can come up with an angle in the form of a visual aid which helps to graphically demonstrate the library's need. The library director in Dekalb County, Georgia, literally cut an old book in half and waved it around at every campaign gathering she attended to demonstrate graphically that the library only had half-a-book per capita. This illustration appealed directly to the community's sense of civic pride and was rather difficult to ignore. Another example of a gimmick is the photograph in Figure 4-4 of the Volkswagen parked in front of the library in Grafton, Ohio, which demonstrated how small the existing library really was since it was barely wider that the length of the car.

THE NEED FOR SIMPLICITY

Simplicity in the campaign is important for more that just slogans and logos: the simpler the issue, the better the chance for success. The ballot question itself should be defined so that it is reasonable and easily understood. Multiple library issues on the ballot at the same time can be a problem because of the added complexity and should be avoided if possible. When it is not possible, do everything practical to clearly define each issue. Avoid the use of jargon and complex wording which confuses the electorate. Confusion over a ballot issue is the kiss of death in the voting booth and usually leads to defeat.

Bring the issue down to earth, especially when you are discussing money. Don't mention money at all if you don't have to, but if you must, keep it simple and describe the smallness of

FIGURE 4-3   Library Campaign Logos/Slogans. (See Page vii for Institution/ Organization Courtesy Statements.)

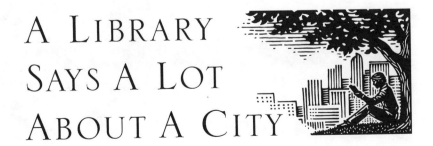

FIGURE 4-4   Volkswagen in Front of the Grafton, Ohio, Library. Provided Courtesy of Grafton–Midview Public Library, Grafton, Ohio.

the tax increase in terms that are easy to grasp. For example, *"the annual increase for the average home owner will equal the cost of a good book,"* or *"for a dime a day, you get a whole new library."* Make certain that your monetary arguments are accurate and don't fudge even a small amount. Always be straight forward and precise when discussing the costs of the library issue, but don't get into long-winded explanations of complex funding formulas.

Do not vacillate. *Find a simple message and deliver it repeatedly and relentlessly.* Major and frequent shifts in strategy throughout the campaign simply confuse the electorate and usually generate questions which translates into a loss of confidence in the library planners and the issue itself. Questions at the polls usually mean negative votes. This is why one overall message and several themes which pull the campaign together into one unified effort should be found early.

ARCHITECTURAL MODELS, PLANS, AND RENDERINGS

Displaying architectural models, plans, and renderings avoids confusion over what the project will be like by providing information about the project and also raises awareness for the impending campaign. Exterior elevations and floor plans of the proposed new building highlighting new or improved services can be displayed in the lobby of the existing library, at City Hall, the County Courthouse, the Post Office or various shopping malls. Figures 4-5, 4-6, and 4-7 present excellent examples of such displays. Library trustees, Friends or other campaign workers can be positioned near the displays during peak foot traffic periods to explain the plans and answer questions. While this is a very good way of informing the public of what the library project will look like, there are potential disadvantages to this approach.

FIGURE 4-5   A Rendering of the Proposed Columbiana Library. Provided Courtesy of Columbiana Public Library, Columbiana, Ohio.

FIGURE 4-6   Exterior Elevation & Floor Plan, Farmingdale, New York. Provided Courtesy of Beatty, Harvey, and Associates.

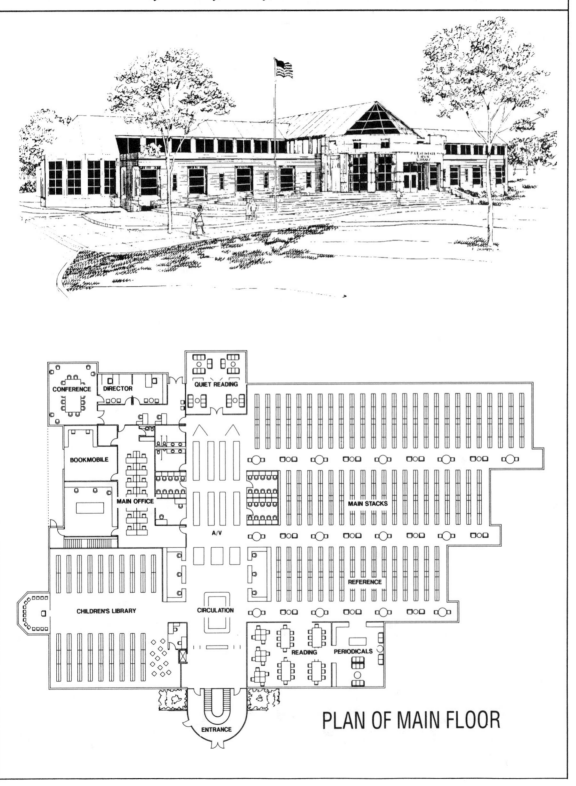

PLAN OF MAIN FLOOR

FIGURE 4-7   Lobby and Reading Area Interior Elevations. Provided Courtesy of Desoto Public Library, DeSoto, Texas.

CONTROVERSY

Sometimes the display of the exterior design of the building in advance of the referendum causes unwelcome controversy. Some people may not like the aesthetics of the design, or some aspect of the plans, like the project's site. If these opponents are vocal and influential, they can place the campaign on the defensive. Planners must ask themselves, *"How much information about the design of the project is it appropriate to disclose in advance of the referendum?"* While the public deserves to be fully informed, the opposition might take some small and relatively insignificant aspect of the design and turn it into a major stumbling block for the campaign. Obviously, each campaign's steering committee must resolve this dilemma for themselves.

Given this kind of potential problem, sometimes it's better not to develop the design in great detail before the election or to simply indicate that it will change. With this approach, the plan should only be developed enough to provide an adequate budget estimate and show the basics regarding the proposed project. For example, it is possible to only distribute a conceptual floor plan which shows the placement of services to be offered if it is felt that showing an elevation will cause problems. What is important is to try to present the building's design, cost, and location in a favorable light with a minimum amount of controversy. Obviously, if the voters feel that the building is one that they, as a community, will feel proud of and one that is not overly expensive or located on an objectionable site, the chances for success are greatly improved. However, mishandling any controversial aspect of the building project can cause the referendum's defeat.

HISTORIC BUILDINGS

It is certainly difficult when the very building or site library planners are trying to improve works against them. However, in some cases where strong opposition groups are present, this may be unavoidable. This may happen when the existing library is historically significant, such as a turn-of-the-century Carnegie library. If the plan is to abandon this facility or to expand it with an ultra-modern design, the resulting public outcry is always difficult to overcome. Regardless how inadequate an old Carnegie building has become, planners must recognize the strong community sentiment for these historic buildings.

Local historical groups who feel strongly about preserving the architectural integrity of these buildings may suddenly become very active in opposing a new library building. If they feel the future of the existing Carnegie building is uncertain, or worse, that it will be torn down, they will undoubtedly oppose the project. This sentiment must be taken into consideration early in the needs assessment process as well as the campaign planning stages or the project may well be in jeopardy. Often all of the possible alternatives for the project must be explained and a satisfactory plan for the disposition of the beloved existing building must be put in place as part of the library project proposal.

PROBLEMS WITH THE LIBRARY SITE

Another potential area of conflict is the selection of a site. Along with historic buildings, library sites have a way of fast becoming forceful emotional issues in a community. It is wise to remember the importance of emotional issues when considering the location of the library site.

If there are strong concerns regarding the site, and they are not satisfactorily addressed, these problems can elicit incredibly powerful negative reactions from the community. Dealing with this conflict can drain a campaign of much time and energy. This is why it is wise to do a careful site selection process well in advance of the campaign and weigh all of the positive and negative aspects of each site carefully.

There are all kinds of site considerations which can come up during a campaign and cause a problem. Is the site located near a jail or prison, a bar or liquor store, a mental health center or halfway house, a major highway or busy intersection, or in an area of town that has a high level of vandalism? Is the site in a flood plain? Are there soil contaminants at or near the site? Is the site located under a flight path of a nearby airport? The list of possible negative emotional issues for a site is seemingly endless. Again, this is why it can be extremely important to do a comprehensive and professional site study well in advance of the campaign.

CENTRAL LIBRARY VERSUS BRANCHES

Another study, the library facilities master plan, will have an impact on the campaign strategy as well. Winning a referendum for a large central library building is difficult. In urban communities that are large enough to need a central and branch libraries, the question of which should be built first, and which can be sold politically is critical. This determination needs to be made early based on competent professional analysis in the form of a master plan. Polling data and/or a market research study can also be helpful.

A number of recent library campaigns recognized that voters might not approve a large central library building distant from the average citizen's immediate neighborhood. In order to convince the electorate to support such large central facilities, it is often necessary to "sweeten the pot" by including branch library projects in the immediate proximity of suburban areas. While increasing the overall cost of a library issue, this approach has proven very effective in many cases, including but not limited to campaigns in cities such as Denver,[7] Los Angeles,[8] and San Francisco.[9]

The concept is simple: spread the wealth and therefore the support around to obtain as broad a constituency base as possible by bringing the question down to each voter's individual level. A ballot measure which provides a number of library branches is inherently "personalized" because it shows each specific voter how they will directly benefit. In this way, the campaign can be localized by bringing it to the neighborhood level. Campaign planners must show what the advantages in the "package" are for each area in the community. Will this area get a new branch or have its beloved branch expanded and renovated? This approach creates a grassroots, vested interest in the campaign which cannot be bought with any amount of campaign advertising and will likely result in success at the ballot box.

If campaign planners are unsure how to proceed with respect to this issue, the concept can be pretested with a market research survey or poll in advance of a campaign. For example, through a questionnaire, the electorate can be asked if they would:

A. Support a $50 million central library project.
B. Support a $75 million central library project with 10 branch libraries in the following areas: (list branches).
C. Support a $25 million package with 10 branch libraries in the following areas: (list branches).

If there are significantly higher favorable response rates for questions "B" and "C" than for question "A", it may be wise to proceed with the "package" approach especially if the central library project is badly needed. If support for the branch libraries is higher than for the central library (which is frequently the case), the steering committee should obviously emphasize the branch library projects during the campaign and deemphasize the central library project except in areas which show the strongest support for the central library project. Voters who use the various branch libraries which will be improved should be targeted, and the campaign message that they receive should clearly and concisely indicate the benefits that they and their branch will receive if the ballot measure passes.

Central libraries in large metropolitan areas are often difficult to sell to the community as a whole especially if the jurisdiction is spread out over many square miles. While the library management knows that a strong central library is critical to a strong branch library program, this fact is often very difficult to communicate to the electorate. While the Dallas Public Library was able finance a large central library facility through a bond issue without simultaneously placing branch libraries on the ballot, this project was the exception and not the rule. Frequently, the *only* way to finance a large central library is by combining it with a number of popular branch library projects.

This is the approach that campaign planners took in the recent Denver campaign. While support for a central library project by itself was less than enthusiastic, a poll showed that support for improving branch library facilities was at the 70 percent level.[10] When the branch libraries and the central library project were combined into one package, the support level came in at 58 percent, which was lower than the support for the branches alone, but still high enough for the campaign planners to feel confident that the issue would pass. Their confidence was well-founded since the ballot measure passed handily.

This approach was also tried in the late 1980s in Los Angeles. Unfortunately, in this case a $90 million package failed when the issue received only 62 percent of the votes (a two-thirds majority is required to pass bond issues in California). A subsequent ballot measure six months later, which removed the central library project and financed 28 branch library projects on their own, passed with 68 percent of the vote. Fortunately, the central library project was later financed through a complicated series of "creative financing techniques."[11] Los Angeles was indeed fortunate because it is frequently the case that if the central library project is not funded either ahead of or with branch library projects, the chances of funding it later are greatly reduced. This was one of the reasons that the Atlanta central library project was placed before the voters in the 1970s prior to a major branch expansion program in the 1980s.

There are numerous reasons why a combined central/branch library package may not pass, but the main reason is that the size of the package simply gets too large for taxpayers to support at one time. However, some of the other reasons may be controversial aspects of different projects. One issue to watch out for is the closing of a library. As many library directors and boards have discovered, closing a branch, no matter how small or how inadequate, can be political dynamite even when a larger "regional" branch is being substituted for the small neighborhood library. Great care must be taken during the facility master planning phase and during preliminary market research surveys and polling to ascertain that the "package deal" will be strong enough to overcome any potential opposition to the closing of any libraries.

There is one way that this strong community identification with branch libraries can be utilized to the benefit of a library package. Assuming residents living around the proposed branch library projects aren't upset about branch closings, library campaigns have been known to successfully target the neighborhoods that are within a few miles of the location of proposed new branches during the campaign. These people, obviously, have reason to be supportive of the issue if they currently drive many miles for library service. These concepts of targeting and timing are important early strategic considerations and the following chapter is dedicated solely to the discussion of both subjects.

REFERENCES

1. Hunt, Sally. "Chronology of a Successful Library Bond Issue: How One Library System Developed Public Support to Pass a Bond Referendum for Badly-needed Facilities." *Virginia Librarian* (March–April, 1986), p. 35.
2. Comments provided to the author in response to the *Library Journal* survey on local referenda for library buildings.
3. "Economic Vitality: How Libraries Can Play a Key Role." *The Bottom Line* 3:1 (1989), p. 19.
4. Hall, Richard B. "The Votes Are In." *Library Journal* 115:11 (June 15, 1990), pp. 42–46.
5. Rickert, Susan. *Campaigning for Libraries*. Wheat Ridge, Colorado: Central Colorado Library System, 1988, p. 3.
6. Hall, Richard B. "The Votes Are In." *Library Journal* 115:11 (June 15, 1990), pp. 42–46.
7. McCune, Bonnie and Molly Squibb. "Denver PL Moves Beyond Slogans" *Library Journal* 117:11 (June 15, 1992), pp. 40–41.
8. Reagan, Robert. "A Tale of Two Bond Campaigns: The Los Angeles Public Library" *Library Journal* 115:11 (June 15, 1990), p. 45.
9. Schneider, Marcia. "The San Francisco Bond Campaign" *Library Journal* 115:11 (June 15, 1990), p. 44.
10. Ciruli, Floyd. Memorandum to Library Bond Election Task Force RE: Report on Polling Concerning Library Issues. Denver, Colorado: *Ciruli Associates*, March 11, 1990.
11. Hall, Richard B. *Financing Public Library Buildings*. New York: Neal-Schuman, 1994, pp. 224–225

5 TARGETING & TIMING

Two of the most important aspects of any campaign strategy are targeting and timing. These both need to be thoroughly discussed by the steering committee and incorporated into the campaign plan. Effective targeting of the electorate, as well as appropriate timing for the campaign, may give library supporters just enough of an advantage to win in an otherwise marginal or even hostile political environment. By using targeting techniques and making good timing decisions, the campaign's leadership can increase the effectiveness of volunteers and save a lot of time and effort to help ensure a victory for the library issue.

TARGETING THE ELECTORATE

Targeting is the technique of picking specific groups of the electorate and making sure that the campaign's message is adequately tailored and delivered to those people to induce them to go to the polls and vote "Yes" for the issue. The trick is to select groups which are naturally inclined to support the library issue at the polls as well as those undecided voters who can be persuaded, with a little help from the campaign, to vote for the library issue. The campaign must focus delivery of its message precisely and repeatedly to these groups. However, the number of voters in these target groups which can be persuaded to go to the polls and vote for the library issue must add up to the majority needed to win the election.

One of the major mistakes that inexperienced campaigners make is trying to communicate the campaign's message to too many people. It is usually too expensive for most grassroots campaigns to communicate with every possible voter, let alone everyone in the community. The first cut that should be made is to recognize that campaign workers should be contacting only registered voters. Unlike routine library public relations programs, campaign planners are not trying to reach the general public. Concentrating on registered voters narrows the field considerably, but the next step in the process is to target those who are most likely to vote for the library issue. Clearly, the challenge is to identify those voters as uninformed, undecided, or favorable toward the library issue and inform them, persuade them, and get them to go to the polls and vote.

TARGET GROUPS

Targeting specific groups within a community is important for any campaign, but it is especially important if campaigns funds, volunteers, and time are short. Targeting is the most cost-effective method of successfully reaching that subset of the electorate that the library needs to win. Discovering target groups is done through careful analysis of the data collected during the project needs assessment process and polling (See "Determination of Target Groups by Cross

Tabulation" in Chapter 3) as well as other campaign information sources. The key is to identify those groups that are needed to win the election, and then to identify what they want to hear about the library issue that will most effectively convince them to vote "Yes." Once this is done, all that remains is to pound that message home repeatedly throughout the campaign.

Planners should make a prioritized list of the target groups which the campaign needs to concentrate on. This is important so that the most important ones will be sure to be covered if funds run short. Further, this priority list will provide a way of knowing which groups should get the most emphasis through repeat contact if funds and time permit a get-out-the-vote effort. Effective, *repetitive* communication with these targeted individuals is the key to winning a campaign.

In looking for target groups to concentrate on, the steering committee should identify people who have the most to gain from the library issue. Those individuals which have some form of vested interest in the library are most likely to support the issue. Obviously, library Friends and patrons who use the library fit this bill as do many other individuals in the community who are interested in education and economic development.

Educators such as secondary school teachers, college professors, and administrators are often supportive (assuming that there is no conflict with a local school referendum). Many communities have very effective Parent Teachers Associations (PTAs) with active political networks which can be accessed to help support library issues. Often the library's own children's librarians are aware of individuals who will be supportive of issues concerning children and the reference staff, especially those who specialize in business information sources, may have some very good contacts with the business community.

HABITUAL VOTERS

Anyone who has voted repeatedly in recent elections is considered a "habitual" voter and is someone that campaign planners want to contact and influence. In some communities, habitual voters total as much as half the number of registered voters; in other communities, their number is significantly less. It is extremely important to identify which of these voters are potential supporters of the library issue as well as which ones are undecided, particularly if a low voter turn out is expected. While habitual voters, by definition, usually don't have to be encouraged to vote, those who are undecided must be convinced to vote "yes." Once undecided habitual voters have been identified by the campaign, they should become one of the top priority target groups that library supporters try to influence through persuasive mailings, telephone calls and, if possible, door-to-door canvassing. The more often these people receive a positive personal contact from library volunteers, the more likely it is that they will vote for the library issue. It is imperative that consistent voters be targeted; since they can be counted on to show up at the polls, they had better be convinced to vote "Yes," or they library issue will be in trouble.

THE UNDECIDED VOTER

In close campaigns, the undecided voter may become the "swing" vote; therefore, targeting, reaching, and convincing the undecided voter can frequently mean the difference between success and failure. In addition to targeting undecided habitual voters, it is often necessary for campaign planners to target undecided "occasional" voters along with occasional "Yes" voters. In very close races, callers should try to determine if undecided voters are "leaning toward," "leaning against," or truly undecided. Subsequently, library supporters should devote much of their persuasive activities toward influencing undecided voters who are either "leaning for" the library issue or who remain undecided. Since door-to-door canvassing brings personal contact with highly committed campaign workers and has a positive impact on voter turn-out, the library campaign should strongly consider implementing door-to-door canvassing in areas with a high concentration of undecided voters. This approach can be supplemented with printed material and media coverage, but there is nothing better than a friendly face and a handshake to tip the scales in the right direction.

The process of identifying who the undecided voters are can be accomplished in a number of ways. It can be done in general through polling, but if the campaign has an active telephone bank or door-to-door canvassing effort, the undecided voters can be more precisely identified. Careful documentation in both of these activities is crucial. As preliminary contact is made, campaign workers simply need to write down those voters who are undecided about the issue. Then later in the campaign, these individuals can be targeted for a repeat "persuasive" contact in a concentrated effort to win them over to the cause (see Chapters 12 and 14 for a detailed description of this process).

THE "YES" VOTER

In addition to reaching undecided voters, it is essential to identify and contact individuals who can be considered potential "Yes" voters. From the very beginning, the identification and contact with the potential "Yes" voter is a critical campaign tactic. The steering committee must know where it is likely to obtain the majority of its support for the library issue, and then contact these individuals, promote their awareness of the issue, gain their confidence, and finally their vote on election day. By definition, it usually doesn't take a lot of persuasive effort to convince potential "Yes" voters to vote for the library issue; however, the library campaign can't take the "Yes" voter for granted. Many individuals in the community may be favorably disposed toward the library issue, but it still may take some convincing to get them to pull out their pocketbooks to pay for a tax increase. Along with persuasive efforts, it is extremely important to target "Yes" voters, and particularly occasional "Yes" voters, during the get-out-the-vote effort to remind them that they need to go to the polls and vote for the library issue. If time and funds permit, it doesn't hurt to remind habitual "Yes" voters to vote as well.

Many campaign volunteers will come from the neighborhoods where a high percentage of voters will be "Yes" voters. This is also true for the library Friends group as well as the registered patrons of the library. Conventional wisdom indicates that the better-educated, affluent, white-collar sector of a community is most likely to approve a library issue. In addition, these people are the most likely to turn out to vote in the first place. In other words, the areas most likely to be favorable to the library issue are also more likely to have a higher turnout. This fact greatly improves the chance for success of library issues, and is one of the main reasons that library ballot measures are as successful as they are. However, it is never wise to take the outcome of a library referendum for granted. One way to make sure this doesn't happen is to understand local voting trends by examining the results of previous local ballot measures and attempting to ascertain the reasons for their success or failure.

ANALYSIS OF PREVIOUS BALLOT MEASURES

Studying the results of recently held referenda in the community is particularly valuable in designing a strategy as well as identifying target groups. Previous referenda which are similar to the library issue should be researched carefully. Campaigns for other educational facilities such as schools as well as those for cultural organizations such as art centers, museums, and civic centers are particularly significant and revealing for library campaign planners. The leaders of these campaigns should be interviewed in order to determine what they felt were the major reasons for success or failure of their efforts. Elections held within the last three to four years will give the most up-to-date and accurate voter behavior information. Analyzing older election results has a higher degree of error because the political climate may have changed significantly and many of the those who voted then will have since died or moved away. Looking at the type of election is important as well. If the library referendum will be held during a special election, the results of previous special elections will be more indicative than the results of general elections.

PRECINCT ANALYSIS

If possible, campaign planners should obtain the voting results for recent elections on a precinct by precinct basis in order to really understand the voting record of the community as a whole. By studying the results of several campaigns and looking at specific geographical areas, it may be possible to identify very specific sectors of the community which are key to the election. By understanding which areas and therefore which voters may be pivotal, the campaign can more effectively direct its energy and resources.

It is essential to understand where "Yes" voters are particularly when campaign resources are limited. This means that precincts where similar issues defeated in a big way should probably be ignored by campaign planners, but precincts which solidly supported similar issues should receive the most campaign attention, time, and effort to make sure that these voters turn out and vote for the library issue. Further, if the election will be close, precincts where the results were close in previous elections may have to be targeted as well, particularly if early campaign polling shows that there are a high number of undecided voters in these areas.

Based on the analysis of similar kinds of elections, and assuming a similar turnout, campaign planners should be able to analyze past elections and determine how many votes they are likely to get in the current election. In order to be successful, campaign planners must determine the number of votes needed to win the election. This means determining how many votes are needed in each precinct as well as which precincts will likely provide the most votes for the library issue. Through an analysis of the percentage of potential "Yes" and undecided voters, voter turn-out percentages, and the actual number of voters in each precinct, planners should be able to target the specific precincts where the campaign's activities will be most effective.

Campaign planners must look at all of the above factors together in order to determine the precinct's relative importance to the campaign as well as assess which activities should be performed in each precinct. As part of the campaign plan, the steering committee can subsequently rank both precincts and the various campaign activities in the order of importance to the campaign in the following manner:

1. Get-out-the-vote telephone bank in precinct 5
2. Door-to-door persuasive canvassing in precinct 7
3. Telephone persuasive canvassing in precinct 1
Etc.

Again, if funds run short, prioritizing will be invaluable to ensuring that essential activities get done before the money or time runs out.

Campaign planners should set up a map of the community at the campaign headquarters and identify the key precincts where most of the campaign efforts will be targeted. Voter profiles should be created which clearly identify what the "typical" voter looks like in each important precinct by attempting to correlate the precinct with census information, voter identification data, and any other community information available. This profile should be constantly tested against polling results and feedback from campaign workers going door-to-door or staffing the telephone bank. How is the campaign message being received by these people? Are there any major issues in these areas which the campaign is not adequately addressing? Is the campaign getting a good number of volunteers from these areas? Are they willing to put up yard signs? If these people are not supportive, campaign planners may need to do some more research into why and adjust the campaign strategy. One way to reach the voters in a specific area is to tweak the message slightly and tailor it to the target group.

INDIVIDUALIZE THE MESSAGE

One of the advantages to identifying specific target groups is that individualized versions of the main campaign message can be transmitted to these people. With the advantages of today's computerized databases, it is possible to disseminate very precisely tailored messages to very specific subgroups in a community. This is the science of telling people what they want to hear about the library issue, no more and no less from the beginning of the campaign right up to the last day before the election. By effectively delivering the desired message to each targeted subgroup, campaigns greatly increased their chances of success.

In addition to modifying the message sent to each target group, it may be necessary to change the delivery method depending upon the makeup of the target group. Mass mailings may work in some areas, but door-to-door contact may be more effective in others. For example, a last minute mailing of a postcard may be a good method to remind solid "Yes" voters to vote, while the personal contact of a door-to-door canvassing effort is better for precincts with a high number of undecided voters. Frequently, it is important to make sure that the right person or persons are delivering the message. The issue here is credibility. It is important that the targeted subgroup is able to identify with the message provider. For example, cultural similarity can be important. It is helpful if a respected member of the Latino community communicates the library issue to the Latino neighborhoods targeted by the steering committee.

Frequently ethnic neighborhoods are important to library campaigns because minorities often have a very high support level for library issues. Unfortunately, neighborhoods with a high percentage of ethnic minorities residing in them also frequently have a very low voter registration level. If an area has been determined to be supportive of the library issue, it will obviously be helpful to make sure that as many of the individuals in the precinct are registered to vote as possible before election day.

VOTER REGISTRATION DRIVES

Providing information and raising awareness in the community in general is helpful to kick off a campaign, but once the campaign gets into full gear, it is important not to waste time on people who aren't even registered to vote. *Campaigns must concentrate on registered voters*, since after all they are the individuals who will decide the ballot issue. Sometimes it is helpful to help "stack the deck" in supportive areas of the community through early voter registration drives. Usually a very high percentage of voters registered by a campaign organization subsequently vote favorably for the issue.

Voter registration efforts can take many forms. In many states, it is permissible to have public libraries be voter registration sites. This can be a very good way of introducing people to the library as well as getting them registered. An active campaign may want to go further and be even more aggressive in registering voters particularly in critical precincts. Voter registration sites can be set up in shopping centers or in other areas where people congregate in the targeted precincts. Another approach is to begin the training of the campaign's volunteers by having them go door-to-door in very important neighborhoods with registration forms. Not only does this get people registered to vote, but it also provides experience for campaign volunteers in meeting the public and starting the all-important process of engaging the public through personal contact. Voter registration drives are also a good method of identifying potential future volunteers for the campaign. Anyone who appears to be enthusiastic about the library issue should be noted and contacted later when the volunteer recruitment drive is in full swing.

VOTER REGISTRATION LISTS

In order to make sure that the campaign message gets out to registered voters, obtain a current registered voter list from the jurisdiction's local election office (County or City Clerk's office, Board of Elections, or comparable local elections office). This list can be particularly useful when attempting to contact registered voters and can be used very effectively by the campaign workers who are organizing the telephone banks, direct mailings, and the door-to-door neighborhood canvassing. However, registered voter lists sometimes need to be "cleaned-up" and/or enhanced by campaign planners to be used more effectively. For example, it is helpful if all those individuals who have died or moved since the last election are removed from the list. Further, it is advantageous if the lists have been "householded" which means that if there are multiple voters living at the same address, that the list is modified to avoid multiple contacts by telephone or mail.

Frequently, massaging voter registration lists means creating a campaign voter file on a microcomputer so that various sorts and selects can be performed. If it is not feasible for a campaign to set up its own voter list file in this manner, it may be possible to obtain these kinds of lists and services from political consulting firms; however, the campaign will have to pay for the services. Regardless, there are many advantages to having clean lists which can be processed quickly and effectively for campaign purposes. Telephone banks need telephone numbers, but many voters won't divulge their telephone number when they register to vote (in most states it is optional). Therefore, these numbers have to be looked up. Accurate street addresses are important if door-to-door canvassing will be performed, and it is helpful if the list can be manipulated so that odd and even street number lists can be generated for each street to make the canvassing easier by being able to go down one side of a street and not crossing back and forth. For mailings, it will be helpful to have the carrier routes and other necessary postal information needed to reduce mailing costs. Manipulating voter registration lists in these various ways frequently saves the campaign time and money.

CAMPAIGN TIMING

Along with targeting, timing is one of the more important factors affecting a campaign's success or failure. Research has shown that library administrators felt the timing of the vote was a very important factor in successful library referenda campaigns.[1] Many aspects of timing are important and finding the best time to hold the ballot issue is a major consideration.

Should the library issue go on the ballot during a general or special election? What time of the year is best? Should the library issue compete against a number of other ballot issues or should campaign planners bide their time and pick an election with no competition? Timing with respect to the economic climate, recent tax increases, or increased activities among opposition groups can all be important considerations. If the campaign starts too early, the opposition will have time to organize. If the campaign starts too late and is not well organized, the results may be disappointing. There may also be the perception that the library supporters are trying to "sneak the issue through" without proper public discussion.

WHEN TO HOLD THE REFERENDUM

The date of the referendum is one of the most important decisions that campaign planners will make and should be carefully chosen by those who know the community's political and economic climate. However, the library management and supporters must be aware that the political pundits in some communities may never think that the time is right to place the library issue on the ballot. If this is the case, campaign planners may have to try to assess their chances on their own and commit to a campaign based on their own knowledge of their constituency.

In some states, specific dates for general or special tax referenda are set by state law and there is little or no flexibility; many states, however, permit a great deal of flexibility. If the library planners have good relations with those responsible for setting the ballot agenda for various elections, and are fortunate enough to be able to select the best possible date to place the issue before the voters, many factors must be considered. The date of the referendum should be chosen to give the campaign planners their best shot at success. Unfortunately, setting the date is not always in the hands of the steering committee. In most cases, the elected politicians representing the funding agency that will authorize the referendum are in control of when the referendum will be held. In many jurisdictions, there is also an unofficial "queuing" mechanism in place which means that the library project may need to "stand in line" behind a school or a roads issue which needs to be presented first. Sensitivity to this process can be very important so as not to ruffle the proverbial feathers of any group or to appear to be non-cooperative with the power structure's "political agenda."

SPECIAL VERSUS GENERAL ELECTION

If the steering committee does control placing the issue on the ballot, its first decision will be choosing between a special or general election. There are several things to consider when determining whether to hold the referendum during a regularly scheduled election or to call a special election. Since special elections are expensive, this approach will not be looked upon favorably unless there is a very good reason to hold a separate referendum. While it may cost the taxpayers more to hold a special election, this is counter-balanced somewhat by the fact that campaign costs in a special election are usually lower because less people typically vote in special elections (sometimes as low as 20 percent of the registered voters); therefore, less people must be targeted by the campaign. In some cases, library supporters may even want to offer to pay for the cost of a special election.

In a special election, it will be particularly important to communicate with habitual voters. Frequently, the lower turn out special elections bring out a high percentage of senior citizens. If this age group is a campaign target group so much the better, but if this group is notorious for turning down tax measures, a special election may be a definite disadvantage for the library issue.

It is commonly believed that the smaller turnout of a special election enhances the chance for success of local referenda. As discussed in Chapter 1, data collected nationally for library referenda shows that those held during special elections have a slight edge over those held during general elections. Many political consultants advise library supporters to plan referenda during special elections or off year elections which have lower voter turn outs. This is because the biggest concern that is present for most campaign planners with general elections, and especially Fall (even more so, presidential) general elections, is that because the size of the voter turn out is much higher, it means that library planners must organize and finance a much larger campaign effort than if the library issue were decided during a relatively low turn out election held during the "off-season."

Using national statistics alone to determine whether to hold a special election or a general election is probably not wise since there are simply too many local considerations which must be brought to bear on the decision that are far more important than what has occurred in other communities across the country. Planners must look at who the typical voters are in both special and general elections in their communities. They must assess whether or not these voters are targeted by the library campaign and what it will take to communicate with the target groups in the different types of elections. Although special elections may to have a slight advantage over general elections for library capital campaigns, the time of the year the election is held appears to contribute more significantly to the probability of success.

SUCCESS RATES BY SEASON AND BALLOT COMPETITION

Table 1-5 in Chapter 1, shows the national success rates of library referenda by season. It is obvious from this table that library planners should be careful about planning referenda in the Spring particularly during Spring general elections. The chances for success appear to be significantly lower during the Spring than any other time of the year, and the national data has reflected this trend for several years. Still, many local library referenda which have passed in the

Spring, and library planners shouldn't be afraid of holding a referendum during this season if poll results show a good chance of success. It is up to the steering committee to assess when the best time is to place the library issue on the ballot, and that includes looking at what the potential ballot competition may be for any given election.

Many library supporters who have lost a ballot issue have concluded that one of the reasons that they lost was because of other issues on the ballot at the same time. Sometimes ballot competition comes by coincidence and sometimes by design. Local funding agencies have a habit of placing library issues on the ballot at the same time as other less popular issues in the hope that the library issue will pull a sewer or prison bond issue through on its coat tails. This generally doesn't happen and frequently the reverse occurs with the library issue failing as well. Because of this, it is often felt that library issues do better without any competition or "help" from other issues.

The effect of competing items on the ballot has long been controversial. Contrary to popular belief, recent research shows that competing items on the ballot are not perceived by most library directors to be a great detriment to the chances of success.[2] Looking back over the years, it does not appear that competition on the ballot (or the lack thereof) is particularly significant in predicting the success or failure of the library referendum. *The real issue is probably the tenor of the competing issues and their potential impact on the library issue.* It appears that competition on the ballot only hurts library issues when there is a negative reaction to or controversy associated with one or more of the other issues which subsequently spills over and hurts the library issue. Because this kind of problem is frequently cited as a significant reason for failure of a library referendum, very careful attention should be given to the popular sentiment of voters toward other issues which will also be on the ballot.

Negative issues and controversy may bring out a high percentage of "No" voters who vote against any and all items on a ballot, including a popular, and what would normally be, successful library issue. As a result, the real issue may be the kind of competition, and not necessarily that there is competition on the ballot. Competition with other educational or cultural projects such as schools, museums, or art centers may actually enhance the chances of a library issue since those campaigns may help to bring the type of voter to the polls who is already inclined toward the library issue. Being associated with other ballot issues that have a strongly negative sentiment should probably be avoided because of the potential for a spillover effect, but association with other positively perceived issues may actually be helpful by providing the opportunity to form coalitions.

COALITIONS

Just as having several branch libraries on a library ballot question can help the various library supporters of a community pull together, numerous capital improvement issues on the ballot at the same time can sometimes be beneficial for all of the issues. This is especially true if the authorizing agency has worked with the community to develop political consensus on the "package" in advance of the election. In addition to providing the political support from the authorizing agency, it also develops a sense of teamwork and a community spirit of "one for all, and all for one." A good example of this approach was the 1993 campaign for a $15.9 million library which was part of a $238 million package in Oklahoma City, Oklahoma.[3]

There are numerous advantages to building coalitions with other groups in the community. During the heat of the campaign when funds are short, it may be possible to double up on mailings for ballot issues which have the same target groups. For example, it may be possible to mail campaign literature for the library issue along with literature for an arts center or a civic center. The same approach may work for door-to-door campaign literature distribution and even telephone banking. Further, speakers who visit community groups can plug more than one issue at a time. This allows for a wider dissemination of information as well as some important repetition of the message if certain community groups hear from more than one speaker. If this kind of coalition building is important, or even critical, to the success of a library campaign, it may be best to hold off on a library campaign until other issues are ready to be placed on the ballot, and then approach the voters in a unified and cooperative manner.

ORGANIZED OPPOSITION, THE ECONOMY, AND TAXATION

The economic climate of the times was not ranked particularly high by library directors that recently held successful campaigns, but it comes as no surprise that it was one of the highest factors ranked by those whose referenda failed.[4] This is presumably because the local economy was not good during the campaign and as a result people were afraid to approve a tax increase. One campaign in Shreveport, Louisiana, noted that budget cuts announced by the Governor one week before the referendum helped to defeat the issue, even though the cuts were later restored. There is no question that negative economic news (either nationally or locally) can negatively impact referenda. Further, opposition groups can use poor economic conditions or anti-tax sentiment against a library issue.

Organized opposition is also one of the highest ranked concerns by those whose referenda failed in recent years.[5] However, for those referenda that passed, it was ranked at the bottom of the scale. Generally, those campaigns that result in success don't encounter much, if any, organized opposition. For those that fail, organized opposition is not only a threat, but a very intimidating fact which has to be contended with on a day-by-day basis. Any campaign committee that has suffered through a campaign with a community group questioning and opposing its every move knows how difficult this kind of problem can be and how important it is to consider these groups in planning the campaign strategy.

Organized opposition can develop quickly in response to an emotional issue, such as the perceived waste of tax funds. If an opposition group has recently stirred up emotions in the community, it may be wise to wait for the furor to die down before proceeding with a ballot issue. If this is not possible, campaign planners must anticipate the group's strategies and work to discredit or defeat the opposition. If a campaign does face well-organized opposition, the chances of success are lower, and a good portion of the campaign strategy sessions will need to be directed toward trying to diffuse, circumvent, or somehow overcome the opposition. It is important not to get the opposition riled up or, worse, give them an issue that they can effectively use against the library campaign. Caution should be exercised to defend the campaign against tactics that are frequently used by opposition groups. As mentioned earlier, one commonly used technique is to attack an issue very late in the campaign, providing inaccurate and damaging information that grabs headlines and gains voters' attention just before the polls open.

There are several approaches to dealing with attacks from the opposition. One line of thought is to simply ignore the attacks. It takes campaign resources to respond to an attack which can be better expended elsewhere getting the vote out. If a campaign must defend itself against an attack, it is usually best to respond quickly and in a similar manner. In other words, if the attack is in the newspapers, quickly respond in the newspapers. The quicker the response, the better, because it doesn't give the opposition's invalid information time to grow and take on a life of its own. Sometimes the best library defense is to prepare a good offense. While responding to an attack, it is frequently a good tactic to simultaneously attack the opposition on some vulnerable issue, and then do it again before they get done responding to the initial attack. This approach keeps the opposition on the defensive instead of the other way around.

Finally, it should be recognized that the loyal opposition does not always play fair. Never underestimate the political tactics of a fervent and vocal opposition group including even potential efforts to infiltrate the library campaign's headquarters in an effort to learn about the campaign plan as well as the library issue's weaknesses. There may even be times when library supporters may need to consider planting a "mole" in the opposition group's camp. While this may seem extreme to some, it may pay tremendous dividends if the library camp is aware of the nature of any last minute smear tactics which are going to be used by the opposition so that there is time to plan an adequate response. Nothing should be taken for granted or excluded when strong opposition is encountered in a campaign.

Sometimes all out fights with the opposition can be avoided through talking with the opposition early on when it is forming and attempting to find some common ground. In this approach, it may be possible to forge a "deal" through political compromise. This approach may not only be expedient but smart, especially if the opposition is formidable or if they are only objecting to one relatively minor aspect of the library issue which can be changed or adjusted without great damage to the project. Opposing viewpoints are sometimes simply not that far apart and if the two sides can talk and work together in the beginning before they "dig in their heels" and start exchanging barrages, it may be possible to save a great deal of time, effort, and anxiety. There are occasions when, regardless of the willingness to talk and compromise, the opposition will not cooperate and cannot be preempted. This is frequently the case when a significant tax increase is necessary.

Ballot measure opposition groups have historically rallied against increased taxation. The primary reason given for library referenda that failed in recent years was the increase in taxation.[6] Few taxpayers are excited about seeing their tax bills increase, but if they perceive that the tax increase is not really needed, or that previous funds have been wasted, the chances of getting a positive result at the polls diminish significantly. Nothing brings people to the polls faster than an unwanted tax increase. This is particularly true in communities where the tax base is already stressed due to earlier tax increases. Even a small increase in a community that is already highly taxed may produce a very negative reaction.

Herein lies the challenge for campaign planners in communities where a tax increase is an extremely sensitive issue. Campaign planners *must* make a direct and highly emotional connection between the library issue and a majority of the voting taxpayers. Campaign workers must get beyond campaign rhetoric and reach the voters through down-to-earth, no-nonsense persuasive contact. The campaign must establish trust with the electorate or the issue will be defeated. There are definite similarities between the emotional pitch made during private fund raising drives and public referenda especially in a campaign where there is strong opposition to any kind of tax increase.

Campaign planners must carefully consider timing when looking at the referendum's impact on the tax base and the current climate among the taxpaying public. It is unwise to place a referendum before the voters if they have recently had a tax increase or if a property tax reappraisal, which has the net effect of raising their taxes, has just been completed. Further, if there is an operating budget deficit (for the library or the library's funding agency) when the issue is being presented to the voters, this will also frequently sidetrack a referendum that might have otherwise passed.

In any campaign there is a natural conservatism on the part of most voters toward any issue which involves increased taxes. This is nothing new, nor is it likely to ever change. Further, it's not really a bad thing, but it does need to be understood and taken into consideration when planning the campaign. It is best overcome if the referendum can be held when the economy is good, and there is no controversy in the community over taxation. Unfortunately, these opportunities seem few and far between. The steering committee must determine to the best of its abilities if the timing is right and then proceed armed with the knowledge that not all people will see the library issue as worthy of an increase in their taxes. Library supporters will simply not be able to convince some people to support the library issue regardless of how badly needed the improvement is or what methods are utilized during the campaign. In other words, some people will be "No" voters regardless of the efforts of the campaign planners and workers.

THE "NO" VOTER

When preparing the campaign plan, remember that historically between one-fourth and one-third of the electorate will automatically vote "No" on most ballot issues. Those who are uninformed about an issue will tend to vote "No," but some individuals will vote "No" regardless of how much information they are given about the library issue. In short, don't waste time on the "No" voters—ignore them, if possible, and more importantly, don't antagonize them! Don't give them an issue which might get them organized and harm the campaign. The best thing that the campaign planners can do with most "No" voters is to get them to stay home and not vote.

If any "No" voter is worth campaign time, it is the influential "No" voter. It may be worth some time to attempt to get these individuals to support the library issue, or more likely to not actively oppose it. This can be an extremely difficult challenge and the key is usually asking campaign supporters who are personal friends, business associates, or political allies to try neutralizing the threat through personal appeal. As with private funding, it is important to send the right person regardless if one is asking for money or political support. Regardless of who approaches the "No" voter, remember that "If your goal is to change attitudes . . . . you have your work cut out for you. As a general rule, a political campaign is not the place to attempt to do this, because attitudes change slowly, and a low-level campaign simply does not have the money or time to produce such permanent change."[7]

All throughout the campaign, campaign workers will come in contact with "No" voters. Sometimes it will be face-to-face during door-to-door canvassing, sometimes on the telephone during telephone canvassing, or occasionally in person during presentations in the community. Regardless of the point of contact, the "No" voter should be treated politely and with respect, but the campaign worker should attempt to disengage as quickly as possible and move on to more positive and fertile ground. Generally, campaign resources are too limited to expend valuable time and effort on these individuals, and there is too much likelihood that the effort will boomerang and become more of a problem which will place the campaign in a defensive position. Even in very close campaigns, it is not wise to try to change the minds of "No" voters. It is much better to try to find more "Yes" voters or to concentrate on the undecided voter and get these last two categories to the polls to vote in favor of the issue.

KICK-OFF EVENT

Concentrating on the positive and bringing out the supporters for the library campaign is important at the beginning of the campaign as well as at the end. The kick-off event is an opportunity for the library campaign to have an official start for the campaign (even though many campaign activities have already begun behind the scenes) and present a "show of support" by bringing out endorsees of the library issue. In addition to showing the community who is behind the library issue, this is an opportunity to start informing the electorate of the library issue and for motivating campaign volunteers and supporters. The kick-off event is a mechanism to get the electorate's attention early on through some kind of publicity event such as a celebrity appearance.

The kick-off event should be scheduled no earlier than two months before the election (usually just after Labor Day for November general elections). This first announcement of the campaign is critical because some voters make up their minds about a campaign issue based upon their first impression. The media as well as local political and community leaders should be well represented at this event. Obviously, this is a time that the campaign must avoid controversy at all costs.

After the initial kick-off announcement, campaign momentum should be built up gradually until it peaks in the last few weeks just before the vote. This final run for the goal line should bring the voters literally "to their feet" in support of the issue. The campaign should whip its troops and supporters into a frenzy in these last few days. This is when campaign workers will be working literally day and night to implement the campaign plans laid out earlier by the steering committee. One of the most important activities which will be performed in the waning days and hours of the campaign is the get-out-the-vote effort.

GET-OUT-THE-VOTE (GOTV)

In addition to convincing the people to vote for the issue, library supporters must also be encouraged to actually go to the polls and vote. This activity usually occurs in the last few days of the campaign and is commonly referred to as GOTV or "get-out-the-vote." While much of the campaign's effort to date has been directed toward trying to persuade undecided voters to vote "Yes" and to identify potential "Yes" voters, the final days of the campaign should be almost exclusively spent getting previously identified supporters out to vote.

There are many ways to implement a GOTV effort. One of the most common GOTV techniques is using the telephone bank to call previously identified "Yes" voters to remind them to go and vote on election day. Postcards with the same message can be mailed just before the election, and door hangers can be dropped by the door-to-door canvassers the day before or the day of the election. In close elections, library supporters need to recognize that "Door to door canvassing has a greater influence on turnout than mail or telephone contact."[8] Whatever the mechanism used to get-out-the-vote, the main thing that should be kept in mind is that the point of the effort is to remind supporters to vote and to make it as easy for them to do so as possible.

Another GOTV method is the use of absentee ballots. The requirements for absentee voting, or "vote by mail," vary tremendously from state to state. While many professional campaign consultants encourage increased use of absentee ballots, the process is frequently complicated and expensive. If this approach is to be used, it is important to get down to the local elections office early in the campaign, understand the requirements, and learn the deadlines. The key to success with absentee ballots is targeting voters who are known library supporters and who would not normally vote (e.g., shut-ins, members of the military, or people who will be traveling during the election). Most absentee voter efforts are done through the mail and over the telephone and often combined with the telephone voter identification process. Once the absentee ballot has been mailed, multiple contacts are usually needed to get the ballot signed and returned. This process can require precious campaign resources, but may be worthwhile in close elections and particularly in special elections, where absentee voting is usually higher.

Timing is critical in the GOTV effort. While the campaign's last week will be heavily involved with GOTV efforts, most of the actual contact should be made within the last two to three days prior to election day. This last week "big push" is when most media advertising funds will be spent in a blitz to make voters feel good about voting "Yes" and supporting the library. Promoting the library issue vigorously during the last few days of the campaign is important because this is when the majority of undecided voters make up their minds on a ballot question. Regardless of the form of contact, the more frequently the electorate is contacted by the campaign, the more likely the message will connect, and the more likely the electorate will vote and vote affirmatively for the library issue.

Getting as many potential supporters to the polls to vote "Yes" for the library issue must be *the* major goal of the campaign in the last few days. All of the campaign's earlier efforts lead up to and rely on this last minute activity, and nothing should be allowed to stand in the way of implementing the GOTV effort. There is nothing more disheartening than to hear library supporters cry the morning after a close loss: "We thought the issue would pass. If we had only known how close it was, we would have gone and voted." Professed support doesn't mean a thing unless supporters go to the polls and vote.

CAMPAIGN DURATION

The one remaining aspect of timing to consider is the length of the campaign. It is usually better to run a well-planned and prepared campaign that is relatively short and intense. While campaign planning and preparation may go on for several months, the actual campaign for a library referendum should probably not be any longer than a few months. This approach is more effective than a long drawn-out campaign which drains the energies of the campaign workers and isn't ever focused enough to gain the attention of the electorate. If the campaign runs too long, campaign volunteers may get tired and leave the campaign just when they are needed the most. In order to make certain that a short term campaign is effective, it is necessary to carefully orchestrate each step in the campaign. The best way to do this is to create a campaign calendar which is one of the subjects of the next chapter.

REFERENCES

1. Hall, Richard B. "The Votes Are In." *Library Journal* 115:11 (June 15, 1990), pp. 42–46.
2. Ibid.
3. Hall, Richard B. "The Vote Is In: Undeniably Operational" *Library Journal* 120:11 (June 15, 1995), p. 45.
4. Hall, 1990, pp. 42–46.
5. Ibid.
6. Ibid.
7. Fishel, Murray. "Strategic Thinking and the Low-Budget Campaign." *Campaigns & Elections* 7:5 (January/February, 1987), p. 21.
8. Jean Drodshaug Dugan et. al. *Campaigning to Win: A Workbook for Women in Politics.* Washington, D.C.: National Women's Political Caucus, 1993, pp. x-3.

CAMPAIGN CALENDAR & BUDGET

THE CAMPAIGN CALENDAR

The campaign calendar is one of the most important planning documents that the steering committee will put together because it will become a "road map" for the rest of the campaign effort. The calendar should specify all of the major campaign activities in chronological order like the model "Hypothetical Library Campaign Calendar" shown at the end of this section. It is essential for campaign planners to carefully detail the timing of each and every important step in the campaign through the use of a campaign calendar.

FLEXIBILITY

The calendar should provide as much detail as early as possible but, like the campaign plan, will also need to be flexible. Because they are easy to change, calendar software packages or good word processing packages are ideal for preparing a campaign calendar. Regardless of how well campaigns are planned, things change, go wrong, or sometimes it simply takes longer to do things than it should. Because of this, extra time should be periodically built into the calendar and the time allotted for each activity should be generous. The steering committee should identify any critical deadlines as early as possible.

WORK BACKWARDS FROM ELECTION DAY

Steering committee members will be wise to develop the campaign calendar by working backwards from the election day to the present date. Not only does this help planners focus on the critical dates, but it puts the campaign emphasis where it should be—at the end of the campaign. It is essential that the campaign leadership precisely detail the last two weeks of the campaign or else much of the efforts up to that time will be wasted. Using this general approach of planning backwards, campaign planners frequently discover they wish they had started earlier. Because of this fact, *it is strongly recommended that the campaign leadership start the process of creating a campaign calendar just as soon as possible*. Nothing puts a campaign in perspective better than laying each activity out on paper in chronological order. The amount of time available (or lack thereof) to perform each step becomes all too clear and, more importantly, this process helps the steering committee eliminate time consuming activities which really don't have to be done in order to win the campaign.

COMMITTEE CALENDARS

Because the "master" campaign calendar can become very cluttered if too much detail is shown, it can be helpful to create "subcalendars" for specific activities which incorporate this detail. When the campaign master calendar showing the major activities has been drafted, it will be useful for each committee to develop these individual "subcalendars" or committee calendars. For day-to-day planning, these may include a scheduling system with "To Do" lists for each month, week, day and, toward the end of the campaign, even every hour of the campaign.

Based upon the in-depth committee calendars, descriptions of associated tasks can be developed and assigned to each individual on the various committees. In this way, everyone in the campaign is informed of the campaign plan and is working in unison toward a common goal through well-coordinated and defined duties. This approach underscores the term "organization" in campaign organization and reduces the problem of campaign workers not knowing what to do or when to do it. Developing a campaign calendar also tends to draw library supporters together and foster their commitment to the campaign.

A HYPOTHETICAL LIBRARY CAMPAIGN CALENDAR

Figure 6-1 is a hypothetical calendar that is being offered as a guide for library planners to use when creating their own campaign calendar. However, several disclaimers are in order. First, it is not essential that the items listed below be performed in the exact order specified. In fact, some may need to be sequenced differently depending upon the campaign plan. In addition, some activities will actually run concurrently over several weeks or even months. The hypothetical calendar is offered only as a rough framework.

Further, few campaigns will actually undertake each and every step listed. The hypothetical calendar simply presents a relative chronology; each community must develop its own campaign plan to determine which steps are necessary and which are not. Only then can a campaign calendar be developed which is specific to the individual community.

Finally, the hypothetical calendar assumes a fairly lengthy time period to allow for project planning, general awareness raising, and preliminary campaign planning and organization. Although it is certainly desirable to lay the groundwork for the campaign over a period of months and even years instead of days and weeks, many campaigns frequently are planned and implemented within only a few months because local funding agencies simply don't give library planners enough time. This is all too frequently a major pitfall that can sometimes be avoided by being aware of the political realities in the community, knowing deadlines for placing issues on the ballot, and planning ahead.

The hypothetical calendar displays the number of months, weeks, and days prior to election day and is broken down into three major parts:

I.   Laying the Foundation
II. Getting the Issue on the Ballot & Campaign Organization
III. Implementing the Campaign

The first section, "Laying the Foundation," can start as early as a year or two or more prior to election day. During this phase, library supporters plan the library project and do the preliminary planning necessary for the project. The second phase, getting the campaign off the

FIGURE 6-1   Hypothetical Planning Calendar

HYPOTHETICAL LIBRARY CAMPAIGN CALENDAR
(Time Periods Indicated are Prior to Election Day)

I. LAYING THE FOUNDATION

2 YEARS TO 6 MONTHS

Start Preliminary Awareness Raising Activities
Try for Extra Newspaper Coverage of Library Programs
Start Identifying Planning/Campaign Leadership & Volunteers
Acquire 501(c)(3) Requirements & Form Library Friends Group
Formation of Library Planning Team & Planning Committees
Fundraising by Friends for Costs of Project Planning Documents
Perform Market Research Survey
Develop a Needs Assessment
Hold Community Input Forums
Try for Extra Newspaper Coverage of Library Project
If Applicable, Develop a Library Facility Master Plan
If Applicable, Develop Library Building Program(s)
If Applicable, Perform Library Site Selection Study(ies)
If Applicable, Hire Architect to Develop Preliminary Architectural Plans
If Applicable, Develop Preliminary Project Budget(s)
If Applicable, Display Architectural Plans, Models or Renderings

II. GETTING THE ISSUE ON THE BALLOT & CAMPAIGN ORGANIZATION

6 MONTHS

Preliminary Contact with Community and Political Leaders
Assess the Possibilities for a Referendum
Assess Employee/Union Commitment to Campaign
Acquisition of Campaign Laws from the Secretary of State
Contact Local Elections Agency RE: Campaign Requirements
Legal Review of Campaign Laws & Requirements
Formation of the Campaign Steering Committee
Selection of the Campaign Manager
Selection of a Campaign Treasurer
Selection of Campaign Committee Chairpersons
Establish Campaign Political Action Committee (PAC)
Establish a Campaign Account
Preliminary Fundraising for Campaign Start-up Costs
Hire a Political Consultant & Pollster
Research Major Campaign Issues
Draft a Campaign Position Paper on the Need for the Project
Newspaper Article Coverage of Formation of Library Campaign

Continued

FIGURE 6-1 *Continued*

5 MONTHS

> Analyze Recent Election Results (By Precinct)
> Perform a Poll to Determine Support for the Library Issue & the
>   Most Effective Campaign Arguments
> Revise Campaign Position Paper on Need for the Project
> Analyze Results of Political Poll
> Hold Public Forums & Focus Groups on Campaign Position Paper
> Assess Major Issues and Develop Campaign Strategy
> Identify and Prioritize Target Groups
> Lobby Politicians to get Library Issue on Ballot
> Publish Campaign Position Paper in Library/Friends Newsletter
> Encourage Supporters to Attend Funding Agency Meeting Re: Ballot Determination
> Assist with Preparation of Ballot Language for Library Issue

4 MONTHS (16 WEEKS)

> Develop Campaign Message, Themes & Logo
> Develop Campaign Calendar & Budget
> Develop Fundraising Plan
> Develop Committee Calendars & Budgets
> Develop Committee Task and Staffing Assignments
> Develop Volunteer Budget

III. IMPLEMENTING THE CAMPAIGN

15 WEEKS

> Start Major Campaign Fundraising Effort
> Start Recruitment of Campaign Volunteer Workers
> Plan Public Service Announcements for Radio & TV
> Start Planning for Campaign Literature & Paraphernalia
> Contact Chamber of Commerce, Board of Realtors, Homeowners Associations, Etc.
> Start Voter Registration Drive

14 WEEKS

> Start First Stage (Identification) of Telephone Bank
> Continue Campaign Fundraising & Volunteer Recruitment
> Start Acquiring Early Personal/Organizational Endorsements
> Seek and Start Forging Campaign Coalitions
> Prepare Ballot Arguments for Library Issue

13 WEEKS

> Produce Public Service Announcements for Radio & TV
> Start Development of Campaign Literature & Paraphernalia

FIGURE 6-1 *Continued*

Continue Voter Registration Drive
Submit Ballot Arguments to Local Election Officials

12 WEEKS (3 MONTHS)

Start Running Public Service Announcements for Radio & TV
Plan Campaign Advertisements for Newspapers, TV & Radio
Verify Radio & TV Media Buy Times for Political Ads
Continue Recruitment of Campaign Volunteers & Fundraising
Continue First Stage (Identification) of Telephone Bank
Organize Speakers Bureau

11 WEEKS

Start to Organize Second Stage (Persuasion) Telephone Bank
Start to Organize Up-Coming Door-to-Door Canvassing Effort
Continue to Run Public Service Announcements for Radio & TV
Continue Voter Registration Drive
Plan Absentee Voter Effort (Determine Time Tables & Procedure)

10 WEEKS

Produce/Acquire Campaign Literature & Paraphernalia
Continue to Recruit Campaign Volunteers & Fundraise
Plan Kick-off and Media Events, Press Conferences & Rallies
Plan Breakfasts and Luncheons with Community Organizations & Businesses
Contact Other Campaigns & Candidates to Distribute Literature

9 WEEKS

Prepare Information Packets for Businesses, Community Organizations,
    Library Friends & Patrons
Plan Letter Writing Campaign to Newspaper Editors
Continue to Run Public Service Announcements for Radio & TV
Acquire More Personal & Organizational Endorsements
Develop & Produce AV Presentation
Step-up Voter Registration Drive
Continue First Stage (Identification) of Telephone Bank
Reserve Media Buys for Campaign Ads with Radio and TV Stations

8 WEEKS (2 MONTHS)

Start "Letters to the Editor" Writing Campaign
Distribute Buttons & Stickers to Campaign Volunteers
Hold Campaign Kick-off Event
Send Campaign Packets to Businesses & Community Organizations

Continued

FIGURE 6-1   *Continued*

Start AV Speaker Presentations to Community Organizations & Businesses
Start Seeking Media Endorsements (Newspaper, Radio & TV)
Mail Campaign Information Packet to Friends & Patrons
Step-up Recruitment of Campaign Volunteers & Fundraising
Start Absentee Voter Effort

7 WEEKS

Start Distribution of Informational Fact Sheets & Bookmarks in Libraries
Try for Extra Newspaper Article Coverage of Library Campaign
Get Campaign Information in Chamber of Commerce & Corporate Newsletters
Continue Voter Registration Drive
Finish First Stage (Identification) of Telephone Bank

6 WEEKS

Start Second Stage (Persuasion) of Telephone Bank
Concentrate on Endorsements of Newspaper, Radio and TV
Continue to Run Radio & TV Public Service Announcements
Continue to Recruit Campaign Volunteers & Fundraise
Prepare Press Kits for Press Conferences / Media Events

5 WEEKS

Step-up AV Speaker Presentations to Community Organizations & Businesses
Hold Press Conferences/Media Events as Needed
Finish Voter Registration Drive
Mailing of Informational Campaign Literature to Target Groups

4 WEEKS (1 MONTH)

Start Broad Distribution of Yard Signs & Posters
Continue Second Stage (Persuasion) Telephone Bank
Hold Library Open House
Try for Extra Newspaper Article Coverage of Library Campaign
Heavily Run Radio & TV Public Service Announcements
Perform & Analyze Results of Tracking Poll
Step-up Letter Writing Campaign to the Editor
Step-up Absentee Voter Effort
Continue to Recruit Campaign Volunteers & Fundraise

3 WEEKS

Start Door-to-Door Canvassing in Target Neighborhoods
Start Holding Block Parties in Target Neighborhoods
Step-up Second Stage (Persuasion) Telephone Bank

FIGURE 6-1 *Continued*

Publish "Library Buildings" Issue of Library Newsletter
Produce Persuasive Campaign Ads for TV & Radio
Secure Endorsements of Newspaper, Radio and TV
File Campaign Finance Reports as Necessary
Mailing of Persuasive Campaign Literature to Target Groups

2 WEEKS

Produce Persuasive Campaign Ads for Newspapers
Distribute Majority of Yard Signs & Posters
Continue Second Stage (Persuasion) Telephone Bank
Continue Door-to-Door Canvassing & Block Parties
Perform & Analyze Results of Optional Tracking Poll
Last Minute Volunteer Recruitment & Fundraising
Finish AV Speaker Presentations to Community Organizations & Businesses

1 WEEK

Step-up Door-to-Door Canvassing
Start Third Stage (GOTV) Telephone Bank
Run Newspaper, TV & Radio Persuasive Campaign Ads
Hold Press Conferences/Media Events as Necessary
Send Last Minute "Letters to the Editor"
Hand out Campaign Literature at Malls & Downtown
Place Remaining Yard Signs & Posters at Major Intersections
Last Mailing of Campaign Literature (GOTV) to Target Groups
    (To arrive a day or two prior to Election Day)

2–3 DAYS

Heavily Run Newspaper, TV & Radio Persuasive Campaign Ads
Step-up Third Stage (GOTV) Telephone Bank
Last Minute Shopping Mall & Downtown Leafleting
Place a Special "Sunday" Supplement in Newspaper
Hold Election Eve Special Event / Campaign Rally

ELECTION DAY

Poster & Sign Waving at Major Intersections and Overpasses
Poll Greeters Strategically Place Yard Signs on Way to Polls
Perform Poll Greeting & Watching Activities
Provide Transportation and Baby Sitting Service
Car Caravans with Loud Speakers and Streamers Cruise Downtown
Do All Last Minute GOTV Efforts (Telephone, Door Drop, etc.)
Finish Absentee Voter Effort
Hold Victory Party & Celebrate!

Continued

FIGURE 6-1 *Continued*

AFTER ELECTION

Send Written Thank You's to Campaign Supporters
Campaign "Clean Up", i.e., Take Down Yard Signs etc.
File Campaign Finance Reports
Write Final Campaign Report Summarizing All Activities

---

ground, involves convincing local officials to place the measure on the ballot as well understanding and complying with campaign laws and filing requirements. This stage will also include the actual formation of the campaign leadership and the preliminary campaign planning. Its preferable to start this phase about six months prior to the election, although it is frequently done later.

The final phase is the process of implementing the campaign. This is the most labor intensive stage, but will go smoother if the first two steps have been performed in a timely manner. Steering committee coordination will be essential since many campaign activities will occur simultaneously during the last few weeks before the election. This last stage will usually start three to four months prior to election day depending upon the size of the campaign, its strategy, as well as the amount of money and the number of volunteers that can be raised.

THE CAMPAIGN BUDGET

When the master calendar has been completed, the steering committee needs to develop a campaign budget. Just as the campaign calendar is based upon the campaign strategy, the budget is based upon specific activities in the calendar. Further, each potential activity specified in the calendar must be scrutinized to ensure that it is essential for getting "Yes" votes for the library. Beaudry and Schaeffer's excellent book, *Winning State and Local Elections: The Guide to Organizing You Campaign*, suggests developing three types of budgets: a program budget, a cash flow budget, and a volunteer budget.

PROGRAM BUDGET

For political campaigns, the budget's format is as important as its content. There is a strong temptation to create a traditional budget showing funds to be expended by category (such as printing, postage, advertising, etc.). However, this approach should be avoided because it is cumbersome for campaigns to use and lacks the degree of detail and flexibility needed in campaigning. Instead, the steering committee should develop a budget based on the various activities called for in the calendar. In other words, once all the activities have been planned, the steering committee must work with each committee to *develop an accurate and realistic cost estimate for each specific activity to be performed by each committee.*

This approach is called an "activity" or "program" budget and has been used effectively in all types of campaigns. Readers seeking more in-depth, professional advice on campaign budgeting are referred to *Winning Local and State Elections: The Guide to Organizing Your*

Campaigns by Ann Beaudry and Bob Schaeffer (Free Press, Macmillan, 1986). Beaudry and Schaeffer point out that "The program budget is derived by projecting expenses for each activity in the campaign plan. If you have described each activity in detail, estimating costs should not be difficult. . . . Go through the entire list of program activities detailed in your campaign plan. Estimate the cost for each."[1] For example, if one wanted to print 5,000 flyers that cost ten cents each, the printing costs would be $500. If you estimated design costs at $100 and typesetting at $50, the total cost for the activity would be $650. If the flyers are handed out by campaign volunteers, there is no cost for postage. In short, the activity budget lists various campaign activities and their costs.

The advantage to this approach is that if projected funds are not raised, the budget can be easily adjusted by eliminating or downsizing one or more activities. For example, a last minute newspaper ad may be dropped or the media budget trimmed so that only twenty radio commercials are run instead of the planned forty. Further, if more funds come in than expected, activities can be easily added or those already listed can be enhanced or expanded, for example, funding a better quality brochure promoting the library issue or more copies of it to be printed and distributed. As a result, the budget can be refined and modified as the campaign progresses and tactics shift.

Implementing this approach to budgeting gives the steering committee a very powerful tool for documenting priorities. Seasoned campaigners know that "Each potential expenditure should be questioned for its value in getting votes."[2] Those activities which have the highest potential to bring in "Yes" votes are the most essential, and *the steering committee must make certain that these get done before any others are undertaken.* This is where the precinct analysis which produced a priority list of activities in each priority precinct (See Chapter 5, pages 90-91) will come into use. The campaign's leadership must decide which activities are absolutely essential to pass the referendum and develop a rock bottom budget to support those activities.

The amount of money necessary to support this budget is the very least amount that must be raised or the campaign will not be viable. Once this bottom line budget is established, the steering committee can then develop "budget blocks" for important, but not essential, activities. If additional funds do become available, these blocks can then be added to the original budget projection to provide some insurance for success. In this manner, the steering committee can more effectively manage money as it becomes available.

Contingency

It is always good to keep a five to ten percent contingency in reserve for any budget, if possible, right up to the end of the campaign. This keeps funds available to take advantage of good ideas which come up during the campaign or for last minute unexpected activities such as responding to an attack by the opposition with an additional newspaper or radio ad. If no opposition forms and there is no last minute need for the funds, one last mailing can be made (or expanded) or the final GOTV effort can be stepped up a notch to help insure that supporters get to the polls.

CASH FLOW BUDGET

In addition to the activity or program budget, Beaudry and Schaeffer recommend that a "cash flow budget"[3] be developed. A cash flow budget provides campaign planners with an analysis of when funds will be needed to support the various activities planned in the program budget.

It is simply a chronological listing of when the various campaign activities in the program budget will take place (based on the campaign calendar) along with a statement of the cost of each activity. When creating a cash flow budget, make sure you keep in mind when the funds will be needed to meet production costs (designing and printing a brochure) as well as actually performing the activity (mailing the brochure).

A cash flow budget is critical to make certain that funds are raised in a timely manner to support campaign activities. It will be used by the finance committee to schedule various fund raising activities. This is particularly important since most campaign expenses must be paid in advance. Without an effective cash flow budget, campaign planners may find themselves in the desperate position of having a planned activity ready to go with volunteers on hand, but without the necessary funds to implement the activity. It is particularly important that this be avoided especially for activities which are critical to the success of the campaign. Figure 6-2 is a cash flow budget for a hypothetical library campaign.

VOLUNTEER BUDGET

The third type of budget Beaudry and Schaeffer recommend is a volunteer budget which takes each of the activities listed in the program budget and assigns the number of volunteers necessary to perform the task. For example, if the campaign needs to construct and place 500 yard signs in the supporters' yards, the volunteer budget would identify how many volunteers would be needed and for how many hours to perform the task. The volunteer budget is a form of resource allocation and management and along with the fiscal budget provides the steering committee with an overview of how all campaign resources are being allocated.

Volunteer recruitment and management is discussed in detail in Chapter 8.

THE SIZE OF LIBRARY CAMPAIGN BUDGETS

The size and characteristics of each library campaign budget will vary depending upon what is needed to achieve the desired goal of a successful referendum. Some campaigns may be successful with shoe-string budgets, while others which spend a great deal may not. Simply spending a large amount of money is not the answer. What matters is how effectively the funds are expended in conjunction with the appropriateness of the campaign strategy. Generally, campaigns in smaller communities will tend to cost less than campaigns in larger, more sophisticated markets. This is true for a number of reasons, not the least of which is that urban campaigns must reach more people with their message. This frequently means that these campaigns must resort to expensive mass marketing techniques such as media advertising. Fortunately, there is also more money available in urban areas than in rural areas. The challenge is to find a way to reach enough voters to pass the measure without spending any more money than necessary.

Data has never been consistently collected on the amount that libraries spend on referenda campaigns. Because of this, there is no "standard" expenditure; however, in recent sampling of library referenda campaigns, the average campaign expenditure was somewhere between $5,000 and $10,000. The majority of budgets were under $10,000, because the majority of campaigns sampled were small and did do not use a political consultant or pollster. Some campaigns went into the $40,000 to $50,000 range and a few major metropolitan campaigns were reported to have spent as much as $100,000 or more.

FIGURE 6-2   Hypothetical Campaign Cash Flow Budget

HYPOTHETICAL LIBRARY CAMPAIGN CASH FLOW BUDGET

JUNE

Commission Voter Opinion Poll	$$$$$$

JULY

Political Consultant's Analysis of Poll Results & Advise on Campaign Plan	$$$$$$

AUGUST

Produce Public Service Announcements for Radio & TV	$$$$$$
Acquire Fact Sheets & Bookmarks for Library Distribution	$$$$$$

SEPTEMBER

Produce AV Presentation for Community Organizations	$$$$$$
Acquire Campaign Buttons with Library Logo/Slogan	$$$$$$
Campaign Kick-Off Event	$$$$$$
Acquire Informational Literature for Targeted Mailing	$$$$$$

OCTOBER — 1ST WEEK

Mailing of Informational Literature to Target Groups	$$$$$$
AV Presentations to Community Groups	$$$$$$

OCTOBER — 2ND WEEK

Tracking Poll	$$$$$$
Political Consultant's Analysis of Tracking Poll & Advise on Adjustments in Campaign Plan	$$$$$$
Acquire Yard Signs & Posters	$$$$$$
Acquire Literature for Door-to-Door Canvassing	$$$$$$
Acquire Persuasive Campaign Flyer for Targeted Mailing	$$$$$$

OCTOBER — 3RD WEEK

Produce Persuasive Campaign Radio Ads	$$$$$$
Construct & Distribute Yard Signs & Posters	$$$$$$
Door-to-Door Canvassing in Target Neighborhoods	$$$$$$
Mailing of Persuasive Campaign Flyer to Target Groups	$$$$$$
Acquire GOTV Postcard for Mailing to Target Groups	$$$$$$

OCTOBER — 4TH WEEK

Purchase Radio Time for Persuasive Radio Ads	$$$$$$
Perform GOTV Telephone Bank	$$$$$$
Last Minute Mailing of GOTV Postcard to Target Groups	$$$$$$
Produce Newspaper Persuasive Campaign Ad	$$$$$$

NOVEMBER

Purchase Newspaper Space for Persuasive Campaign Ads	$$$$$$
Campaign Rally	$$$$$$
Acquire Poll Greeters Flyer	$$$$$$
Victory Party	$$$$$$

The amount of funds available for library campaigns is lower that it really should be to guarantee success, and frankly it is a wonder that as many library issues succeed as the record shows. This in itself is testament to the high level of esteem that the electorate holds public libraries. However, recently there have been signs that this may not be enough to continue to insure success. Competition for the public tax dollar, especially at the ballot box, is increasing each year, and it is becoming obvious that libraries will have to be significantly more aggressive in the future to maintain their enviable success rate with referenda.

One of the ways that libraries have kept the need to raise substantial sums of money down is to turn out significant numbers of volunteers at the grassroots level. As Chapter 8 will discuss, organizing volunteers is critical to the success of most library referenda campaigns. Library planners may also need to use professional campaign fundraisers. Particularly in large campaigns, it is important for the campaign leadership to have assistance from not only able fundraisers, but also lawyers to make sure that the campaign treasurer—and the campaign in general—stays legal and out of trouble.

REFERENCES

1. Beaudry, Ann E. and Bob Schaeffer. *Winning Local and State Elections*. New York: The Free Press, Macmillan, 1986, p. 50.
2. Dugan, Jean Brodshaug. *Campaigning to Win: A Workbook for Women in Politics*. Washington, D.C.: National Women's Political Caucus, 1993, p. VI-2.
3. Beaudry and Schaeffer, p. 51.

7 LEGAL ISSUES & FUNDRAISING

LEGAL ISSUES

LEGAL COUNSEL

There are numerous occasions when campaign planners will need the advice of legal counsel regarding campaign practices. It will be necessary to obtain competent legal advice at a reasonable cost throughout the campaign. Occasionally, the legal counsel will be provided by the attorney for the local jurisdiction, but frequently campaigns must rely on the services of outside attorneys. While it may be possible to obtain legal services free of charge as an in-kind contribution by legal firms, campaign budgets should frequently include a line item for legal fees. This is particularly true if there is likely to be a lot of legal work necessary because of prospective opposition or if a very quick response time to issues which come up in the heat of the campaign is necessary. The major campaign legal issues for which an attorney may be needed are as follows:

- Ballot or resolution language
- Involvement of library staff, facilities, equipment, and supplies
- The printing and distribution of factual and campaign information
- Confidentiality laws regarding use of patron records
- Campaign financial accounting and reporting requirements
- Formation of a Political Action Committee (PAC)
- 501(c)(3) requirements for the Friends group or Foundation
- The petition process.

It is always important to be careful about legal issues when campaigning, but it is particularly important to document all campaign activities that have legal implications when there is strong opposition. Frequently, the opposition will attempt to discredit a campaign based upon legal issues. It does not matter how well meaning library supporters are: if they place the campaign in a compromising position because of lack of attention to legal matters, the campaign could experience an insurmountable setback. It is better to be safe than sorry when it comes to campaign procedures prescribed by law. There is nothing more frustrating than to win a campaign and then have the referendum overturned because of a technical violation of election laws.

SECRETARY OF STATE & LOCAL CAMPAIGN OFFICIALS

The Secretary of State's Office in each state is responsible for providing information on campaign laws and procedures. In addition, local City and County Clerk's offices frequently distribute information regarding any local election ordinances. These laws and ordinances usually cover such subjects as the proper disclosure of campaign contributions and expenditures, filing deadlines, and general ballot requirements. It is helpful to obtain the assistance of the Secretary of State's Office and the local elections official's office early in the campaign so that no mistakes are made in handling of campaign funds. Again, legal counsel will be necessary in order to help understand and interpret some of the requirements. Also, it can be helpful to contact the Treasurer of other recently held campaigns. Because of their recent experience, these individuals should be fairly well versed in the practical considerations of campaign financial accounting and reporting. It is extremely important to clearly understand the campaign laws in order to avoid what could be a very embarrassing situation caused by non-compliance, or worse, punitive consequences resulting from a violation of the law.

THE DECISION TO PLACE THE LIBRARY QUESTION ON THE BALLOT

When campaign planners have retained legal counsel and researched the necessary campaign issues, the first legal step in the referendum process is to get the library issue placed on the ballot for an election. Although there are important legal issues involved in this step, usually the most important aspect of this step is political. Local political officials are generally not predisposed towards putting a lot of issues on the ballot mainly because it costs the local jurisdiction, and therefore the taxpayers, money. Therefore one of the first hurdles for library planners is to convince local politicians that the library issue should be placed on the ballot.

If library supporters can't get past this first step, they won't have to worry about selling the issue to the electorate because there won't be any campaign. So what is needed to convince politicians that the library issue should be on the ballot? First, library supporters must be able to show local politicians that the library issue won't cause problems for them with their constituents. To do this, it is helpful to demonstrate to the elected officials what's in the library issue for them (like a new branch, better service for their constituents, etc.). Library planners should remember that all politicians want to be reelected, and in order to be reelected, they must keep the people in the districts they represent satisfied that they are doing a good job.

So what else can library supporters do to make certain that their library issue will be considered favorably for placement on the ballot? For the most part, *local officials will be looking for a demonstration of broad community support for the issue,* which is another reason why it is important to have performed a good deal of awareness raising prior to the actual campaign. It is also helpful to have raised some campaign donations so that the elected officials know that the community is willing to "vote with their pocketbook" and that library supporters are sincere in their intent to campaign for the issue. Any issue that increases taxes is important to politicians. Unless the electorate perceives the library issue as important and worthy of a tax increase, it is usually not beneficial for an elected official to take a position of raising taxes for the library project. Before library supporters can obtain the privilege of campaigning for the library issue, they must convince the elected officials that the public is already supportive of the issue. This logic sounds a little circular, but it is exactly what needs to happen in order to get the library question on the ballot.

In order to do this, the library supporters will have to show the extent of political support already present in the community. This is when it is important to have already lined up influential endorsees and a substantial number of bodies that can be sent to the council or commission meeting. Packing the meeting room is a tried and true strategy which often works. It is much more impressive to have a room full of supporters, rather than just one or two individuals, asking for the issue to be placed on the ballot. A crowd also demonstrates the likelihood of passing the ballot measure. If any preliminary polls or surveys have been taken, the results may be presented. In addition, it is important to be able to accurately talk about the costs of the project. This includes the capital budget as well as the long term operating budget. Library planners must be able to defend any project cost estimates, and, therefore, should have prepared a preliminary estimate which is as accurate as possible. Finally, the case for the need must be carefully presented as succinctly and dramatically as possible along with a brief description of the improved services for the community. Also any economic benefits should be mentioned at this time and quantified if possible.

In order to "grease the skids" for the issue, it is usually wise to talk with the elected officials well in advance of the meeting where the decision will be made. This will not only help avoid any surprises for the politicians, but will also provide an early warning system if any of the officials are unfavorable. In combination with the "show of force" at the main meeting, it is useful to have the official's constituents and particularly major campaign contributors make contact in advance of the meeting and demonstrate their support of the library issue. If this doesn't happen in advance of the decision, the issue can sometimes be "dead on arrival."

One of the most important things to learn about dealing with politicians is not to embarrass them in public if at all possible. Keep them well informed about the library issue as the campaign progresses, but most importantly try to get their advice and active support for the issue. Elected officials, by the very nature of their job, come into contact with a large number of people on a daily basis. If they are willing to support the issue at public presentations or contact others in their political network, then so much the better. Finally, it is usually extremely beneficial if the steering committee can actually get a majority of the governing body to publicly endorse the library issue. Along with advising on the campaign strategy, if elected officials are willing to actively campaign for the library issue, library supporters will have powerful allies assuming the officials are in good standing with the community.

THE PETITION PROCESS

In most communities, a majority of the governing body of the local funding agency can authorize the placement of a question on a ballot. However, sometimes it is not possible to obtain this support. If this is the case, in most states the only recourse available to library supporters is the petition process which requires library supporters to gather a substantial number (whatever is required by law) of signatures and have them validated by a specified deadline.

Be forewarned, this is not easy. Before it is attempted, library supporters must understand the effort involved. Winning a referendum in a reasonably good political environment is difficult enough, but doing it with the "City Fathers" in opposition is an uphill battle and just that much harder. Being the outsiders in the political arena is not pleasant, but if the petition process is the only option available, library supporters will be wise to obtain legal advice on the petition process and its language.

BALLOT LANGUAGE

Once the measure is approved for placement on the ballot, the next step is to draft the ballot language. The local jurisdiction that places the question on the ballot, usually has its attorney draft the ballot question. However, it may be possible to have input into the language of the ballot question or even the opportunity to draft the language. It will be beneficial to work with the funding agency's attorney to make sure that the wording is understandable, and as much as legally possible, to the library's benefit.

How the ballot question is worded can often make a great deal of difference in the outcome of the vote. This can really make a difference! It is amazing how negative ballot language, especially ballot language dealing with debt, can sound to the general electorate when written up in the required legalese. Legal counsel for the campaign should attempt to have the intent of language stated as positively as possible. Further, it is helpful if the language is as clear and non-technical as possible.

Finally, it is important to write the ballot language as broadly as possible to allow for maximum flexibility in the use of the funds. An example of this is ballot language for a referendum which would allow any funds left over from the main project or projects being proposed to be expended on other library projects, such as the ballot language used by the Palos Verdes Library District:

"PROPOSITION D. For the purpose of adding to and renovating library facilities to increase educational, informational and recreational opportunities of residents and to make health and safety improvements including seismic, fire protection, asbestos removal, and disabled access, shall the Palos Verdes Library District incur a bonded indebtedness in the maximum amount of $16,000,000?"

The referendum was for the remodeling and expansion of the central library building, but any funds left over could have been used to expand and remodel branch libraries as well. A similar approach could be taken to allow for the expenditure of remaining funds for books if this activity is allowable under state laws.

LOCATION ON THE BALLOT

Campaign planners will also want to have their attorney review the location of the library question on the ballot. If input is allowed, it is important to avoid following any controversial and potentially negative campaign questions. Of course, it is better to avoid being on the ballot with a large number of negative issues at all, but this is frequently not possible. Further, it is usually better to be placed as high on the ballot as possible. This is because voters often get tired and turn negative the farther down the ballot they get. If letters are used to identify ballot items in the jurisdiction, try to get one that can be used effectively in campaigning. For example, even though their ballot measure was low on the ballot, the Rockridge, California, campaign supporters were able to obtain the letter "L" and turned it into a campaign advantage by promoting "L is for Library."

BALLOT ARGUMENTS

Ballot arguments should be carefully prepared in order to make the case for the library issue in a positive and forceful manner. If campaign planners do nothing else well, they need to make sure that they do a good job on the ballot arguments especially if funds necessitate a limited campaign. In many campaigns, the ballot arguments are the main method of communicating the library's message as these will be read by almost every potential voter just before going to the polls. In some cases, this may be the only message the voter gets about the library issue. Obviously, it had better be a persuasive one.

The individuals who sign the ballot arguments are also extremely important because they are essentially providing an endorsement, and like any endorsement, the status of the endorsee is very important. Civic leaders and respected members of the community should be sought out to sign the ballot arguments. Once the ballot language and arguments are finalized, it is often a good move to display them in the library or hand them out at various activities to get the electorate used to the language as well as raising awareness of the library issue. Again, it would be helpful to have an attorney review any ballot arguments to make certain they are accurate and legally acceptable.

THE USE OF LIBRARY PATRON RECORDS

Another area which needs legal review is the sensitive issue of the use of library patron records during a campaign. The first and most obvious issue is that of the confidentiality of the patron records. While it is extremely important that libraries be able to utilize the influence and support provided by their patrons, it is also imperative that the campaign does not abridge any laws. Before using any patron records as part of the campaign, the steering committee should consult with an attorney. This should be done early in the campaign in order to determine the potential use of the records so that the legal interpretation can be considered during strategic planning. In most cases, library patron records can probably be used for activities such as informational mailings (newsletters, fact sheets etc.), but mailings which are persuasive in nature (i.e., political campaign materials) may fall into a different category and may not be permitted.

The use of patron records for political purposes must be approached with great care and caution. If the current patron records are restricted from use by the campaign, it may be possible for the library management to consider a course of action which will provide some future access to the records without abridging confidentiality laws; however, any such attempt should be performed with the understanding that proponents may be on questionable ethical ground. In order to avoid problems with confidentiality laws, it may be possible to provide access to some patron records for political purposes if certain steps are taken at the time of the next patron registration effort. It may be possible, for example, in some states and locales to provide space on the patron registration form to ask the following question:

"Will you allow the library management to provide your name, address, and telephone number to a campaign committee for the express purpose of seeking your support for any upcoming library ballot issues?"

Based on the answer to this question, the library management could generate a list of patrons who have given their permission to have their records utilized for any library campaign. This would be especially easy if the patron registration activity is automated. However, it should be noted that the paper record of these transactions should be kept in case there is ever any question regarding the activity. Further, if this approach is attempted, it should be done under the review of an attorney, and if there is any concern on the part of the attorney or library management regarding the legal or ethical propriety of the approach, the more conservative and safe interpretation should be followed by campaign planners. Remember, it only takes one irate and vocal library patron who doesn't support the referendum issue to create a lot of bad press at the worst possible time in a campaign.

With this disclaimer in mind, it is also obvious that the library's own patrons will be one of the main sources of volunteers, financial support, and votes. If there is any legal and ethical way to access these individuals, it is extremely important to do so efficiently and effectively. There is absolutely nothing wrong with asking those who benefit most from the service to become advocates for that service as long as it is done on firm legal ground. Library campaigners should use any and all means legally at their disposal in their attempt to win the campaign. They should not be expected to fight the battle without their primary support group at their side. Those library managers and supporters too timid to ask their patrons to advocate for the library will find any campaign effort extremely difficult. If these people are not willing to support the library question, it is difficult to conceive how the issue will succeed at the polls.

If it is determined that library patron records can be accessed for campaign purposes, the information has many potential uses. Patrons can be contacted as any other target group. Besides providing a source of potential volunteers, patron records can provide a way to reach library patrons through informational and persuasive campaign mailings. Patrons can be contacted by telephone banks and asked for campaign donations and support at the polls. The use of patron records can be an important tool, especially if they can be cross-referenced with a voter registration list. This group is a prime target group of sympathetic "Yes" voters, and they are also individuals who tend to have a relatively high voter registration rate. Regardless of the process used, they *must* be aware of the library's issue and encouraged to vote for it.

LIBRARY STAFF INVOLVEMENT

Another sensitive campaign issue is the involvement of the library staff. In many states, the use of public facilities, staff, or supplies for campaign purposes is restricted or prohibited. Generally, only an informational role is allowed, although some states' campaign laws are more lenient. It is best, early in the campaign, to check with local elections officials and the Secretary of State's Office to determine the permissible level and extent of staff involvement and facility use. The campaign's legal counsel can then determine the extent of staff involvement in the campaign. However, it should be recognized that the campaign laws in many states may be open to interpretation; again, it is usually best to be safe and act conservatively.

In any case, staff should be informed and trained as to how they should respond when asked about the referendum while they are on duty. This is important particularly if there are specific things that they must not say or do when asked about the library's need and/or referendum issue. Train staff how to respond positively to inquiries or else they may be uncomfortable and generally be non-responsive to the public on the issue. To be positive ambassadors for the library, they must know what is expected of them, what is appropriate, and what is not.

Any restrictions placed on staff involvement while on duty are frequently lifted when they are off duty. Again, this must be reviewed by an attorney. If the perceived "vested interest" is of concern and has the potential for becoming a significant negative campaign issue, it may be best to limit the campaign activities of the staff regardless of the legality of such activity. However, if this is not a problem, the staff's involvement can be of considerable help since they will probably be highly motivated workers and potential campaign donors. Further, because of their intimate knowledge of the library issue, they can be very good promoters and can often be an effective sounding board during development of the campaign plan as long as they do so on their own time. If there are no legal or practical restrictions to staff involvement, it is generally good to have active staff support for the campaign, but be sure not to put any pressure on them to campaign for the issue if they do not want to.

Even if use of the library's staff and facilities will be limited to providing information only, this in itself can be a very effective method of raising awareness. For example, the library can distribute informational fact sheets and bookmarks explaining the situation and the need to patrons. This can be done not only across the circulation desk, but also during programs scheduled in the library's meeting room which can be a particularly effective way of reaching community groups which use the library's meeting room facilities. Just be certain that these materials only provide information and do not attempt to persuade a "Yes" vote in any way. Further, the library's logo can be effectively incorporated into book bags, buttons, and balloons given out at special activities. As mentioned earlier, staff can also increase library awareness through special programming for adults or children during the campaign.

FUNDRAISING

POLITICAL ACTION COMMITTEES (PACS) & FINANCIAL REPORTING

Legal advice is also needed on the campaign's organization and finances. Based upon the legal review of the information collected from the Secretary of State's Office, the campaign's legal counsel can recommend a course of action regarding establishing a political action committee (PAC) for the library campaign as well as a separate campaign account. In some states, this step may not be required depending upon the amount of funds collected and expended for campaign purposes, but in most, it will be necessary to set up one or more PACs for the campaign. Usually, PACs are established under specific campaign laws so that the public interest is protected from abusive campaign practices.

Proper handling of campaign contributions and expenditures is a major concern. Because of specified reporting procedures, a PAC's financial transactions are open for public inspection. In many states, campaign disclosure laws limit how campaign contributions can be made (by check versus cash), define whether or not in-kind contributions must be reported, and specify the date by which campaign finances must be reported. Further, most states require that all campaign commercials or literature be identified by a statement which identifies that the commercial or literature was paid for by the name of the campaign committee along with the name of its treasurer. In many states, the campaign treasurer is responsible for filing all required campaign financial reports.

THE CAMPAIGN TREASURER AND THE FINANCE COMMITTEE

Because election laws must be observed, it will be necessary for the steering committee to select a treasurer who will be responsible for accounting for the receipt and disbursement of all campaign funds as well as complying with all codes regarding financial reporting. Obviously, someone with accounting skills who has served as a campaign treasurer before would be a good choice. The treasurer should work carefully with the campaign's legal counsel to make sure that all campaign laws are fully complied with. Further, the treasurer is responsible for providing campaign financial statements to the campaign manager on a regular basis as well as keeping all steering committee members informed on the balance of funds allocated to their individual committee activity "accounts."

This is an extremely important position and the treasurer must be selected carefully. Fundraising skills are also needed if the person is also be responsible for campaign fundraising. In many cases (unless prohibited by state law), the campaign treasurer will also serve as head of the finance committee.

Since the finance committee must raise the funds necessary to operate the campaign, each committee member should have experience at fundraising and be able to deliver funds from specific sectors of the community. The committee should be made up of well-respected local people who have money, who know people who have money, and are used to handling money in some manner. Committee members will assist in identifying prospective donors as well as participate in the solicitation of the money. They should be able to ask for money and should usually belong to or be in some way associated with professional, business, or technical groups which have funds available for campaign donations. While campaign donations can to some extent be generated on an broad basis from the community as a whole, the majority of private contributions will normally be obtained from a relatively few individuals or organizations in the community. This fact reinforces the necessity to make certain that finance committee members have good access to those individuals and organizations who regularly donate funds.

FUNDRAISING FOR START-UP COSTS

Any campaign fundraising effort will have a few start-up expenses for which funds will need to be found just to get started with any serious fundraising. This is fundraising in order to fundraise. Start-up campaign costs can include expenses for such things as letterhead, envelopes, mailing labels, postage, a graphic artist, printing for some preliminary campaign literature, and potentially a microcomputer with software to develop donor lists and profiles as well as provide assistance in mailings if one isn't owned by a campaign steering committee member and available for the campaign. For large campaigns, funds may be needed up front for space rental, along with telephones, desks, file cabinets, as well as paid personnel. Once a minimal amount of start-up funding is obtained, the finance committee can gear up for a serious fundraising effort.

Start-up funds usually come from one highly motivated individual or from the campaign committee insiders. This "anteing up" can be very good because it demonstrates commitment and allows fundraisers to be able to say to prospective donors that they have already given to the campaign. One way to raise $10,000 quickly from close campaign supporters is to use techniques such as Beaudry and Schaeffer's "Ten for Ten" program which is essentially a pyramid scheme in which ten volunteers form a Ten for Ten Committee. Each of these Committee members recruits ten people to give a party for ten guests.

"Your goal: a hundred hosts and hostesses, each of whom will invite ten guests. Each invitee (or couple, family, etc.) is asked to contribute $10. At 1,000 guests times $10 each, that's $10,000 in campaign contributions. The parties can be held over a period of several weeks, or all in one week, as your campaign calendar dictates. . . . The individual hosting each party contributes the food and refreshments and provides the entertainment. Party themes can be as varied as dinner by a gourmet cook, a backyard picnic, cards and games, or an evening of old movies played on a video recorder."[1]

FUNDRAISING PLAN

The finance committee is responsible for developing a plan to support the projected campaign budget. This should be a written plan which lists and describes the fundraising activities in detail, sets up a timetable for each activity, and establishes deadlines by which specific amounts of money must be raised (the cash flow budget discussed in Chapter 6) in order to meet the campaign's plan requirements. The plan must set specific amounts of money to be raised by each activity in the financial plan, i.e., how much will be raised by direct mail, special events, direct one-on-one solicitation, etc. The financial plan should also document how the campaign will keep donor records. This is necessary to comply with campaign reporting requirements, to make sure that every donor is properly thanked, as well as to provide a list of donors which can be approached a second or third time later in the campaign if funds run short.

One part of the financial plan is to establish a structure for identifying potential donors and then determining how much they will give and why they will give it. Donor prospects must be identified and classified by the amount of money they may be expected to give. This can be done by the fundraising committee during a prospect evaluation meeting where each potential donor is assigned to a specific donation category like $50, $100, $500, $1,000, etc. Like most private fundraising efforts, this approach will establish a fundraising pyramid with a specific number of large donors at the top, a higher number of medium donors in the middle, and an even larger number of small donors at the bottom of the pyramid.

Campaign solicitors need to seek the right amount from each prospective donor. Information about the potential donor's previous giving history will help to size the amount of the request so that fundraisers don't ask for too little or too much and offend the prospect. When asking for campaign donations, it is critical to ask for a specific amount as well as providing donors with a good reason why they should give money to the campaign. Most people won't give to a campaign unless they feel they have something to gain. Campaign solicitors have got to make a personal connection between the prospective donor and the library issue. One frequently used pitch is to demonstrate to the potential donor how their donation can be viewed as an investment in the community because of the benefits provided to all people in the area by an information source such as a public library. Always remember: the primary reason people don't give is that they are never asked.

CAMPAIGN FUNDRAISING: METHODS & SOURCES

Incredible amounts of money are raised every year for political campaigns, but raising money for a library campaign takes perseverance and dedication as well as believing in the library issue. A lot of people are going to have to commit time, money, or both. Many people find it easier to ask someone to donate time to a campaign than they do asking for money, but in today's society "time is money," so it's not much of a stretch to learn to become comfortable with asking for funds as well. If the campaign is having difficulty getting contributions, this may be a sign that its planners are not really committed to the library issue. If this is the case, the steering committee may need to reexamine the issue before they proceed with the campaign. Once it is decided to proceed, it is usually a good idea to get as many people involved in fundraising as possible since this will create a sense of ownership and increase the likelihood of those people, and the people they come in contact with, actually voting for the issue. A broad-based fundraising effort also demonstrates support for the library issue to elected officials and the media. It is universally understood that people who donate even $20 to a campaign are very likely to vote in favor of the issue.

One of the first questions that is often asked is "How much money will we need to raise for the campaign?" The answer to this lies in the campaign strategy and plan as well as the amounts typically spent on other recent campaigns held in the community. It is a good idea to talk with the treasurer of other recently held campaigns to get an idea of what the costs were, as well as obtain a copy of the donor list of those who contributed to the campaign. If there is any hesitancy to ask for this information, remember it can be obtained from the Secretary of State's Office since it is public information available because of campaign financial reporting requirements. Donor lists from several recent local campaigns can be worth their weight in gold, because they represent known donors. Those individuals who have donated to a campaign before have a higher probability of donating to a campaign again; it is relatively easy to raise money from these individuals if they are sympathetic to the library issue.

Donors come in all shapes and sizes. Small donors usually provide contributions of less than $50, but enough of them will make a difference in a campaign, especially if fundraisers can set up a monthly donation system. The first step in any campaign fundraising effort is to set up a donor database system. This can be done with file cards or on a microcomputer. Basic information should be entered which identifies the donor by name, address, and telephone. Other information that may be helpful is any previous history on the frequency and amount of political contributions. Further, a system should be set up to track when the donor has been contacted, by whom, how much was given, and how many times the donor has given. This should be done for both small and large donors if possible.

Most campaigns find that it is more difficult to raise money early in the campaign than it is later. This is because people are not aware of the campaign in the early stages, but as they become familiar with it, they are often more likely to support it financially. This can create problems when setting up a budget at the beginning of a campaign. The more money that is raised early, the easier it is to plan the campaign strategy and establish the budget. Further, it is often true that the more money a campaign raises in the early days, the easier it is to convince others to follow suit thereby making it easier to raise additional funds later in the campaign. By creating a donor list and database, campaign fundraisers have a tool which can be used in the later stages of the campaign in order to go back and resolicit funds for last minute campaign activities, like that one last newspaper ad or mailing just before the election.

Individuals who have given once to a campaign are very likely to give again, if they perceive that the money is needed and that it will make a difference. In these cases, it is particularly important to solicit the funds for a specific purpose. There are many methods of raising funds for a campaign, but one of the most effective is to solicit funds for a specific activity. While some individuals or organizations are willing to give funds to a campaign in general, it is usually easier to get money if it can be tied to a specific need such as a mailing, printing campaign literature, or a radio ad. Basically, this approach works because donors like to know what their money is going for. When asking for money in this manner, be as specific as possible about both the amount needed as well as the activity.

There are many ways to solicit campaign contributions, but one of the most effective is direct personal solicitation. Experience has shown that regardless of the method used to ask for funds, the personal touch is extremely important. There is no better approach than a direct appeal from a highly motivated individual who believes in the campaign and can convince his or her friends, associates, or colleagues that the cause is worth donating money toward. Usually, contributions from large donors are obtained from face-to-face sessions. Essentially, the solicitor should be prepared to tell the library's story in a compelling manner and provide the potential donor with an outline of the campaign's plan. A specific amount should be requested. If a pledge cannot be obtained on the spot, a deadline by which the funds are needed should be given.

Every individual who has donated to the campaign should be thanked in some manner no matter how small their donation. A personal note from the campaign manager, treasurer, library director, or board chairperson will go a long way toward making the donor feel appreciated. Donors who feel that their contribution was valued will be more receptive if a second request for funds becomes necessary later in the campaign. If donors are made to feel special, they will usually open the pocketbook wider as well. This is particularly important for campaigns which are held during general elections when the competition for political contributions is high.

Fundraising should go on throughout the campaign and be performed by as many individuals as possible. In a sense, everyone active in the campaign can be a fundraiser and every campaign activity can have a fundraising aspect associated with it. Campaign workers should always have "contribution cards" ready. Solicitation letters can be sent out after a telephone contact or provided during a door-to-door canvassing contact. Many campaigns raise money using direct mail techniques. Direct mail can be expensive and frequently about two-thirds of every dollar raised is used to pay for the cost of the mailing. Return rates are often low, usually only around two to three percent, but these rates can be increased significantly if the mailing is followed up with a telephone call by a campaign volunteer. As with other campaign methods, it is best to target prospective direct mail donors. This approach allows for solicitation letters to be tailored to the target group as well as personalized by campaign supporters. There is a real art to developing effective direct mail solicitation letters. They should appeal to potential donors on an emotional level and make them feel like their personal contribution is essential to the library issue.

This is true of any fundraising effort because once again it demonstrates how important the personal aspect of fundraising and campaigning is to the success of the endeavor. Regardless if it is an appeal to an individual or to an organization, the personal aspect of the appeal is essential and should not be underestimated. Simply blanketing the public with letters asking for money rarely produces the desired effect. While it is extremely tedious, it is best to have campaign committee members sign letters, add personal notes, and direct them to people that they know personally or have some association within the community. Because of the

FIGURE 7-1 Fundraising Envelope. Provided Courtesy of Spokane Public Library, Spokane, Washington.

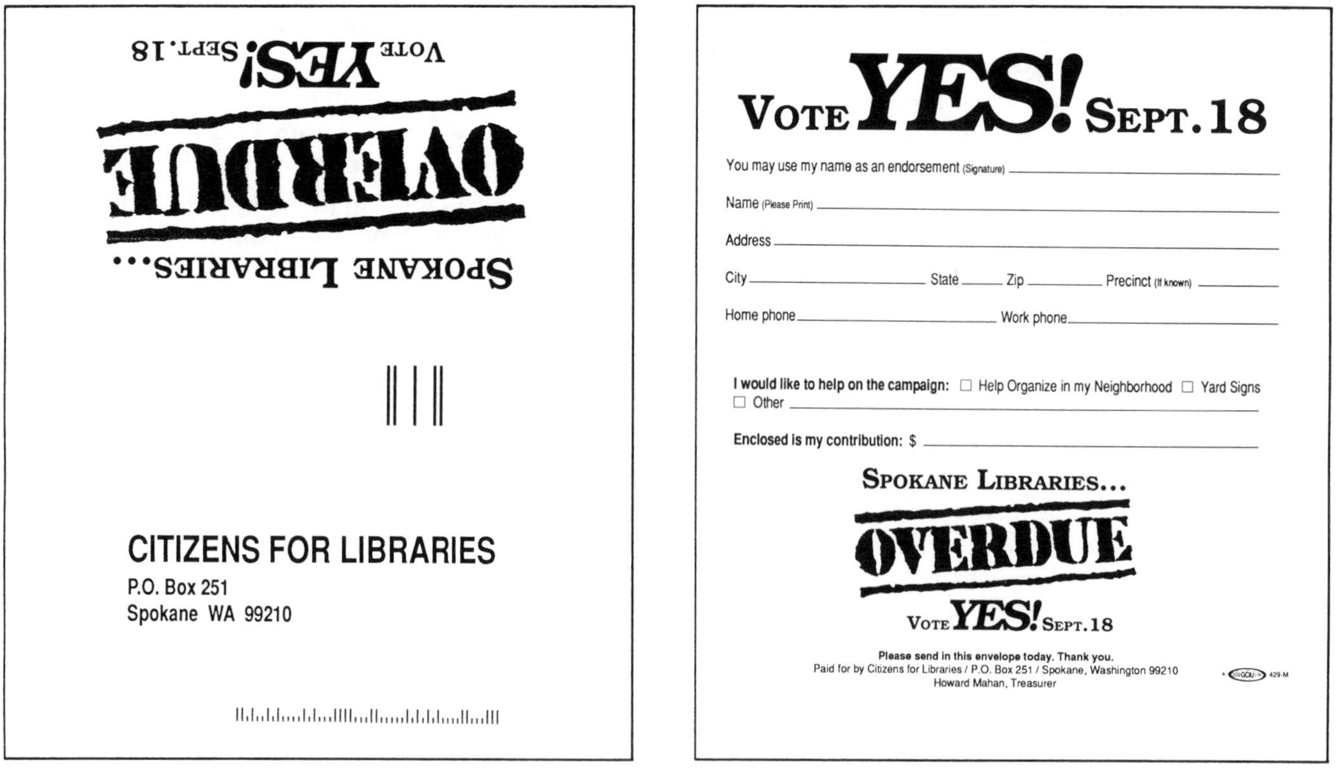

importance of personal contact during fundraising, it is extremely helpful if the library has an already established Friends group.

THE ROLE OF THE LIBRARY FRIENDS GROUP IN FUNDRAISING

A large and active Friends group with the inclination and ability to actively raise funds can tremendously benefit a library campaign because they provide an expanded contact base into the community at large. Frequently, many of the campaign workers and even the steering committee members will also be members of the Friends. However, the financial relationship between the two organizations should be carefully reviewed by an attorney to make sure that there are no problems with either campaign laws or the 501(c)(3) status of the Friends group. There are limits on the amount of funds that can be raised for lobbying (including local ballot measures) by 501 (c)(3) organizations such as the library Friends group.

With the Tax Reform Act of 1976, Congress provided a way for tax-exempt organizations to utilize a "substantial part" test. One of the best source documents on this matter is the *Friends of Libraries Sourcebook*, edited by Sandy Dolnick. Chapter 5 on the "Tax-exempt Status" and Chapter 12 on "Lobbying and Legislation" provide excellent overviews of the subject. While tax laws are always changing, and there should be proper local legal review of this matter for each campaign, the following information is pertinent:

"A tax-exempt organization may now spend 20 percent of the first $500,000 of its tax-exempt purpose expenditure for purposes of influencing legislation. If the exempt purpose expenditure is more than $500,000, this percentage decreases for each additional $500,000. Within these limits, a separate limitation is placed on so-called "grass roots lobbying," that is, attempts to influence the general public on legislative matters. Expenditures for grass roots lobbying may not exceed one-fourth of the general limitation described above. Also, any out-of-pocket expenditure that an individual (such as a member of the Friends) incurs in lobbying on behalf of the Friends must be included in determining the Friends' lobbying expenditures, even if the individual is not reimbursed for the expenditure.

If an organization exceeds its permissible limits (either the general limit or the grass roots limit), it will be taxed 25 percent of the amount by which it has exceeded the allowed amount. If a group exceeds its limits by an average of 150 percent over a four-year period, it will lose its tax-exempt status."[2]

David J. Guy, Attorney-at-Law, and President of the Friends of the Sacramento Public Library provides a good example of the application of the law, as follows:

"As an example, if a Friends organization spends $10,000 in a given year for books and other library programs, then under the expenditure test, this organization can spend $2,000 (20%) total on all lobbying, and $500 (25% of $2,000) on grass-roots lobbying, without paying taxes. If the Friends then spent $3,000 on total lobbying, they would be required to pay $250 (25% of $1,000) in excise taxes."[3]

Again, reviewing this matter with the appropriate legal counsel and tax consultant is necessary in order to ensure that the Friends group doesn't end up having to pay unexpected taxes, or worse, jeopardizing their tax-exempt status.

FOUNDATIONS

In addition to Friends groups, the library foundation and other local or regional community foundations may be a good source of campaign funds, although as 501(c)(3) entities, they have limitations regarding political contributions as well. Foundations which provide local assistance for educational or community development purposes are the best ones to target, assuming they are willing to contribute to political campaigns. Make a particular effort to approach foundations with board members or administrative officers who are known personally by members of the finance committee or the campaign steering committee. Asking for funds from a foundation involves more than just personal contact, although frequently personal contact with foundation board members can make the difference between getting the request or not.

Foundations, like major corporations, usually require organizations to make a formal application for funds. This is necessary because the requested amount is usually substantial and they get many more requests than they grant. In addition, they have to have a basis upon which to evaluate the various applications. Many foundations have a specific format for their application, but if not, the finance committee should submit a comprehensive proposal which specifies the reason for the request and how the funds will be spent. The documentation should describe the campaign's organization and plan. Essentially, it should convince the foundation that the campaign will be successful and that its purpose is compatible with the foundation's interests.

CORPORATIONS & SMALL BUSINESSES

Like foundations, corporations usually require substantial documentation when funds are requested. When requesting funds from corporations, be specific, and be sure to submit the request through the proper channels. It is essential to convince the proper corporate representatives that they should provide funds for the campaign. This may take a sophisticated effort because along with convincing the corporation of the library's value to the community, and therefore its worthiness of financial support, it will be necessary to demonstrate to the corporation why supporting the campaign is in its own best interest. Corporations which have their headquarters in the community will often be more receptive than those who do not, unless the corporation has reason to be looking for a good public relations investment. Don't forget the Chamber of Commerce as a source for campaign funds. The Dekalb County Library in Decatur, Georgia, got most of its campaign financing for a $29 million referendum from their local Chamber.

Fundraisers will frequently have better luck with small businesses than large ones. This is because small business usually are more community-based. The closer a business is to individuals in the community, the more open it tends to be with contributions. Unfortunately, smaller businesses usually tend to make smaller contributions than larger corporations. Smaller businesses will often assist the campaign by providing counter space for campaign literature and even posting yard signs. Sometimes small businesses will add a message like "Vote Yes for the Library" to their monthly statements to customers along with a small piece of campaign literature inserted in each of their regular mailings. These kinds of "mom and pop" operations can be a very effective way of reaching the grassroots of a community. If campaign workers can sell one local business person, they may have sold ten, twenty, or a hundred or more of that business's patrons.

Often corporations and small businesses who won't make an actual monetary contribution, will provide some kind of in-kind service to support the campaign effort. Again, it's good to try to be specific about what is needed and attempt to tie the in-kind contribution to a product or service which is already provided by the business. For example, printing shops may be willing to print some campaign literature for free or at a discounted price. Office supply stores may contribute supplies. Advertising companies may provide assistance with the preparation of campaign ads. Catering services or restaurants may provide food and drinks for receptions or dinners. Novelty stores might provide balloons, buttons, or stickers. The possibilities are endless, it just takes someone on the finance committee to sit down with a list local businesses and organize an in-kind contribution list. Finally, if a specific product can't be identified, it is always worthwhile to talk local companies into allowing campaign mailings to be run through their postage machines. The postage for a 10,000 piece mailing can be a significant in-kind contribution. Don't forget that in many states it is necessary to report in-kind as well as cash contributions.

PACS AS CAMPAIGN CONTRIBUTORS

Organizations of all types form PACs to support political activities, and some of these may be willing to contribute to the library campaign. In some states, there are PACs in the educational community such as for secondary education, colleges and universities, teachers, etc. Corporate PACs sometimes make very generous contributions. Labor unions also frequently form PACs. Obtain a list of registered PACs from your state's Secretary of State's Office, review it, and identify likely prospects.

Understanding why the PAC was formed and what its financial resources are is critical to receiving money or in-kind support. By their very nature PACs are political animals. Individuals associated with them know how campaigns are run. They will want to know that the donation is going to be well spent and will not be impressed by an incomplete or sloppy presentation. A "PAC kit"[4] should be put together and used when presentations are made to PACs. This kit, similar to proposals sent to corporations and foundations, should include an overview description of the campaign organization, fundraising plan, polling data, and strategic plan.

PACs can contribute to campaigns in more ways than just giving money. They may be able to help with in-kind contributions such as assistance with mailings, volunteer lists, voter lists, donor lists, research, polling, or just good campaign advice.[5] If a PAC is strongly supportive of the library issue, they may be willing to organize a special event and provide the library campaign with some additional visibility or even assist with the production of campaign media ads if library campaign planners don't have experience in this area. PAC endorsements also help campaigns because they usually mean that the PAC's membership will support the issue with their own time, money, and votes.

REFERENCES

1. Beaudry, Ann E. and Bob Schaeffer. *Winning Local and State Elections*. New York: Macmillian, 1986, p. 178.
2. Hite, Sarah C. "Lobbying and Legislation." in Dolnick, Sandy, Ed. *Friends of Libraries Sourcebook*, Second Edition. Chicago: American Library Association, 1990, p. 135.
3. David J. Guy. "Legal Limits on Lobbying: Library Advocacy." *The FOLIO* (Winter, 1995), pp. 1 & 6.
4. Ruppert, Paul "How to Attract PAC Support." *Campaigns & Elections* 7:1 (May–June, 1986), p. 8.
5. Rickert, Susan. *Campaigning for Libraries*. Wheat Ridge, Colorado: Central Colorado Library System, 1988, p. 12.

8 CAMPAIGN VOLUNTEERS

A good volunteer organization is critical to the referendum's success because volunteers are one of the primary ways that the campaign will get its message out to the voters. This personal approach is very important in most grassroots campaigns which rely more on campaign workers than money to spread the word. It is never too early to start working to acquire a sufficient number of campaign workers to support the planned campaign activities.

VOLUNTEER COMMITTEE

The way to do this is to form a volunteer committee early in the campaign. Without this committee, most campaign efforts would grind to an immediate halt. This committee is charged with recruiting volunteers, matching them with tasks they are interested in, and assigning them to the appropriate committees such as door-to-door canvassing, telephone banking, etc. After identifying potential sources of volunteers, the volunteer committee must develop a list of volunteers along with a profile of interests. Some volunteers will be willing to work on only one limited aspect of the campaign, while others will be interested in several roles and willing to put in a considerable amount of time and effort.

It is essential for the volunteer committee to keep a current list of volunteers so that individuals can be quickly and efficiently assigned to campaign committees on an as needed basis. Sometimes emergency situations will arise and volunteers will have to be recalled from one assignment to assist with some other committee activity. If the volunteer committee is set up well, this can be accomplished smoothly and without upsetting committee members and volunteers. However, occasionally an emergency situation will come up and there simply won't be enough volunteers available to be reallocated to cover the situation. In these cases, it will be necessary to ask the steering committee and the campaign manager to determine priorities and provide guidance on handling the situation.

VOLUNTEER MOTIVATION

What motivates an individual to want to become a volunteer campaign worker? Usually, it is because the volunteer is getting something out of the experience. Motivating volunteers is like motivating voters only more so; there must be some kind of emotional connection between the individual and the campaign. Either the individual is community-minded and feels that libraries are good for the community in general, they use the library a lot themselves, or they have a child, spouse, parent or friend who does. In other words, they have a vested interest in the library issue. Creating a vested interest in the library project and then tapping that interest brings volunteers into the campaign's fold; the stronger the connection, the more dedicated the volunteer will be.

FIGURE 8-1   Campaign Thank You Postcard. Provided Courtesy of Dekalb County
Public Library, Decatur, Georgia.

.......for the great support you gave your public library
by your Volunteer Telephone Calling, winning for us all
more Books and Libraries

WE COULDN'T HAVE DONE IT WITHOUT YOU!

With sincere appreciation,

Barbara Loar

Library Director
DeKalb Public Library

Building on and solidifying this interest is crucial for the library management in order to keep volunteers working for the library after the campaign is over. New library buildings especially need all the support they can get because there will undoubtedly be an operating budget increase needed to staff the new facility. In order to insure this ongoing support, make certain that volunteers feel that their work is appreciated. Holding a victory party, writing thank you notes (such as the one in Figure 8-1 above), providing special access to celebrities endorsing the campaign, or placing a plaque in the library with the names of all of the campaign volunteers are all inexpensive, tried-and-true recognition techniques. Remember that it is important to thank volunteers whether the referendum is approved or not, since they may be needed again if a subsequent campaign is attempted. The bottom line is to make sure that volunteers feel appreciated.

SOURCES OF VOLUNTEERS

Where do volunteer committees turn to find good volunteers? Most start with their own friends, family, and neighbors and then to build a broader organization. Volunteers from previous community campaigns will be a good source of seasoned workers. Try to identify those who have been particularly active and effective. Contacts in other community organizations often are very fertile ground for finding volunteers for the library campaign mainly because there is a very high correlation between library use and membership in a volunteer association.[1]

There are many potential sources of volunteers in every community including but not limited to:

- Library Friends Group
- Library Patrons
- League of Women Voters
- American Association of University Women
- American Association of Retired People
- Historical Society
- Sportsman Clubs
- Parent Teachers Association
- Teacher's Unions
- Junior Service League
- United Way Agencies
- Cultural Societies
- Chamber of Commerce and Economic Development Groups
- Kiwanis Club
- Lions Club
- Rotary Club
- Key Club
- Homeowners Associations
- The Masons
- The Grange
- Future Farmers of America
- Cub & Boy Scouts
- Brownie & Girl Scouts
- 4H Club
- Optimists Club
- Jaycees Club
- Elks Club
- Churches
- Veterans Groups
- Optimists Club

THE LIBRARY FRIENDS

Obviously, the Library's Friends group is one of the best sources of volunteers, since by charter it exists to assist the library. If a Friends group is not already in place, it should be formed well before campaign activities start. Assistance in forming a Friends group can be found in the *Friends of Libraries Sourcebook*.[2] In most campaigns, the library's Friends group provides the muscle behind the steering committee.

Along with recruiting and organizing volunteer activities, the Friends group can also be a very effective way of raising funds for the campaign. For those recent library referenda campaigns which were successful, the participation of the Library's Friends group in numerous campaign activities was considered very important by the library director.[3] Library Friends often make the best advocates for the library issue because they are committed, active, and usually well-informed.

VOLUNTEER RECRUITMENT

Volunteers will be needed for many things; from processing mailings to contacting targeted groups through telephone banks or door-to-door canvassing. Volunteers are the "troopers" necessary to run any campaign. Without enthusiastic volunteers much of the work of a campaign will not get done and the chances of success will be decreased. Sometimes the amount of effort that can be obtained from enthusiastic and committed volunteers is truly amazing. This kind of participation and effort cannot be bought at any price because it comes from the heart not a paycheck. Volunteers are more precious than money. See the discussion of a "volunteer budget" on page 112 for one way of allocating this precious campaign resource.

It is always wise to recruit more volunteers and to assign a few more volunteers to any given task than actually needed just to make up for "no shows." Volunteer recruitment should start early and go on continuously throughout the campaign, not only because more volunteers will be needed toward the end of the campaign during the get-out-the-vote effort, but also because some volunteers will tire halfway through the campaign and will need to be replaced by new volunteers with plenty of energy and enthusiasm. But what is the best way of recruiting and organizing volunteers?

One way to recruit volunteers is to use "volunteer pledge cards" which provide space for the potential recruit's name, address, and telephone number along with possibly a short list of possible volunteer activities. All campaign committee members and any speakers should keep an ample supply of these cards handy at all times. Both fundraising and volunteer pledge cards should be passed out at all campaign activities and included in any target group mailing (they may even be combined into one card if advantageous). Many volunteers will come from target neighborhoods identified as having a high number of potential "Yes" voters. When door-to-door canvassing begins in these areas, campaign workers should provide volunteer pledge cards to interested individuals and encourage them to "sign-up" that day. The volunteer coordinator should contact the potential volunteer within a few days of receiving a card, thank them, and asked for more indepth information regarding how they would like to assist with the campaign.

During this "interview," the coordinator should develop a "volunteer profile" and try to obtain a commitment for specific activities. Developing and using a volunteer questionnaire during the telephone interview, recruitment open houses, meetings, or even through the mail can assist in preparing this profile. The questionnaire should include as much information as necessary to be able to identify volunteers' interests, when they can work, approximately how much time per week they are willing to work, and how to contact them.

When this information is collected, it must be effectively organized. Although paper-based systems will work, one of the best ways to organize the data is to enter it into a computer database so that the volunteer coordinator can use various sorts and selects to develop lists of potential volunteers for various campaign activities. For example, the process of computerizing

YES! I will help us *Grow!*

Name: _____

Address: _____

_____

Phone: (H) _____ (W) _____

☐ Mailing
☐ Telephone
☐ Distribute literature
☐ Distribute lawn signs
☐ Display a lawn sign
☐ Work in a booth at a public event
☐ Help with campaign kick-off
☐ You may use my name as an endorsement
   signature: _____
☐ I can also help by contributing money

Committee for the Library, Vernon Bowlby, Treasurer, 310 N.W. 5th

the volunteer list facilities quickly generating separate lists for telephone banking or door-to-door canvassing as well as improved organization and communication, particularly if postcards need to be mailed as reminders to volunteers.

VOLUNTEER ORGANIZATION, ORIENTATION, & TRAINING

Volunteer effectiveness can be increased if the campaign is well-organized; no volunteer should feel like their talents and time are being wasted. One way to ensure that volunteers are being effectively used is to develop a volunteer orientation and training program. All new volunteers should also be thoroughly briefed on the library issue, the campaign strategy, and the importance of the various tasks which they will be asked to perform. In short, they should be given a concise overview of the campaign effort, the reasons behind the campaign, and a clear understanding of their role in the campaign. A good way to start this process is to review and discuss the "Fact Sheet" developed for the public. If campaign workers don't understand the facts about the library project, they won't be able to effectively communicate them to the voter. Volunteers should also be informed about the areas they are not to attempt to handle (because these problem questions need to be referred to others in the campaign). Finally, they should be encouraged to provide input into the campaign based upon their understanding of the commu-

FIGURE 8-3   Sample Volunteer Questionnaire

Volunteer Questionnaire

Volunteers Name: _____
Address: _____
_____
_____
_____

Precinct #: _____
Telephone (Home): _____
Telephone (Office): _____
Volunteer can work:

	Mon	Tue	Wed	Thur	Fri	Sat	Sun
Morning	___	___	___	___	___	___	___
Afternoon	___	___	___	___	___	___	___
Evening	___	___	___	___	___	___	___

Approximately _____ Hours per Week.

Campaign Activities:
 Assist with Any Activity Needed   ___
Particularly interested in the following:
 Campaign Fundraising   ___
 Door-to-door Canvassing   ___
 Telephone Bank Calls   ___
 Poster and Yard Sign Placement   ___
 Assist with Special Events (Receptions, etc)   ___
 Write Letters (To Editors, Elected Officials, etc)   ___
 Assist with Operation of a Microcomputer   ___
 Assist with Mailings   ___
 Assist with Campaign Literature Preparation   ___
 Assist with Media Ads & PSA Production   ___
 Assist with Production of AV Presentation   ___
 Be a Speaker for the Speaker's Bureau   ___
 Serve as a Poll Greeter   ___
 Provide Transportation to Polls   ___
 Provide Child Care on Election Day   ___
 Art Work (Flyers, Banners, etc.)   ___
 Construction Activities (Signs, etc.)   ___
 Other Activities
   (Specify) _____
   (Specify) _____

nity and their own neighborhoods as well as any information they gain through carrying out their assigned duties.

Volunteers should understand what is expected of them and why. When volunteers are assigned a task, they should be given training on how to perform the task. For relatively simple tasks, a written "package" or "kit" can be developed which explains the activity and provides all of the necessary materials and reporting forms. Other tasks, like speaking for community, radio, or TV presentations and interviews, may require more in-depth training sessions including role playing and even practicing before a video camera. The better prepared volunteers are to do their work, the more confident and effective they will be. This will increase the library's chances for success at the polls. It is always best to give campaign workers well-defined quantities of work (deliver 200 door hangers to the attached list of registered voters in precinct 2) as well as precise deadlines (complete the task by noon on Saturday). Finally, the volunteer committee members must set up a monitoring and reporting system so that they know if the work is being done and so they can communicate its status to the steering committee. Whatever the campaign's techniques, the use of well-organized, trained volunteers will probably mean a much more effective campaign.

REFERENCES

1. Westin, Alan F. and Anne L. Finger. *Using the Public Library in the Computer Age.* Chicago: American Library Association, 1991, p. 18.
2. Dolnick, Sandy, Editor. *Friends of Libraries Sourcebook.* 2nd Edition, Chicago: American Library Association, 1990.
3. Hall, Richard B. "The Votes Are In" *Library Journal* 115:11 (June 15, 1990), pp. 42–46.
4. Beaudry, Ann E. and Bob Schaeffer. *Winning Local and State Elections.* New York: Macmillian, New York, 1986, p. 47.

9 THE MEDIA

Although most library campaigns are low-budget grassroots volunteer efforts, the use of the media, particularly the electronic media, cannot be ignored in today's society. Effectively using the media is extremely important, especially in large campaigns where campaign planners must make a connection with large numbers of people. There is no better way to reach a substantial number of people quickly than through the media, whether print or electronic.

To deliver a well-planned, emotionally charged campaign message, planners need to develop a series of "sound bites," or short punchy "message packets," which can be used repeatedly to deliver the campaign's main message without the audience having to think about it much. For example, real life stories about how the library has changed people's lives are more effective than dry statistics. This approach is particularly effective with paid advertisements, but is equally useful with "free" media such as interviews with reporters.

One of the best and most effective strategies is to be proactive and engage the media rather than waiting for reporters to approach campaign leaders. Hopefully, the library management has developed a good rapport with the media over the years and has personal relationships with reporters and even editors. If not, the campaign's leadership should start by setting up interviews with key reporters who cover the political scene and develop a file on each one. Try to understand what motivates them, what their political "slant" is, and then try to find some common ground between their perspective and the campaign issue. Cultivating the media early is important because preliminary campaign coverage is helpful with fundraising for the campaign. Get the media to cover fundraising activities, particularly special events or activities which need to be "advertised." Not only will this coverage help raise the awareness of the community that there is an impending library campaign, but it will assist in acquiring early endorsements and volunteers as well as increase the amount of money coming into the campaign.

PRESS RELEASES

Early in the campaign, it is helpful to start sending information to the media regarding awareness raising activities of all kinds at the library. The campaign should start in a low key and informal way to feed information to the press in the beginning, but as the campaign builds momentum, these communications should become more formal and "official." This can be accomplished by issuing formal press releases. Press releases can be made to look official and more important if they are printed on paper specifically designed for the purpose. Campaign letterhead (with campaign colors and logo) created by a graphic artist can be modified slightly to work well. Make sure that there is a "For Immediate Release" or "Embargoed" line which indicates the date the information can be used by the media as well as a "For Information Contact:" line with the name and telephone number of the campaign's press contact person provided. Press releases are not dissertations and should be no longer than one to two pages. Be sure to type "end" at the bottom of the last page to indicate the conclusion of the news release. News releases should have a headline designed for maximum impact and provide short "bullets" of additional information which grabs the attention of the media and provides the necessary "Who, what, when, where, how, and why" regarding the matter at hand. Try faxing particularly important press releases to emphasize their importance or timeliness.

Providing frequent press releases to the media and cultivating editorial staff will hopefully bring the positive press coverage necessary to help win the campaign. Be sure to send press releases to *all* of the media outlets in the community and surrounding areas where coverage is desirable. It is also helpful if the chairperson of the public relations committee follows up each press release with a telephone call to each media organization in the community. This not only ensures that the press release got to the proper person, but it also allows campaign officials the opportunity to expand on the press release, see if there are any questions which need to be answered, and increase the chances that some form of media coverage will actually take place.

PRESS KITS

Along with press releases, it is sometimes helpful to create a "press kit" which can be used to provide reporters and editors with general background information on the library issue and the campaign. Along with providing the obligatory fact sheets and campaign literature, press kits should have materials which are visually appealing such as a rendering of the new library building or pictures of the current building with books stacked on the floor, in the window wells, etc. This is an opportunity to provide a lot of material in one package, and it should be carefully thought out to emphasize the campaign's main message and themes. Humorous items like funny pictures or quotes are very likely to be used by the press and usually tend to get the audience's attention as well as put the library issue in a positive light. Remember, that in the early stages of a library campaign, the emphasis should be on building issue recognition for the library, just as a politician must develop name recognition. Press kits and media events provide a mechanism for the public relations committee to place the library issue before the media and ultimately the voter.

MEDIA EVENTS

Special media events draw attention to the library issue, but they must be handled with creativity and savvy if they are to be effective. In most campaigns, the first media event will probably be the "kick-off" event for the campaign. This is news in most communities. It is when the library as a public institution announces its plans for a capital campaign. By making a "big deal" out of this action, the campaign can focus media attention on the library and its need. This initial event is an opportunity to disseminate fact sheets to the media and bring forward any endorsements which have been acquired by the campaign at this time. The intent of this media "blitz" is to garner as much publicity for the campaign as possible to gain the attention of the voters.

Between the first campaign "kick-off" event and the last election eve event, the public relations committee should plan frequent events or "publicity stunts" which create interest in the library issue and provide visibility for the campaign. It may be possible to hold an event at some point in the campaign to announce additional endorsements by particularly influential individuals or groups such as the local taxpayer's opposition group, an influential conservative banker, a respected politician, the League of Women Voters, etc. A good technique is to create a "photo opportunity" with all the endorsers up on a platform holding hands in a sign of unity under the library banner. Anything that is particularly noteworthy can be cause for a media event. A major leak in the library's roof which destroys part of the collection can turn misfortune into opportunity. Any campaign milestone, like the campaign reaching its fundraising goal or having recruited its first one hundred volunteers, can work.

The more impact the event has, the better its chances for coverage. If it is important to have the event covered by the television media, the public relations committee will need to "frame" the event in a visually attractive manner and provide "action shots." It is always helpful to make the event easy for the media to cover, by making the location easy to find and timing the event so that it will make the evening news show or main edition of the paper without a major effort on the part of the reporters involved. Providing busy reporters with a box lunch or some kind of food is a good idea because this will help insure that they come. Further, consider giving them something like a T-shirt for their kids (with the library logo and slogan on it, of course). In addition to media events, campaigns may need to occasionally plan press conferences.

PRESS CONFERENCES

When releasing a "hot news story," invite all of the media to come for the announcement as well as to have an opportunity to ask questions. Dramatizing the action helps to emphasize it with the media and engender better coverage. Press conferences are specifically for the media and should be set up to accommodate them as much as possible. Make certain that there is easy access, that there are adequate power outlets for cameras and microphones, as well as decent lighting and ventilation. Grumpy reporters that have to sit in hot rooms and can't get the camera shots they need usually don't provide advantageous coverage.

When scheduling the press conference, try not to conflict with other major competing events or activities. Schedule the press conference several days in advance and always call the day before to remind reporters of the conference and confirm their attendance. When the press conference begins, it is impressive to "make an entrance" and then have several specific but short statements announcing the important news supported by visual aids before opening the meeting up to questions. A press conference should be fairly short—don't waste a reporter's time. Distribute a written statement and have campaign spokespersons available after the conference if any reporters have additional in-depth questions. Sometimes it is helpful prior to a press conference to create a list of the most likely asked questions and be well-prepared to respond to them. Practicing the response by rehearsing with campaign volunteers is often helpful and might raise additional questions not thought of previously. The public relations committee should make certain that they are well-prepared and have identified specific people who are to be the campaign's spokespersons.

In addition to promoting the library issue, press conferences can also be used to battle the opposition. Sometimes it is helpful to schedule a last minute press conference right before the election to help dispel inaccurate information and rebut false rumors being spread by the opposition. If so, be careful not to give the rumors more coverage and credibility than they would have otherwise. There are many opportunities where press conferences can be used during a campaign; however, it is important not to overuse the technique or it will lose its effectiveness.

PUBLIC RELATIONS COMMITTEE

In small campaigns, the campaign manager will handle the media under the guidance of the steering committee, but larger campaigns will probably need to assign media coverage to a committee. The public relations committee monitors media coverage, develops press releases, coordinates media events and press conferences, and produces advertising. They may engage a public relations firm to assist in these activities or to simply advise. Regardless of the approach, all major public relations activities should be brought before the steering committee for review, discussion, and approval. This not only allows all segments of the campaign to be informed of the public relations activities, but it also keeps control of the campaign's "public voice" in the hands of the steering committee where it belongs.

In order to avoid confusion, it is usually best to have one person whose primary responsibility is talking to the media. This can be the public relations committee chairperson or the campaign manager, but if more than one person is dispatching information to the media, slip-ups and inconsistencies are bound to occur. The primary contact person, or "press secretary," should have some experience in dealing with the media, and preferably has either worked in the media or at least has good contacts there. This person should always be accessible to the media and informed on all campaign issues. Dealing with the media can be trying, and it helps to "know the ropes." The media should be treated equally, and never lied to—if the campaign spokesperson doesn't know the answer to a question, they should say so and promise to get back to the reporter. A person with a positive attitude who can give concise answers to reporter's questions while avoiding library jargon will make a good impression for the campaign.

In addition to providing the main spokesperson for the campaign, the public relations committee has numerous additional duties. One of these is monitoring the news media during the campaign. Campaign volunteers will need to be organized to monitor radio and television stations as well as the local newspapers. The media should be monitored to see if there are new developments in campaign issues, advertising campaigns by the opposition, and if and how the media is covering the campaign's press releases, media events, and press conferences. Sometimes an early warning system provided by such monitoring can save a campaign if the information can be reported to the steering committee quickly and a timely and effective response created. The public relations committee will also have a hand in creating campaign advertisements.

MEDIA ADVERTISING

Many library campaigns don't have adequate funds for media advertising, especially radio and television commercials because of their cost and the relatively high level of sophistication needed to produce them. However, large and well-funded campaigns may find this approach to be cost-effective if the ads can be delivered to appropriate target audience. "In most local races, television advertising can be compared to rolling out a cannon to kill a gnat. Don't waste the campaign's money reaching a high percentage of people who can't or won't vote for your candidate [or issue]. It's easier to target a specific audience with radio, cable TV, special interest print publications or direct mail. Most local campaigns use a combination of paid media such as radio ads, yard signs and direct mail."[1]

Identifying the best time to run ads and which media to use is critical to reaching the intended audience. Public relations firms or advertising agencies usually understand through market research which media sources can reach which target audiences. For example, trying to reach adults by advertising on Saturday morning television is not an effective approach. However, advertising during the local evening television news or on an all-news radio station will probably reach many well-educated, socially-responsible adults in the community.

While planners should use Public Service Announcements (PSAs) early in the campaign to build goodwill and issue recognition, most paid advertising should be reserved until the last week prior to the election (particularly the last few days). This is when most undecided voters make up their minds. Radio ads can be particularly effectively during the GOTV effort.

If the budget allows, it is useful to run several versions of media ads. It's good to have a common beginning and/or ending that reinforces the main message, but the body of the advertisement may be varied in order to deliver information on the campaign's various themes. The public relations committee, steering committee, library management, and staff should review "draft" advertisements regardless of the media to be used prior to release. Writing and producing campaign ads is not easy and, since they are expensive, care should be taken to promote the main campaign message in a clear, uncomplicated manner. Remember, the format of the ad is just as important as the content of what is said. The best radio and television ads strike a "responsive chord"[2] in the electorate by recognizing that the electronic medium is most effective when an emotional response is elicited from the audience. Obviously, professional assistance can be of tremendous help as well as make the money spent on media advertising even more effective.

As much repetition in the media of these ads as the campaign can afford is desirable, but a balance with other campaign needs must be maintained. Decide which media will provide the most potential votes for every campaign dollar spent. In most communities, newspaper advertising is at the top of this list, but cable television and particularly radio advertising can be very effective. While newspapers ads can be designed to deliver an emotional impact, the print media is a more "rational" media and is most frequently used to make a logical case for the library. The electronic media is most effective at persuading the electorate to vote for the library issue, primarily because it is an emotional media. "A radio ad can 'move' a person in a way that is nearly impossible in a newspaper ad and actually quite difficult in television."[3]

Regardless of the method used, the public relations committee must work closely with the advertising departments of the various media so that ad submittal deadlines are not missed. While production assistance can be obtained from a number of sources, final responsibility for the ad rests with the campaign. Don't forget that all political advertisements, like persuasive campaign literature, must have a political disclaimer.

NEWSPAPERS

Of the three main media, print is by far the most frequently used in library campaigns.[4] The local newspaper is one of the most consistent source of news and information that residents in any community turn to especially during elections. Newspaper coverage can be instrumental to the success of a campaign; the library campaign must plan to effectively exploit this fact. If a good relationship already exists between the newspaper and the library so much the better. If not, one must be forged during the campaign. The public relations committee must provide the press with a constant stream of information and ideas for articles about the library and the campaign. It is particularly important to work with the newspaper to plan for a special feature article. A feature article in the Sunday paper on the eve of the referendum is a highly desirable tool that has worked well in many campaigns as a last-minute appeal to bring supporters out to vote. The public relations committee should pull out all the stops to get this kind of coverage. If it is agreed to by the newspaper, the campaign must work hard to make sure that any and all information and assistance necessary is provided to the reporter working on the piece. In addition, don't overlook the weeklies in the area; they will often provide the library with a lot of coverage since they are frequently looking for copy.

Feature articles or articles of any kind are an opportunity for the library to present its case. All of the facts and figures must be brought forward, but they must be presented in an interesting and informative way. In other words, the facts must be present, but there should also be a human interest angle to the story by providing interesting anecdotes. For example, the need for more space, books, and hours may be communicated by comparing the library's situation to other nearby comparable communities because being at the bottom of various statistical lists is news. However, this approach will be even more effective if a story can be developed around how it affects the everyday life of individuals in the community. A picture of students sitting on the floor trying to study because all of the library's chairs are full can speak volumes to the electorate. Unusual or funny articles and photos like a python wrapped around a bookstack can create interest in the library as well.

Along with newspaper articles, campaigns should seek exposure by obtaining editorials, having the library featured in a popular column and in letters to the editor, and finally by obtaining the endorsement of the newspaper's editorial board. All of these efforts will be helpful, but obtaining the paper's endorsement may be the most critical factor in those communities where the newspaper's editor is very influential. These endorsements are particularly important because they impress last minute undecided voters. The campaign steering committee should schedule a meeting with the newspaper's editorial board well in advance of the endorsement decisions. Obtaining this endorsement may be difficult, especially if the newspaper is extremely conservative politically, but it's usually well worth the effort if successful. The presentation to an editorial board should be short and to the point, but include enough detail to address their major questions and concerns. Whoever makes the presentation should be prepared to respond effectively if resistance is encountered. One meeting may not do the trick; it also helps to have as many influential campaign supporters as possible contact the editor prior to the decision.

Sometimes a newspaper will come out against a library issue, or a letter to the editor will appear which raises controversy. The steering committee should not panic and overreact. The event should be carefully and objectively discussed and an appropriate response should be hammered out before any response is made. Far more damage can be done by releasing a quick and inappropriate response than by saying nothing at all. If confronted by a reporter in the heat of battle on a particularly hot topic, it is often better to indicate that one is not prepared to respond until further review of the matter, than to have headlines the next day which create even more controversy because of an "off-the-cuff" comment which was inaccurate, inappropriate or, at best, not well thought out. Campaign supporters should realize that not all controversy is bad. Sometimes a little controversy can move the library issue up from a "ho-hum" status into the spotlight. The public relations committee can capitalize on controversy and turn it around so that it actually benefits the campaign. At a minimum, controversy does at least raise the awareness of the library issue with the electorate and if the project makes sense to begin with, library supporters should be able to take this opportunity to convince the community that the project is in its best interest.

NEWSPAPER ADVERTISING

Newspaper advertising is the most commonly used form of advertising for library campaigns primarily because local newspapers tend to deliver the message to a more geographically limited target audience than other media and because it is a medium that most campaign volunteers feel comfortable with. If there are competing newspapers in the area, circulation figures and reader profiles should be compared to the advertising rates. It may be that the least expensive newspaper is reaching more of the campaign's target audience than the most prominent paper. Keep in mind that "Some weekly newspapers or 'shoppers' charge a reasonable fee for inserts. Inserting a brochure or other campaign literature in a weekly newspaper can be especially effective in rural areas or districts with community newspapers. Advertising in weekly newspapers can be more effective than advertising in daily papers because the readership is more targeted and they have a longer shelf life."[5]

One way to get "free" newspaper advertising is to ask local supportive businesses to take out an ad for the library campaign or to simply add the library slogan to any ads that they would normally run prior to the election. For a nominal cost the library gets some visibility and an implicit endorsement from the business owner. This was done effectively in the Rapides Parish, Louisiana, campaign where many local businesses added the following to each of their business ads:

"Libraries Change Lives—Vote YES January 15."

The public relations committee should contact the ad department of any newspapers which will be carrying ads and discuss the details of the advertisement early so that deadlines are not missed. Those working with the ad department must clearly understand the paper's camera ready copy requirements, the cost of ad space and applicable volume discounts, along with the advantages and costs of the positioning of the ad in the paper. The best location is the upper half of the paper where it will be seen most readily by those who are skimming the paper as well as those who are reading it. The public relations committee will have to decide if the best approach is to run a number of smaller ads or one or two larger ads. Full or double paged ads can be very dramatic and sometimes particularly effective, but they are also the most costly—make sure they are worth it.

Regardless of the size or cost, remember that the purpose of the ad is to "sell" the library issue. This is not the time to beat around the bush. While a "soft sell" works best in some communities, in most cases the ad should specifically ask for a "Yes" vote with the campaign's logo, slogan, and message dramatically pitched to the reader. If funds are not available to hire a public relations firm, it may be helpful to look at ads published in previous years' newspapers around election times. Lots of ideas can be gained from this research. The campaign can adapt those ads which are best remembered or which solicited the most positive response to the library's ad copy, but be careful about abridging copyright. Ad ideas can be obtained from many sources. Brainstorming with the steering committee and/or public relations committee often helps, but be receptive to creative ideas from volunteers and library staff who are on the "front lines" of the campaign. Frequently some of the best ideas come from the grassroots level—those closest to the voters usually have the best idea of what will influence them.

RADIO

Radio is the second most frequently used media for distributing the library's message in capital campaigns.[6] Public Service Announcements can be produced relatively inexpensively. They are particularly effective if they engage the voter emotionally and communicate the library's story without being an obvious campaign ad. PSAs are very effective if the radio station can be convinced to run them during high listening periods such as when people are going to and from work. Some radio stations will take stands on political issues and endorse specific campaigns, but less commonly than newspapers.

Frequently the campaign leadership can communicate with the electorate through the use of radio interviews or "actualities" which can be easily taped over the telephone. This approach is particularly effective with small radio stations looking for news. The library's campaign manager or press secretary can call radio stations and request air time to make a statement about the campaign or provide comment on a major campaign issue. "Even small campaigns can afford to do radio actualities since all they require is:

A telephone,

A tape recorder with a high bias cassette to reduce hiss,

A voice coupler that the campaign can buy at any audio equipment store and a cord to connect the tape recorder to the telephone, and

A list of radio news directors and their telephone numbers."[7]

With a little work, the public relations committee can probably get the campaign manager or campaign spokesperson on popular radio talk shows where he or she will be interviewed and given the opportunity to explain the library's issue. This technique is very effective, especially if there is one particular show that everyone in town listens to regularly. However, a word of caution is in order—KNOW THE AUDIENCE OF THE TALK SHOW. Talk shows with a conservative audience may not be ideal for the library issue if a tax increase is necessary. Call-in shows also can give the opposition an audience at the campaign's expense, even if friendly call-ins are carefully orchestrated. Because of this problem, this approach is not recommended if a strong opposition group is active in the community.

Some radio stations specialize in remote broadcasts at specific locations. Car dealers and other retailers often hold such promotions when they are opening up for business or running special sales. However, some radio stations, especially in small towns, will perform these kinds of "benefit broadcasts" for non-profit organizations. It may be possible to get the radio station to spend a day broadcasting in the library's parking lot or in a mall where a special library campaign event is taking place. Special "library-related" prizes such as children's books can be given to listeners who call in or show up. Usually, the more outrageous the activities, the better to attract people. Even a "dunk the librarian or board president" event can draw a surprising crowd if the individuals are well-known (it really is amazing what some people will do for libraries). Fast-talking disc jockeys who can provide a little good-natured ribbing about the library's image, and at the same time sincerely pitch the library's cause, can be very effective.

Radio Advertising

Radio "spots" can be a very cost-effective method of reaching voters, particularly since the targeted segment of the community can often be reached directly. When trying to decide whether to advertise on a radio station, the first thing to understand is its audience. Are the people who are listening to the station the ones the campaign is trying to reach? If there is only one radio station in town, the decision is easy, but if the campaign is being held in a large metropolitan area, there may be multiple stations and formats to choose from. If the campaign is trying to reach an older, more mature target group, an "oldies" station may be a good choice. If the station is trying to reach highly educated individuals, the local public broadcasting radio station or all news format station may be the best decision.

If two stations appear to target the same market, compare their market shares (percentage of available listeners) with their rates when expending hard-earned campaign funds. National media ratings services (Arbitron and Nielsen) provide demographic information for each station for every hour of the day and should be consulted when attempting to target specific audiences. Again, once a radio station is selected, the public relations committee must work closely with the ad department to insure that the ad is produced on time and in a format which is acceptable to the station.

As mentioned, utilizing drive times is one of the most effective ways of reaching large numbers of people. One good way for libraries to appeal to drive time listeners is by using the books on tape pitch: "Did you know that the library has books on tape? (Background announcer naming easily recognized titles.) If you'd stopped by the library and picked one up yesterday, you wouldn't be so bored stuck in traffic right now. Help us provide more of this kind of service at your local public library. Vote "Yes" on Measure K!" Airing numerous ten second ads like this just before the election can work wonders.

Radio ads can be effectively utilized even for "silent" campaigns which are trying to get their message out, but without raising a lot of general awareness and possibly opposition. "Radio is invisible. It works at its best in a guerrilla tactical warfare. Often an opponent, political insiders, and news media will remain totally unaware until its impact has already been achieved. Radio is your secret weapon to make critical and effective tactical moves."[8] Further, if the opposition does attack the library issue (and particularly if they attack late in the campaign with misinformation), radio is the ideal medium for the campaign to respond quickly and effectively if funds have been held in reserve.

TELEVISION

While television is one of least used methods in library campaigns, it is one of the most important sources of political information in our society. For this reason, some library campaigns must make effective use of television in order to be successful. If there are good connections with the local television station(s), even small campaigns can benefit from a well-produced public service announcement. Cable television stations and public broadcasting stations often tend to be more receptive to working with libraries because of their public service policies. Some of these stations will even provide a good deal of assistance in producing a PSA. This can be an invaluable service since television tape production is difficult and costly.

Like radio stations, some television stations air editorials, endorse local issues, and produce talk shows. If the station invites the campaign manager or spokesperson on a talk show, it is wise to provide the interviewer with a complete description of the project's need and the major campaign issues in advance. If possible, it is good to discuss well in advance of the "on-air" interview the questions which will be asked so that appropriate and to-the-point responses can be delivered in a smooth and professional manner. While some interviewers may be generally sympathetic toward the library issue, it is their job to make the interview interesting and newsworthy. There may be surprises and questions which are not always easy or comfortable to answer. Interviewees will have to stay alert. Remember, image is everything in this medium. It is usually the case that the way one comes across is more important that what one says. *Be positive*, never repeat an interviewer's negative question, and stick to the preestablished script as much as possible.

Occasionally, local television stations will sponsor debates about hotly contested campaign issues. If there is strong opposition to the library issue, this "opportunity" may be extended to the library campaign. It is not always necessary to accept these invitations, but it is usually better to accept and have the opportunity to present the library's position, than to have the show go on with only the opposition present. If the campaign accepts the invitation, understand the ground rules for the debate and prepare well. Practice for such an event by role playing with a "live" audience of campaign supporters who can provide objective and constructive criticism before the actual event. It is also a good idea to videotape the role playing so that the debaters can see their own performances. This makes the debaters more confident, smoothes out points of rough delivery, and sharpens responses to any hostile arguments.

Television Advertising

Generally, television ads are a relatively small part of most library campaigns because of their great expense and the fact that it is difficult to target the audience when television stations broadcast to very large numbers of people in metropolitan areas. If a television station reaches five or six counties in an urban area, but the library campaign is only in one county, the ad will be delivered at a substantial cost to many people who have no interest in it. However, if the television station is relatively small and most of the people it reaches are in the jurisdiction, television advertisements can potentially be very effective campaign tools if produced with a reasonable degree of sophistication and finesse.

Cable television, with its ability to provide targeting, should also be considered by library campaigns because advertisements may be able to be delivered in a cost-effective manner to specific target groups. "According to Mediamark Research Inc., cable subscribers are 14 percent more likely to vote than non-cable subscribers. Also, MRI reports they are 36 percent more inclined to be involved in political fund raising and 28 percent more likely to actively work for a political candidate or party than people in non-cable households."[9] Another advantage to using Cable TV is that it has more competitive advertising rates than broadcast television.

How does one go about buying television time? The first thing that needs to be understood is the importance of a rating point. If a television show has a 50 rating for adults age 35 and older, then 50 percent of those people with television sets watch the show. "Conventional wisdom has it that an ad's message will not register until the viewer has seen it at least three times. Since you want 100 percent of the audience to see your spot three times, you'll need a minimum of 300 points. Media buyers tend to want to buy closer to 500 points, because we know the electorate tends to head for the fridge during at least one of the precise moments you have purchased to prod its political consciousness."[10] Since different programs have different ratings, they also have different costs for a thirty second spot. Careful review of the station's rates and program ratings will uncover cost-effective purchases which have lower costs per point. The cost per point (CPP) is obtained by dividing the cost of the ad by the rating.

Different rate schedules are available. Commercial rates are the most expensive, but stations often offer much lower "political" rates. These lower rates may help the budget, but be careful because ads can be "bumped" at these lower rates and never appear. Again, volunteer media monitoring can be important since the campaign is due a refund for any ad that is bumped. As with radio ads, be sure to plan ahead and schedule television ads early because availability may be limited in an active election year. Contact the television station and find out the earliest date that the ads for the last week of the campaign can be scheduled. Early scheduling will often produce the best and most cost-effective results.

Prime time slots reach a very large number of people and may be one of the best last minute methods of reaching and influencing the voter in a close election. Campaign planners should carefully analyze the costs of television ads versus other techniques such as a last minute mailing. Although a television ad may cost a lot more, it may well reach far more people and be much more effective. Campaign planners should not be afraid of television advertising just because they haven't had a lot of experience with it. Professional assistance is available from a number of sources. Well-done, well-placed television ads may be a campaign's single most important technique for influencing the electorate. However, each campaign's public relations committee must evaluate their ability to produce television ads and the cost effectiveness of these ads in relation to the other planned activities. While it is true that many library campaigns don't produce television ads, they all create some form of campaign literature, the subject of the next chapter.

REFERENCES

1. Jean Drodshaug Dugan et. al. *Campaigning to Win: A Workbook for Women in Politics.* Washington, DC: National Women's Political Caucus, 1993, pp. ix–16.
2. Tony Schwartz. *The Responsive Chord.* Garden City, New York: Anchor Press/Doubleday, 1973.
3. Joe Slade White. "Wavelength Winners: 12 Rules for Better Political Radio Ads." *Campaigns & Elections* June/July, 1993, Vol. 14, No. 2. p. 46.
4. Hall, Richard B. "The Votes Are In." *Library Journal* 115:11 (June 15, 1990), pp. 42–46.
5. Dugan et. al., pp. ix–21.
6. Hall, pp. 42–46
7. Dugan et. al., pp. ix–9.
8. White, p. 45.
9. Michael Labriola. "Campaigning on Cable." *Campaigns & Elections..* 14:3 (August, 1993), p. 35.
10. Beall, Pat. "Buy Your Own Time" *Campaigns & Elections* 12:2 (July, 1991), p. 48.

10 CAMPAIGN LITERATURE & PARAPHERNALIA

CAMPAIGN LITERATURE

The most commonly used campaign method in recent library referenda campaigns is the creation and distribution of campaign literature such as pamphlets, fact sheets, and bookmarks.[1] These are simple, effective, and relatively inexpensive ways to communicate the library's message to voters. This is particularly true if substantial numbers of the various campaign pieces can be printed up at one time. The unit cost of any form of campaign literature or paraphernalia goes down significantly as the number of pieces printed or manufactured goes up. Significant savings can be realized if volume discounts can be negotiated; it may be better to print a larger number of three pieces of literature than smaller numbers of four or five different pieces.

Many forms of campaign literature can be developed; some campaigns will need to use all formats and others will select only a few. The choice depends primarily on the campaign's strategy and budget. Regardless of the methods selected, campaign literature must be effectively designed, produced, and distributed.

CAMPAIGN LITERATURE COMMITTEE

Unless handled by the public relations committee, the campaign literature committee needs to brainstorm and come up with effective forms of campaign literature which matches the overall campaign strategy. They should be presented to the steering committee for review, discussion, and further brainstorming. If funds allow, some campaigns will want to hire public relations firms or advertising agencies to assist with this process from the very beginning. Regardless of the method used, the steering committee should give the final go ahead approval for production of the campaign literature unless it is willing to delegate this authority to the campaign literature committee. After the steering committee has approved the general concept for the campaign literature, it is important to have graphic artists develop mock-ups. After thorough review by the campaign literature committee, these "drafts" of the campaign literature can be presented in the form of concept boards to the steering committee for final approval. The campaign literature committee should obtain accurate cost estimates for production within the stated budget allocations.

When the campaign literature has been designed and produced, it must be distributed. In most cases, fact sheets and bookmarks can usually be distributed through the central library and branches as long as the literature is informative and not persuasive. In other cases, persuasive campaign literature will be mailed out to selected target groups or distributed through door-to-door canvassing of specific neighborhoods. This latter approach is one of the most time consuming, but is also one of the most effective, especially if there is direct personal contact between the campaign workers and the potential voters.

Private schools, day care centers, and small businesses will often distribute information about the library issue. Look in a local business directory, or simply look down main street and identify those businesses which are visited most frequently during the public's normal daily routines. These small businesses are some of the best outlets for campaign literature. Bookmarks placed on the counter of the local coffee shop can reach an amazing number of people over a month's time. Retail stores can sometimes be convinced to put campaign information in sales sacks or even print up special bags to help raise awareness for the library issue. It is often effective to have campaign volunteers work mass transit stations and major shopping malls in targeted areas just before the election by handing out or placing pieces on the windshields of vehicles in the parking lot. Don't forget football games, other sporting events, and community festivals. Campaign literature can also be distributed through the newsletters of companies and associations such as the Chamber of Commerce, the Board of Realtors, etc.

Sometimes library campaign planners cooperate with other campaigns to distribute one another's literature during mailings and speaking engagements. These kinds of coalitions can be very helpful and build a spirit of cooperation instead of competition. It may be that the local jurisdiction has decided upon a "package" referendum where numerous ballot issues for capital funds will be decided by the voters at one time. These package deals offer a good opportunity to build coalitions which can be used to support one another during literature distribution, for example. One large mailing could be planned with each campaign's literature. This may work well and save mailing costs; however, the danger is that the library's message will get lost in all of the information arriving at one time. Another caution comes with using the distribution systems of political parties. Though they are very good, the library should avoid any taint of partisan politics. This method should be used only if both political parties agree to distribute literature for the campaign.

The campaign literature committee has a big job because there are so many potential ways to distribute campaign literature. In larger campaigns, literature distribution may become too much for one committee. It may be necessary to set up several committees or there may at least need to be subcommittees assigned to specific distribution tasks. This means that there could be individual committees assigned to mailings, door-to-door canvassing, posters, and yard signs. Campaign planners will organize the campaign based upon the size of the effort as well as the strategic plan.

Timing is as important as the distribution method. Literature distributed early in the campaign will be informational. Informational flyers explaining the library's position should be filled with facts and figures. Later in the campaign, however, the literature will be more persuasive and emotional, i.e., "*Vote 'Yes' for new libraries because our kids need them.*" While informational literature distribution may go on for several months, persuasive literature will be distributed primarily in the last month before the election with an extra special effort made in the last two weeks prior to the election.

INFORMATIONAL VERSUS POLITICAL LITERATURE

As has already been pointed out, campaign literature comes in two forms. The first is informational and the second is persuasive or "political." Informational literature is neutral. It provides facts and explains the issue objectively. It does not espouse any position or opinion.

Informational literature may suggest that individuals vote on an issue, but not how they should vote. Political literature is intended to persuade and takes a position in favor of or opposed to an issue. It attempts to convince the reader to vote "for" or "against" an issue, is not objective, and frequently has highly emotional content. Campaign literature that endorses the library issue *is* political.

In most states, public agencies such as the library can distribute informational literature, but they are usually prohibited from disseminating persuasive or political literature. It may be possible for the library to produce (graphic design, layout, and printing) campaign literature as long as it charges the campaign for the activity, but this is often a gray area in the law. While producing the materials in-house is often cheaper than going to commercial printing firms, the activity can open the issue of conflict of interest and inappropriate use of public funds. If there is any room for interpretation of the law, it is usually best to be conservative and avoid controversy. Again, it is wise to consult an attorney to determine the proper roles for the production and distribution of campaign literature inside or outside the library.

POLITICAL DISCLAIMERS

It is also important to know when it is necessary to print a disclaimer statement on campaign literature. Usually, informational literature does not need a disclaimer, but political literature does. A disclaimer statement usually consists of a statement that the literature in question was *"Paid for by the Citizens for a Better Library Committee, Joe Book, Treasurer."* Campaign laws vary from state to state, but it is generally accepted practice to provide the name of the political action committee paying for the literature as well as the name of its treasurer.

FACT SHEETS

The most commonly used piece of campaign literature for library referenda is the informational fact sheet.[2] It should be developed early in the campaign and distributed widely throughout the campaign effort. The fact sheet should use a well laid out and attractive graphic presentation to get the voter's attention and hold it long enough to deliver the critical facts. The use of graphic artists or software programs on microcomputers is strongly advised to help make the fact sheet visually appealing and communicate the information more effectively.

It may be wise to develop several versions of the fact sheet. One version of the fact sheet should not be more than one page. It could be printed front and back, but an abbreviated single-sided version is optimal. Remember, the attention span of the prospective voter is often short, and the facts should be presented like the thirty second sound bite—quickly and dramatically. It may also be helpful to have a lengthy, more in-depth version for thoughtful voters who do their research into the issues. A good way to handle this longer fact sheet is to print it on 11" × 17" paper; it can then be folded in half for a booklet effect or two or three times for a mailer. This version could certainly be available at the library or mailed out to targeted voters, but this is probably not the version to be handed out at the malls. The shorter version should be produced in significantly higher numbers than the longer version. Both versions of the fact sheet should be printed on good quality paper and look professionally prepared as is the case with the examples provided in this chapter.

It is important to keep in mind that a fact sheet provides just the facts; it's informational, not political literature. For example, the fact sheet may provide any of the following facts about the project:

DESCRIPTION OF THE SCOPE OF THE PROJECT: The project must be clearly described. Is it a new building or is it a remodeling? Provide an elevation, floor plan, site plan, or interior view of the project.

THE SQUARE FOOTAGE OF THE PROJECT: Along with indicating the size of the project, it may be helpful to also provide comparative square footage for nearby communities. These figures can be contrasted with the existing (and presumably) inadequate library square footage. A comparison to accepted standards (if available) may be helpful as well.

THE PROJECT BUDGET ESTIMATE: It is usually necessary to inform the electorate of the cost of the project. This figure may be shown as a lump sum or it may be itemized. Describe the source of funds for the project budget, i.e., local bonds, in conjunction with state or federal funds, etc. Showing the total project cost with the resulting cost per household, or a similar comparison, is a good way of bringing the cost down to earth and making it seem inconsequential. Along with stating facts, the idea is to make the cost of the new facility sound like a deal that no one can refuse. Some examples of this approach follow:

- "The library project will cost $12 annually per $100,000 of appraised home value."
- "For the price of a good book (or video tape), you can have a new library."
- "For two tickets to the movies and popcorn, you'll get a whole year's worth of access to the new library."
- "For 16 cents a day, you can give your child the world through books."

DESCRIPTION OF USERS & NEW SERVICES: Fact sheets will often describe new or expanded services which will be offered by the library. In other words, what the public will get for their money. Fact sheets also provide information on the users of the library such as children, young adults, senior citizens, businesspeople, etc. Pictures of users in the library may often provide focus for a fact sheet. Also, it is usually helpful to emphasize the growth of the community and the library.

LOCATION OF THE PROJECT(S): Describe where the new library will be located, or, if there are several branches planned, provide a map showing the locations of each branch.

DATE THE ISSUE WILL APPEAR ON THE BALLOT: It is important to inform the electorate when the library issue will appear on the ballot for their consideration. However, do not suggest that they should vote for the library issue in the fact sheet, just that they should vote.

FIGURE 10-1   Fact Sheet: Las Vegas-Clark County Library District Bond Issue.
Provided Courtesy of Las Vegas-Clark County Library District,
Las Vegas, Nevada.

BLUEPRINT FOR THE FUTURE

What is the Las Vegas-Clark County Library District Bond Issue?

May 7, 1991, citizens will have an opportunity to vote on a general obligation bond issue to benefit the Las Vegas-Clark County Library District.

What will it do?

BUILDINGS

Build a 102,000-square-foot library and art museum at W. Sahara and Grand Canyon.

Build a 37,643-square-foot library on the West Charleston Campus of Clark County Community College to replace the over-crowded Charleston Heights Fine Arts Center.

Build a 26,800-square-foot library at Cheyenne and Buffalo to replace the Rainbow Library now in a rented location in a shopping center.

Build a 38,503-square-foot library in the Summerlin community.

Build a 25,000-square-foot library at East Las Vegas to replace the 3,300 square foot library located in a rented storefront.

Build a 14,000-square-foot library in Laughlin.

Build a 25,000-square-foot library in the Enterprise Township.

Expand the Clark County Library by 61,000 square feet to house a larger periodicals department, add a new auditorium, enlarge the Young People's Library and other library service functions.

Expand the West Las Vegas Library by 9,500 square feet to accommodate a 225-seat auditorium.

BOOKS

Buy 444,000 new books to stock the new libraries.

How much will it cost?

BUILDINGS: $70 million
BOOKS: $10 million

TOTAL: $80 million

Why we need more libraries:

ONE MILLION PEOPLE BY 2000. By 2000, Las Vegas can expect to grow to 1.2 million people.

THEY DON'T BRING THEIR LIBRARIES WITH THEM. Growth fuels demand for housing, public services and businesses. Each year 50 thousand new residents settle in Las Vegas, the population served by one branch library.

WE GREW BY 5.7% IN THE 1980s. The 1.2 million figure predicts a modest growth rate of 3% from our present population of 651,859. But from 1980-89 Las Vegas grew by 272,805. Clark County actually grew at an average annual rate of 5.7%, and even that rate fails to show the 10% to 12% growth rate of the late years of the decade. The average was lowered by the recession of the early 1980s, reflected in a 3% growth rate.

WE'RE GROWING TO THE WEST, NORTH AND SOUTH. By 2000, Las Vegas will grow farther north, west and south. Summa Corporation's 24,900-acre Summerlin development could expand all the way to the border of Red Rock

recreation area. Cosmo World's Silver Canyon, south of McCarran International Airport on Henderson's western edge, will attract development. Henderson, tripled by Green Valley, will continue to boom.

Q. Didn't we recently pass a bond?
A. The 1985 bond met the needs of that time. Growth has placed new demands on the library district. The District built for a population of 466,000. Currently 200,000 residents are without library services.

THE PREVIOUS BOND MET THE NEEDS OF 1985. The Las Vegas-Clark County Library District began planning in 1980 to build enough libraries to fulfill existing and projected needs with the 1985 bonds. The final project of that fund was completed in 1990.

THE 1991 BOND MEETS THE NEEDS OF THE 1990s. In 1990 our libraries again are strained to meet the needs of the present population. Without the 1991 bond, which anticipates the needs of the Southern Nevada area to the end of the millineum, we will fall further and further behind.

How will it be paid for?

The owner of a $100,000 house will pay $20 annually at the highest. The average annual payment over the life of the bond will be only $12.

THE 1991 LIBRARY BOND ISSUE

FIGURE 10-2 Fact Sheet: Spokane Public Library Bond Issue. Provided Courtesy of Spokane Public Library, Spokane, Washington.

FIGURE 10-2 Continued

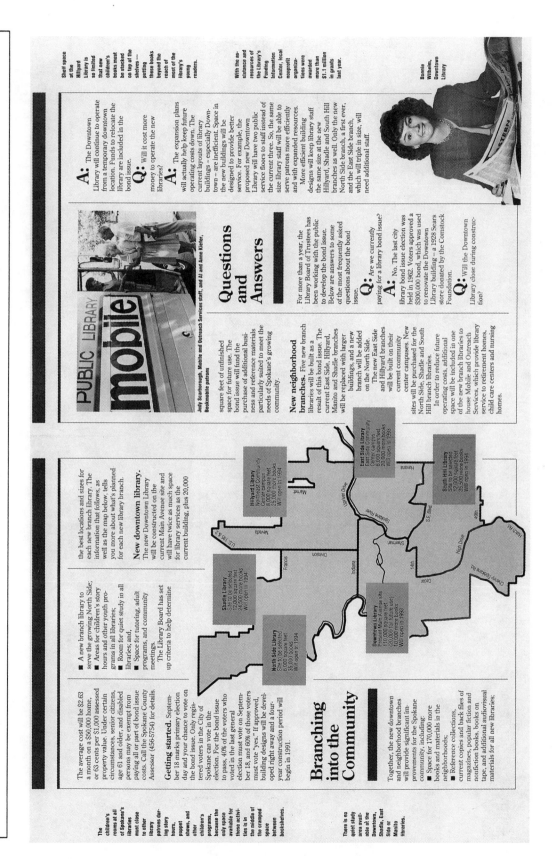

The average cost will be $2.63 a month on a $50,000 home, or 63 cents per $1,000 assessed property value. Under certain circumstances, senior citizens, age 61 and older, and disabled persons may be exempt from paying all or part of bond issue costs. Call the Spokane County Assessor (456-5754) for details.

Getting started. September 18 marks primary election day and your chance to vote on the bond issue. Only registered voters in the City of Spokane can vote in the election. For the bond issue to pass, 40% of the voters who voted in the last general election must vote on September 18, and 60% of those voters must vote "yes." If approved, building designs will be developed right away and a four-year construction period will begin in 1991.

■ A new branch library to serve the growing North Side;
■ Areas for children's story hours and other youth programs in all libraries;
■ Room for quiet study in all libraries; and,
■ Space for tutoring, adult programs, and community meetings.

The Library Board has set up criteria to help determine

the best locations and sizes for each new branch library. The information that follows, as well as the map below, tells you more about what's planned for each new library branch.

New downtown library. The new Downtown Library will be constructed on the current Main Avenue site and will have twice as much space for library services as the current building, plus 20,000

square feet of unfinished space for future use. The bond issue will fund the purchase of additional business and reference materials particularly suited to meet the needs of Spokane's growing community.

New neighborhood branches. Five new branch libraries will be built as a result of this bond issue. The current East Side, Hillyard, Manito and Shadle branches will be replaced with larger buildings, and a new branch will be added on the North Side.

The new East Side and Hillyard branches will be built on their current community center campuses. New sites will be purchased for the North Side, Shadle and South Hill branch libraries.

In order to reduce future operating costs, additional space will be included in one of the new branch libraries to house Mobile and Outreach Services, which provide library service to retirement homes, child care centers and nursing homes.

Branching into the Community

Together, the new downtown and neighborhood branches will provide significant improvements for the Spokane community, including:

■ Space for 170,000 more books and materials in the neighborhoods;
■ Reference collections, current copies and back files of magazines, popular fiction and nonfiction books, books on tape, and additional audiovisual materials for all new libraries;

Questions and Answers

For more than a year, the Library Board of Trustees has been working with the public to develop the bond issue. Below are answers to some of the most frequently asked questions about the bond issue.

Q: Are we currently paying for a library bond issue?

A: No. The last city library bond issue election was held in 1962. Voters approved a $300,000 bond, which was used to renovate the Downtown Library building – a 1928 Sears store donated by the Comstock Foundation.

Q: Will the Downtown Library close during construction?

A: The Downtown Library will continue to operate from a temporary downtown location. Funds to relocate the library are included in the bond issue.

Q: Will it cost more money to operate the new libraries?

A: The expansion plans will actually help keep future operating costs down. The current layouts of library buildings – especially Downtown – are inefficient. Space in the new buildings will be designed to provide better service. For example, the proposed new Downtown Library will have two public service floors to staff instead of the current three. So, the same size library staff will be able to serve patrons more efficiently and with expanded resources.

More efficient building designs will keep library staff the same size at the new Hillyard, Shadle and South Hill branches as well. Only the new North Side branch, a first ever, and the East Side branch, which will triple in size, will need additional staff.

Judy Scarborough, Mobile and Outreach Services staff, and Al and Anne Kiefer, Bookmobile patrons

PUBLIC LIBRARY mobile

The children's rooms at all of Spokane's libraries must close to other library patrons during story hours, puppet shows, and other children's programs, because the only space available for these activities is in the middle of the cramped space between bookshelves.

There is no quiet study area available at the Downtown, Shadle, East Side or Manito libraries.

Shelf space at the Hillyard Library is so limited that new children's books must be stacked on top of the shelves — putting these books beyond the reach of most of the library's young readers.

With the assistance and resources of the Library's Funding Information Center, local nonprofit organizations were awarded more than $1.1 million in grants last year.

Bonnie Wilhelm, Downtown Library

Map labels:

Hillyard Library
Northeast Community Center campus
8,000 square feet
25,000 more books
Will open in 1994

East Side Library
East Side Community Center campus
6,000 square feet
20,000 more books
Will open in 1993

South Hill Library
Site to be selected
12,000 square feet
35,500 more books
Will open in 1994

Shadle Library
Site to be selected
12,000 square feet
24,500 more books
Will open in 1994

North Side Library
Site to be selected
6,000 square feet
35,000 books
Will open in 1994

Downtown Library
Present Main Avenue site
110,000 square feet
(20,000 for future use)
10,000 more books
Will open in 1993

FIGURE 10-3   Fact Sheet: Fairfax County Public Library. Fairfax, Virginia. Provided Courtesy of the Fairfax County Public Library.

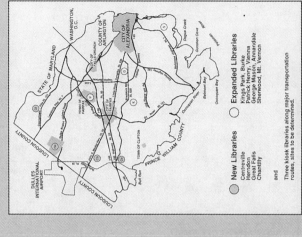

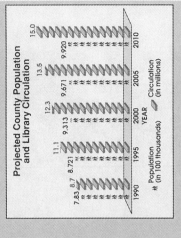

Access to Yesterday
Help for Today
Steps toward Tomorrow
The LIBRARY is a
Good Place to Start

Fairfax County Public Library's 22 branches differ in size, type of collection, services available and patrons served. But they all have one thing in common: a commitment to provide easy access to a multitude of resources for the education, entertainment, business or pleasure of the 746,800 Fairfax County residents.

This fall, the Fairfax County Board of Supervisors will ask voters if they wish to borrow $39.1 million to finance a five-year library capital improvement program. If approved, the bond funds will provide for construction of seven new libraries and expansion of four existing libraries.

Each year the Library's Board of Trustees and staff study and update the five-year capital improvement program (CIP), which is included in the overall Fairfax County CIP. The proposed construction projects are based on such factors as projected population growth, circulation and demand for service. The selection of libraries for renovation is based upon a review of the age, condition and usage at each facility.

County population is projected to increase by more than 148,000 in the next decade. The continued influx of new residents and a rise in birthrates are among the factors contributing to this increase. As population grows so does the need for new or enhanced libraries to meet minimum service standards of .5 sq. ft. of library space per capita. These guidelines, established by the Library's Board of Trustees, follow "Recommended Minimum Standards for Virginia Public Libraries," which sets basic requirements for receiving supplemental state aid.

Facts on the
Library
Bond Referendum

Fairfax County, Virginia
Tuesday, Nov. 7, 1989

Fairfax County Public Library

Library Administration
Greenbriar Corporate Center, Suite 301
13135 Lee Jackson Highway
Fairfax, Virginia 22033

FIGURE 10-3 *Continued*

New Construction

REGIONAL LIBRARIES

Centreville Regional Library

A 30,000 sq. ft. library to be located at the intersection of Lee Highway (Rt. 29) and Machen Road. The library will house the Willoughby Newton Stone, the county's oldest dated artifact (1739) and the area's oldest surviving boundary marker. Projected Opening: January 1992. Estimated Cost: $5,692,000 (design & construction).

Chantilly Regional Library Complex

A 52,000 sq. ft. building to be located at the intersection of Rt. 50 and Stringfellow Road. In addition to a full-service 30,000 sq. ft. library, the building will house the system's Technical Operations and Computer Center which includes cataloging, materials selection, acquisitions and other behind-the-scenes management functions. Projected Opening: November 1992. Estimated Cost: $10,380,000 (land acquisition, design & construction).

Regional Library features:
- open seven days a week
- collection of 125,000 volumes including children's books, large print books, books on tape, video and audio cassettes, compact discs and more than 300 magazine and newspaper titles
- information service, including access to nearly 300 computer databases
- public meeting room, study carrels, lounge seating
- multimedia center with video, audio and cable access
- programs and activities for all ages including children's story times, films and lecture series

COMMUNITY LIBRARIES

Herndon Community Library

A 13,500 sq. ft. building to replace the 2,047 sq. ft. structure built in 1927. The library will be located in downtown Herndon, at a site to be determined. Projected Opening: May 1992. Estimated Cost: $3,390,000 (design & construction).

Great Falls Community Library

A 10,000 sq. ft. building to replace the kiosk mini library. The library will be located near Georgetown Pike, at a site to be determined. Projected Opening: November 1992. Estimated Cost: $4,460,000 (land acquisition, design & construction).

Community Library features:
- collection of 65,000-80,000 volumes including children's books, records, books on tape, video and audio cassettes, in addition to periodicals and newspapers
- consumer information, current financial information, research assistance for students and reader's advisory service
- multimedia center with video, audio and cable access
- public meeting room, study carrels and lounge seating
- programs and activities for all ages including children's story times, films and lecture series

KIOSK LIBRARIES

Three information centers to be located on major transportation routes. These mini-libraries will include collections of approximately 10,000 current and popular books and reading materials. Projected Opening: 1992. Estimated Cost: $660,000 (construction).

"An investment in knowledge pays the best interest."

Benjamin Franklin

"To furnish the means of acquiring knowledge is . . . the greatest benefit that can be conferred."

John Adams, 1846

Expansion

Sherwood Regional Library

A project to expand the current facility, located at 2501 Sherwood Hall Lane in Mt. Vernon, from 21,000 to 37,400 sq. ft. to meet the 5 sq. ft. building space standard. The building's second floor will house two unique services for county residents: InfoLine, a telephone reference providing answers to commonly asked questions and Special Services, materials for the visually and physically handicapped, homebound and deaf. Projected Completion: September 1991. Estimated Cost: $3,330,419 (design & construction).

Kings Park Community Library

A project to fund land acquisition for parking lot and building expansions. The library, located at 9000 Burke Lake Road in Burke, would be enlarged from 11,402 to 17,200 sq. ft. to meet the .5 sq. ft. building space standard. Projected Completion: December 1991. Estimated Cost: $1,107,114 (land acquisition, design & construction).

Patrick Henry Community Library

A project to expand the building, located at 101 Maple Avenue East in Vienna, from 11,000 to 16,912 sq. ft. to meet the .5 sq. ft. building space standard. Projected Completion: April 1992. Estimated Cost: $2,840,000 (design & construction).

George Mason Regional Library

A project to enlarge, renovate and modernize the current structure at 7001 Little River Turnpike in Annandale. The expansion from 24,000 to 30,000 sq. ft. would enable the library to meet the .5 sq. ft. building space standard. Projected Completion: June 1993. Estimated Cost: $3,125,000 (design & construction).

Expanded Library features:
- increased service area with a central information desk
- additional conference room and quiet study area
- additional parking
- enlarged staff workroom

Facts and Firsts

Fairfax County Public Library is the busiest public library in the southern U.S.*

In the last fiscal year, library staff:
- circulated 8.5 million books and other materials
- answered 2.1 million reference questions
- informed nearly 170,000 people through library programs

For every hour of operation, library staff circulated 2,577 items, answered 636 reference questions and presented a program to a group of 50 people!

*annual Memphis/Shelby County survey designated FCPL "most active" of 94 library systems in 15 southern states.

These facts have been published for your information by:

The Fairfax County Public Library Board of Trustees

Linda A. Singer, Chair
Centreville District

Sharon Murphy
At-Large

Phyllis A. Salak
City of Fairfax

Vincent Kashuda
Lee District

Louise L. Meade
Mount Vernon District

Linda Hunt
School Board

Irene Burgess, Vice Chair
Springfield District

Dr. Bruce Richards
Annandale District

Marge Genic
Dranesville District

Gwendalyn F. Cody
Mason District

Herbert A. Doyle, Jr.
Providence District

Administration

Edwin S. Clay, III
Director of Libraries

Patricia M. Paine
Deputy Director

For further details, call the Library's Office of Public Information, 222-3184.

Bonds

The sale of municipal bonds is a form of long-term borrowing that spreads the cost of major capital improvements over a period of years while libraries are being used. Bond sales ensure that both current and future users share in paying for the benefits of new and enhanced libraries.

Funds for major maintenance, minor improvements and selected repairs are included in the annual operating budget. The subsantial cost of building and renewing libraries with operating funds would have severe impact upon library collections and other services.

Since the issuing of bonds results in future obligation for taxpayers, the law requires that bond sales be approved by voters.

Fairfax County is one of only 13 of the nation's 3,106 counties that have the highest credit rating possible for local government. For this reason, Fairfax County bonds always sell at exceptionally low interest rates.

If the referendum is approved on November 7, bonds will be sold to meet cash requirements for specified projects. County bond sales are controlled by the Fairfax County Board of Supervisors within approved financial guidelines to safeguard the coveted Triple-A bond rating. The Board of Supervisors' financial guidelines provide that the annual cost of the county's debt (principle and interest) is no greater than 10 percent of the annual combined general fund disbursements.

The Board of Supervisors maintains the county's net long-term debt at or below 3 percent of the total estimated market value of taxable property in the county.

FIGURE 10-4   Fact Sheet: King County Library System Expansion. Seattle, Washington. Provided Courtesy of the King County Library System.

Community and Library: A Shared Future

On September 20, 1988, voters will decide on a $67 million bond issue for new libraries, expansions of current buildings, and new books and other materials. Here is information to help you make your decision.

🅚 KING COUNTY LIBRARY SYSTEM
300 Eighth Avenue North
Seattle, Washington 98109

King County Library System circulates more items than any library west of the Mississippi or north of Los Angeles, but is unable to keep up with the demand. New and expanded libraries, as well as more books and other materials are needed. Operating funds are inadequate to fund the needed capital expansion.

Population is growing at a rapid rate in the county and library use is growing even faster. Since 1980, library circulation has doubled. Projections indicate that by the year 2000 population in the district's service area is expected to increase from 840,000 to 1.2 million and library use will triple.

What is included in the bond issue?

Approximately two-thirds of the money will be spent for site acquisition and construction of new or expanded libraries. This amount includes the renovation of existing libraries, expanded Traveling Library Center service and a computerized catalog. About one-third of the money will be used to buy new books and other materials.

Where will the new libraries be located? Which ones will be expanded?

New libraries will be built in Woodinville, Pine Lake, Upper Snoqualmie, Shoreline, Carnation/Duvall and two libraries each in East Kent and in Federal Way. Libraries to be expanded: Burien, Newport Way, Redmond, Maple Valley, and Bellevue. The capital plan includes funding for libraries in Juanita, Richmond Beach, Algona/Pacific and Bellevue/Redmond (Overlake/Crossroads) areas. A new service center building for the district will also be built.

What will this cost?

The average annual cost of the 20-year bonds will be 13 cents per $1,000 assessed valuation (or $13 on a $100,000 home). Under certain circumstances, senior citizens and disabled persons may be exempt from paying a bond issue levy. Call the King County Assessor's Office (296-3920) for details.

Are we currently paying for a library district bond issue?

No. The last library district bond issue election was held in 1966; 20 libraries were built and the bonds were paid in full in 1987.

P Proposition 1:
Library Improvement Bonds -
$67,000,000

Who will vote?

Registered voters in unincorporated King County and in Bothell, Bellevue and North Bend (cities which have annexed to the library district) will vote on and pay for the bond issue. (Other cities in the county pay contract fees to the library district, except for Seattle, Renton, Auburn and Enumclaw which operate their own libraries.)

Where can I get more information?

Call the King County Library System Public Information Office, 684-6606.

Mel Huxtable, Shoreline Library
On the cover:
Stephanie Diaz, Federal Way Library

FIGURE 10-4 *Continued*

Improvements will be made in every section of the library district's service area. The building plan will be reviewed annually to best serve the growing population and to meet the demand for library services. (Projected construction dates are shown in parentheses.)

Books and Materials

About one-third of the bond money will be used to buy books and other materials for the new and expanded libraries. All library users will be able to check out these new materials including books, reference titles, magazines, newspapers, audio and video cassettes, compact discs, on-line databases and films.

**Area One:
North King County**

One of the first projects is a new library in Woodinville, a heavily populated area that has no local library service (1990). The Shoreline Library will be replaced with a larger and more efficient building (1993) which will provide more reference services. The building plan includes libraries in Juanita (no library currently) and Richmond Beach (a larger building).

Area Two: Eastside

The Newport Way Library will be expanded to serve the growing Eastgate area (1994). An addition to the Redmond Library is planned (1995). The plan includes a library in the Overlake/Crossroads area to better serve the residents between Bellevue and Redmond

The library system is currently buying half of the Ashwood school property in Bellevue as the site for a 40,000 square foot library funded from annexation revenues. Planning projections indicate that the building needs to be half again as large to meet the demand for services on the eastside. The additional 20,000 square feet will be incorporated into the original building plan and paid for from the bond issue (1991).

**Area Three:
East King County**

New libraries will be built in the growing Pine Lake area (1991), Upper Snoqualmie Valley (1993), and in the Carnation/Duvall area (1997).

**Area Four:
South King County**

Two new libraries are planned in the rapidly growing East Kent area (one in 1991), a second one in 1995). An addition to the Maple Valley Library will extend the services offered to this expanding community (1995).

**Area Five:
Southwest King County**

The Federal Way Library is the smallest of the system's six regional resource libraries and is inadequate to serve the needs of this rapidly growing community. Two new libraries are planned. One, south of the current site, will replace the current building (1990). A second library will be built north of the current site (1996). When the two new libraries are open, the existing building on S. 320th will be sold.

An expansion of the Burien Library is planned to better serve the Highline area and nearby communities (1995). A new library is planned in the Algona/Pacific area.

**District-Wide
Improvements**

The Traveling Library Center (which visits retirement homes, nursing homes and day care facilities) will be expanded to include more stops and services.

Many of the library district's older buildings will be refurbished. These improvements include new furnaces, roofs, carpeting, and shelving. A new computerized catalog system will be installed to replace the microfiche catalog. A new service center (headquarters and central processing facility for the district) will be built; the current service center building and site will be sold.

Dean Phung,
White Center Library

L ibrary Improvement Bonds will provide funds for new and expanded libraries, and new books and other materials.

**King County
Library System**

AREA 1
AREA 2
AREA 3
AREA 4
AREA 5

● **Current libraries**
● **New libraries**
1. Shoreline
2. Federal Way/1
3. Woodinville
4. East Kent/1
5. Pine Lake
6. Upper Snoqualmie
7. East Kent/2
8. Carnation/Duvall
9. Federal Way/2
10. Juanita
11. Crossroads/Overlake
12. Algona/Pacific
13. Richmond Beach

Library expansions
14. Bellevue
15. Burien
16. Maple Valley
17. Newport Way
18. Redmond

(Locations of new libraries represent general areas; public meetings will be held to discuss sites and building designs.)

FIGURE 10-5 Fact Sheet with Architectural Graphics: The New Wyandach Public Library. Wyandach, New York. Provided Courtesy of the Wyandach Public Library.

VOTER INFORMATION

REQUIREMENTS:
- Citizen of United States.
- 18 years or older.
- Registered. (Note that registration for federal, state or school district elections qualifies voters for this vote.)
- Resident of district for at least 30 days prior to the vote.

The following voting activities will take place at the Straight Path Elementary School:

REGISTRATION
Tuesday, October 16, 2PM to 10PM
INFORMATION MEETING
Thursday, October 25, 7PM
LIBRARY VOTE
Monday, October 29, 10AM to 10PM

**For Your Community
For Your Family
For You!
The NEW Wyandanch Public Library**
We're Opening a New Chapter in Our History.
Join Us....

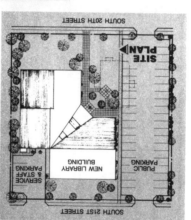

SOUTH 20TH STREET

SITE PLAN

PUBLIC PARKING

NEW LIBRARY BUILDING

SERVICE & STAFF PARKING

SOUTH 21ST STREET

Wyandanch Public Library
14 South 20 Street
Wyandanch, N.Y. 11798

Wyandanch School District
Local Resident and Box Holder
Wyandanch, New York 11798

NON PROFIT ORG.
U.S. POSTAGE
PAID
WYANDANCH, N.Y.
PERMIT NO. 9

Think about a library. It's more than books and periodicals. It's part of the very fiber of a community. A locus of personal growth and enrichment, a center where views and ideas can be examined and exchanged and a partner in the education of our children.

Now look at our new Wyandanch Public Library. It's a modern, brand-new building. It houses an expanded collection of volumes. But, most importantly, it's a facility designed to meet the educational needs of our community today — and for years to come. Spacious meeting and conference rooms will be available for use by Wyandanch community groups. A new media center will give Wyandanch residents hands-on experience with the latest information technology. A new computer will help Wyandanch youngsters gain the competitive edge that our technologically-driven society demands.

Consider the impact of such a library. Consider the role it can play in the quality of life for all of us in Wyandanch. And then consider this: **the total costs of the new Wyandanch Public Library averages out to a mere $1 per week for each household in our community.**

What a small price to pay for an institution that can play such a vital and positive role! So join us as we turn a new page in our community's history. Join us in supporting — and in using — this valuable new resource. Join us as we open the doors of the new Wyandanch Public Library.

Welcome!

FIGURE 10-5 *Continued*

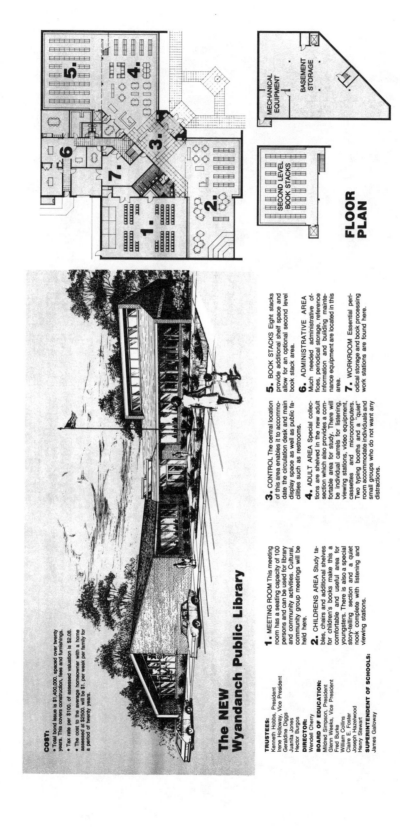

The NEW Wyandanch Public Library

COST:
- Total bond issue is $1,400,000, spaced over twenty years. This covers construction, fees and furnishings.
- Tax rate per $100, of assessed valuation is $2.08.
- The cost to the average homeowner with a home assessed at $2500, will be $1, per week per family for a period of twenty years.

1. MEETING ROOM This meeting room has a seating capacity of 100 persons and can be used for library and community activities. Cultural, community group meetings will be held here.

2. CHILDRENS AREA Study tables, chairs and additional shelves for children's books make this a comfortable and useful area for youngsters. There is also a special story-telling section and a quiet nook complete with listening and viewing stations.

3. CONTROL The central location of this area enables it to accommodate the circulation desk and main display space as well as public facilities such as restrooms.

4. ADULT AREA Special collections are shelved in the new adult section which also provides a comfortable area for study. There will be individual carrels for listening, viewing stations, video equipment, cassettes and microcomputers. Two typing booths and a "quiet" room accommodate individuals and small groups who do not want any distractions.

5. BOOK STACKS Eight stacks provide additional shelf space and allow for an optional second level book stack area.

6. ADMINISTRATIVE AREA Much needed administrative offices, periodical storage, reference information and building maintenance equipment are located in this area.

7. WORKROOM Essential periodical storage and book processing work stations are found here.

FLOOR PLAN

FIGURE 10-6   Fact Sheet with Architectural Graphics: The New Brentwood Public Library. Provided Courtesy of Brentwood Public Library, Brentwood, New York.

FIGURE 10-6   *Continued*

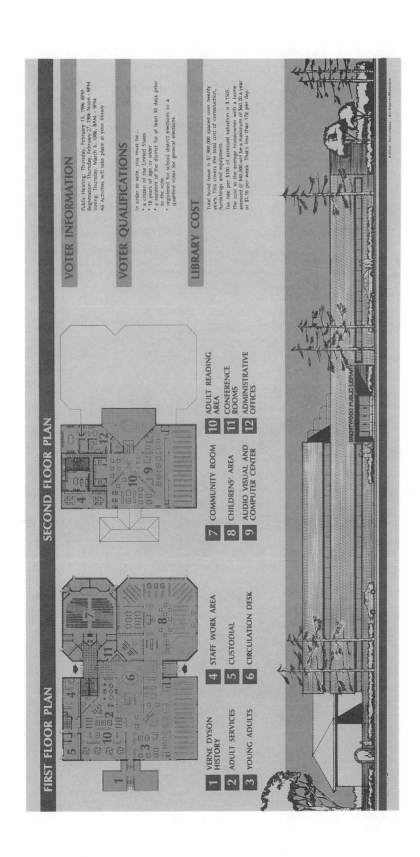

FIGURE 10-7   Dekalb Map of Library Branches. Provided Courtesy of Dekalb County
Public Library, Decatur, Georgia.

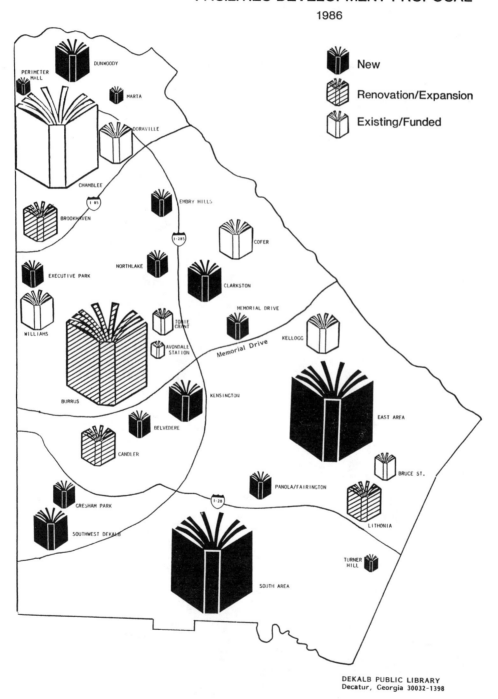

DEKALB PUBLIC LIBRARY
FACILITIES DEVELOPMENT PROPOSAL
1986

DEKALB PUBLIC LIBRARY
Decatur, Georgia 30032-1398

QUESTIONS & ANSWERS

A variation on the fact sheet is the question and answer format. This can be particularly effective in providing information and answers to specific questions which have come up during the campaign. Figure 10-8 demonstrates how the question and answer format works.

BOOKMARKS

It may be useful to have a small "bookmark" version of the fact sheet which can be handed out at the circulation desk with every book circulated. Bookmarks are specific to library campaigns and are usually used to supplement more in-depth fact sheets. Bookmarks are a particularly effective way of communicating with library patrons, a major target audience. If bookmarks are handed out at the library, they must be informational and not political. Bookmarks can be a colorful, easy way to communicate specific facts to library patrons. Again, several versions can be printed and distributed in stages as the campaign develops. The first versions can simply raise awareness of the impending library ballot issue, later ones can explain certain aspects of the library issue, and the final version can simply urge library patrons to get out and vote (without saying "vote for the library").

BROCHURES, PAMPHLETS, FLYERS, & LEAFLETS

In addition to fact sheets, one of the most frequently used "nuts and bolts" campaign methods for library referenda is to print brochures, pamphlets, flyers, and leaflets that put the library issue in a favorable light. This is a straightforward and effective method of communicating with voters. It is usually worthwhile to put a good deal of time and effort into planning the products and employ a graphic artist or public relations firm. Like the fact sheet, these may show elevations and floor plans of the new building, highlight new services, picture children in the library, give the project budget, and demonstrate how little the resulting cost per household will be if the referendum is approved by the voters, but there is one important difference. This material is promotional and therefore political because its goal is to persuade the electorate to vote for the library issue. Further, as opposed to the somewhat dry and objective format of the fact sheet, this material has strong emotional overtones, often reflects the main campaign message, and usually displays the campaign logo and slogan.

There may be numerous versions of this material produced. Each version may emphasize a specific campaign theme and be targeted for a specific sector of the electorate. For example, if service to children is one of the campaign themes, service to this sector will be emphasized and the emotional appeal of the campaign literature will be reinforced by heart-touching pictures of children. This material can then be actively disseminated in neighborhoods which have a high number of school-aged children. Another theme may be service to the business community. Campaign literature may be developed around this theme showing respected businessmen using electronic databases or CD-ROM products in the library. Again, this material can be targeted for use with the Chamber of Commerce, major corporations, and small businesses. Any number of themes may be promoted through this form of campaign literature depending, of course, on the overall campaign strategy.

Remember to keep political brochures and flyers SIMPLE! If they are long and complicated, people won't bother to read them and campaign funds will have been wasted. Further, they should be dramatic and graphically enticing. This material is one of the campaign's best shots

FIGURE 10-8 Question & Answer: Investment Portfolio. Provided Courtesy of City of Port Orange, Florida.

An Investment In Your Future

On Tuesday, April 9, the voters of the City of Port Orange, will have an opportunity to determine if a free standing library will be constructed in Port Orange.

Q. Why is a new Library needed?
A. In 1985, when the City of Port Orange moved into the new City Hall, 10,000 square feet was temporarily allocated to the Library. The agreement was for the Library to occupy the space until such time as the City needed the space. It was anticipated in 1985 that the space would be needed within 5 or 6 years.

Secondly, the library has physically outgrown its space. In 1985, the space allocation to the library could accommodate 50,000 volumes of books, plus space for support programs. Today, the Port Orange Library offers many services that were not anticipated in 1985. For example, the library has a video library with over 1,100 movies available; a record and compact disk library; as well as, a computer center with the latest software programs available for citizen use and a homework center for student use.

All of these plus the need to provide space specifically designed for library use and library programs are why the City of Port Orange Library Advisory Board recommended and the City of Port Orange City Council scheduled a Special Election on April 9, 1991.

Q. How many square feet will be included in the proposed Library?
A. The Library Advisory Board has spent over a year looking at the library needs of our community. The analysis, plus the results of a County commissioned study on library needs, has led the Library Advisory Board to recommend that a 30,000 square foot facility be constructed in Port Orange. This facility will take the City into the next Century in terms of meeting its Library needs.

The 30,000 square feet will allow the library to expand the number of books available to residents to between 100,000 - 150,000 volumes; provide larger reference areas and materials to be used by students; expanded children's library area plus children's programs that include story time, crafts, movies and even an expanded after school program; an adult program space that would allow the library to expand its speakers' program and travel log program; public meeting space.

Q. How much will the Library cost?
A. The total cost of the Library will be 3.25 million.

Q. How will the Library be financed?
A. The Library is proposed to be funded with a special property tax millage. The millage will be dedicated to retire bonds issued to provide funds for construction of the Library.

Q. How will this affect my millage rate?
A. The following table shows how much the average homeowner would pay, if the special millage is approved.

Property Ass. Net of $25,000 Homestead Exempt.	Additional Required Millage Rate	Yearly Cost To Port Orange Property Owner	Monthly Cost to Port Orange Property Owner
25,000	0.344	8.60	0.72
30,000	0.344	10.32	0.86
35,000	0.344	12.04	1.00
40,000	0.344	13.76	1.15
45,000	0.344	15.43	1.29
50,000	0.344	17.20	1.43
55,000	0.344	18.92	1.58
60,000	0.344	20.64	1.72
65,000	0.344	22.36	1.86
70,000	0.344	24.08	2.01
75,000	0.344	25.80	2.15
80,000	0.344	27.52	2.29
85,000	0.344	29.24	2.44
90,000	0.344	30.96	2.58
95,000	0.344	32.68	2.72
100,000	0.344	34.40	2.87

Q. What is the length of the Bond Issue?
A. The Bonds will be issued for a period of 20 years.

Q. Can I purchase one or more of the Library Bonds if the voters approve this issue?
A. Yes. The City of Port Orange has set aside a portion of the Bonds that will be made available to interested citizens. (Normally, municipal bonds are issued in denominations of $5,000. In order to allow more citizens an opportunity to acquire these special Library Bonds, Bonds in denominations as low as $500 will be made available to interested citizens. These Bonds are tax exempt and, therefore, free from Federal Income Tax.

Q. Who will own the new Library building?
A. The building will be owned by the City of Port Orange. Volusia County will continue to provide books and other library materials, as well as staff and operating cost. This is the same arrangement we have now with the County.

Q. What will happen to the existing Library space?
A. As soon as the Library is relocated, the space currently occupied by the Library will be converted to use by the City.

Q. Where will the new Library be constructed?
A. Although the exact site has not been determined, the City's master plan for the Municipal Complex has reserved space south of the City Hall for the Library.
If the voters approve the construction of the Library, detailed site plans will be prepared, working with the residents of the Kingswood area to properly locate the library so as to not disturb their neighborhood.

Q. Has the Library been designed yet?
A. No. The City has used construction costs verified by General Contractors to determine the budget. The building will be designed and constructed within the dollars approved.

Q. Will the 30,000 square feet be enough space?
A. Yes. The 30,000 square feet will be ample space for the future. However, the City has a policy that will require the design of the building so that it can be easily expanded.

Q. Will there be public meeting space in the Library?
A. Yes. The Library Advisory Board in the Facility study has found a need for a large multi-purpose meeting area that will seat about 200 people and a need for two smaller meeting rooms.

Q. How many people have Port Orange Library cards?
A. More than 21,000 residents have library cards issued by the Port Orange Library. This means about 60% of our residents are holders of library cards issued by Port Orange. This number does not include residents whose cards were issued by other libraries in Volusia County cities.

Q. When will the millage be levied?
A. If the voters approve the Library, the first millage would appear on the tax bills that will be mailed this November, 1991.

FIGURE 10-8 *Continued*

FIGURE 10-9 Bookmark: Library Proposition #1. Provided Courtesy of Pierce County Library District, Tacoma, Washington.

IT'S UP TO YOU

LIBRARY PROPOSITION #1

please VOTE
September 16

LIBRARY PROPOSITION #1
would allow sale of 28.9 million in bonds for construction of buildings and the purchase of books and other materials for loan.

It would nearly double the scope of library service in our district, easing present overcrowding and lack of books, and preparing for projected population growth through the start of the next century.

It will add 49¢ per $1,000 assessed value per year in property tax (e.g. about $39 on a home assessed at $80,000) to the existing 50¢ library levy.

The new total would be about 8% of the property tax in an average library district tax code area.

For information call Pierce County Library, 572-6760.

86

FIGURE 10-10a   Bookmark: One Year Only Library Levy. Provided Courtesy of Fort Vancouver Regional Library, Vancouver, Washington.

Fort Vancouver Regional Library

One Year Only

LIBRARY LEVY

September 18, 1990

What For?

- New books
- Computers for circulation and catalogs
- Faster and easier access to books in Clark, Skamania and Klickitat Counties
- Start-up costs
- Staff training (no lay-offs from automation)

Why?

Growth in the last 10 years
- Books checked out up **80%**
- Reference questions up **490%**
- Cards filed now, **6 million per year**

Service Improvements

- Buy more books
- Search catalog by keywords
- Print out reading lists
- Reserve books quickly
- Renew books from all libraries
- Link with schools, other libraries, homes and businesses

F A C T S

Special Capital Levy

- Library funding is limited by state law
- **One Year Only**
- Does not cut back on funds for fire or other service districts

Saves Money

- Cuts book loss
- No bond interest payments
- Creates more staff time for public service

How Much?

- This **one year only** levy will raise $2.6 million
- At 35¢ per $1000 valuation, the **one time cost** would be $24.50 for a $70,000 home
- May be less per $1000 based on 1990 assesment
- Senior citizen exemption applies

What's Required?

- 60% Yes to pass
- 40% to validate

Questions?

- **Call Fort Vancouver Regional Library**

695-1561

One Year Only

LIBRARY LEVY

September 18, 1990

F A C T S

FIGURE 10-10b   Bookmark: Bond Issue at a Glance. Provided Courtesy of Spokane Public Library, Spokane, Washington.

Our Library's Future:

Understanding the Bond Issue

On Tuesday, September 18, Spokane city voters will decide on a proposed $28.8 million bond issue for the **Spokane Public Library** system.

This is the first bond issue in Spokane's history that will address library needs throughout the community by building new libraries in the neighborhoods and downtown.

Through the Library Board of Trustees' careful planning with the community, the library needs became clear: Spokane has outgrown its library system in every neighborhood and downtown.

The bond issue will expand and upgrade library services in all of Spokane's neighborhoods.

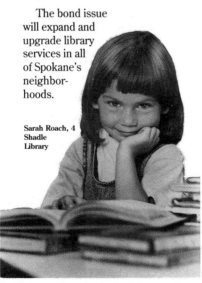

**Sarah Roach, 4
Shadle
Library**

Bond Issue at a Glance

Builds six libraries:
- Downtown
- East Side
- Hillyard
- North Side
- Shadle
- South Hill

Provides:
Books and reference materials, automation, more shelf space, more community meeting space, land acquisition, and construction fees

Bond budget:
$28,883,000 (over 20 years)

Cost to average household:
$2.63 per month (based on $50,000 property value)
63 cents per $1,000 assessed value

Who can vote?
City of Spokane registered voters

When is election day?
September 18

Questions?
If you have questions, please call Lisa Wolfe, Public Information Coordinator, at 838-6757.

SPOKANE
PUBLIC
LIBRARY

Please Vote!

FIGURE 10-11   Bookmarks: The Library Bond. Provided Courtesy of the Chesapeake Public Library, Chesapeake, Virginia. "Yes, we use the library!" Provided Courtesy of the Tulsa City County Library System, Tulsa, Oklahoma.

The Library Bond
Vote November 8.

Not paid for at public expense but by the Citizens for Better Libraries Committee. Frank Gilmore, Treasurer

"Yes,
we use the library!"

Library usage is increasing steadily. Yet, income to operate the Tulsa City-County Library System is decreasing.

Two library propositions will be on the August 23rd Tulsa County election ballot: **Proposition 1** requests a one-mill increase in support for public libraries, **Proposition 2** is a $4.2 million bond issue.

Please remember to VOTE AUGUST 23

at influencing people to vote for the library issue. Again, this is where the emotional "hook" is commonly used to pull the voter into the library's camp and solidify support. All kinds of tactics can be used including appealing to community pride which is often effective. One campaign printed the fact that research had shown that over three-fourths of library capital referenda held nationally had passed in the previous year. The implication being "What kind of community do we live in if we don't pass ours?" The brochures shown here exemplify effective political library campaign material used in recent campaigns.

LETTERS

Writing letters can be a very effective way of communicating with the electorate. There are a number of approaches to letter writing including the following:

Campaign Letterhead

Any campaign will have general correspondence. It is a good idea to print up some campaign letterhead with the campaign logo on it and use it with all official campaign correspondence. The letterhead should be printed in such a manner that the paper and ink will standout prominently. Sometimes it is helpful to place the names of the steering committee members on the letterhead for added impact if they are prominent in the community.

Letters to the Editor

There will undoubtedly be some coverage of the library issue in the local media. An important campaign technique is to have numerous letters written to the editors or the local newspapers as well as the electronic media. Library patrons and Friends can write effective letters stating their support for the library issue as well as disputing inaccurate information put out by opposition groups.

Open Letters to the Community at Large

Sometimes an "open letter to the community" is an effective way of addressing a campaign issue or simply stating the library's case. This letter can be circulated through mailings and other campaign distribution methods, published in the newspaper or read on the radio or television.

Endorsement Letters

Letters of endorsement can be very effective especially when provided by well-respected individuals. They can be circulated with campaign literature, published in the newspaper, or read on the radio or television. Also, it is important for the campaign manager to seek editorials by the local press as well as out-and-out media endorsements. Sometimes endorsement letters can even be used in campaign ads.

Fundraising Letters

Fundraising letters solicit funds for the campaign. They should be straightforward and to the point. They should ask for money and even specify amounts which may be identified with a

FIGURE 10-12   Political Brochure: Spokane Libraries...OVERDUE...Vote YES!
Provided Courtesy of Spokane Public Library, Spokane, Washington.

SPOKANE LIBRARIES...

Vote **YES!** Sept. 18

This September marks the first time in more than a quarter of a century that Spokane voters can
authorize important improvements in library facilities in neighborhoods and downtown. In fact, the
first and last time a library proposal of any type appeared on the ballot was almost 30 years ago.
Judging by these facts, and by the deteriorating condition of existing facilities,
it's hard to deny that Spokane libraries are sadly overdue.
Overdue for renovation. Overdue for expansion. Overdue for our support!

THE PROBLEM.

Put simply, Spokane has outgrown
its present library system.

Over the past several months, many
people – including library patrons of
all ages, city officials, leaders in
education, and members of the
business community – have shared
comments and ideas about Spokane
libraries. In every neighborhood, the
story was the same:

- **Crowded buildings;**
- **Not enough books and resource
  materials;**
- **A severe lack of shelf space;**
- **An outdated public catalogue
  system;**
- **And not nearly enough study
  space, tables or chairs.**

It's hard to argue with this conclusion. A quick inventory of city
libraries not only confirms these facts
– it actually underscores them: Shelf
space at the Hillyard library is so
limited that new children's books
must be stacked on the tops of
shelves, beyond the reach of most
young readers; there is no quiet
study area available at the Downtown, Shadle, East Side or Manito
libraries; the Shadle branch has
room for just three comfortable
chairs where library users can sit
to enjoy a book or magazine. The
examples go on and on.

If you haven't visited a City library
recently, we encourage you to do so
before the September 18 election.
The best way to form an opinion on
this issue, or any issue, is to see for
yourself.

*We think you'll agree
that Spokane City Library
improvements are
seriously overdue.*

THE PROPOSAL.

The bond issue will provide more
space, more books and upgrade
library service in all of Spokane's
neighborhoods. Six new libraries will
be constructed – Downtown, East
Side and Hillyard (on present sites)
and North Side, Shadle and Manito
(on new sites).

The library bond issue amount is
$28,883,000 spread over a period of
20 years. The annual cost to Spokane
home-owners will be 63¢ per $1,000
assessed value ($2.63 per month on a
$50,000 home).   For a new library
system, the owner of a $50,000 home
would pay less than the cost of two
hardcover books a year.

*Senior Citizen Exemptions
Available.*

Under certain circumstances, senior
citizens and disabled persons may be
exempt from paying all or part of bond
issue costs. Call the Spokane County
Assessor for details: 456-5754.

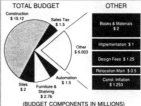

TOTAL BUDGET	OTHER
Construction $ 15.12	Books & Materials $ 2
Sales Tax $ 1.5	Implementation $ 1
Other $ 6.003	Design Fees $ 1.25
Automation $ 1.5	Relocation Main $ 0.5
Sites $ 2	Const. Inflation $ 1.253
Furniture & Shelving $ 2.76	

(BUDGET COMPONENTS IN MILLIONS)

September 18 marks your chance to
vote on the bond issue. For the
proposal to pass, 40% of those voting
in the last general election must cast
a ballot; and 60% of those voters must
vote "yes." If approved, building
designs will be developed immediately
and a four-year construction period
will begin in 1991.

THE PAYBACK!

Together, the new central and
neighborhood library branches will
provide significant improvements in
the following areas:

- **More quiet study seating;**
- **More total floor space;**
- **More books and materials
  available at neighborhood
  branches;**
- **An additional branch to serve
  the growing North Side;**
- **Improved services to children
  and young adults;**
- **And more space for tutoring and
  adult programs.**

Here in Spokane, we are thankful
for a great many unique factors that
contribute to our overall quality-of-
life. Unfortunately, our public library
facilities have not been one of those
factors.
Until now.
When we join together to approve
this proposal, we'll be doing much
more than just giving the nod to new
libraries. We'll be directly supporting
the continued revitalization of the
entire Spokane community:

- **Local libraries play a major role
  in the successful education of
  young people, kindergarten
  through college;**
- **Expanded libraries will mean
  expanded resources for
  Spokane's business community;**
- **Quality library facilities are a
  very sound neighborhood investment. They have a positive
  effect on local property values.**

Please take the time to cast your
ballot on this issue. With your
support, we will all enjoy a larger,
more convenient library system. A
system that is responsive to our
needs, both as individuals and as a
community.

*Thank you for taking the
time to study this issue.*
See you September 18!

BOND ISSUE SUMMARY:

Builds 6 New Libraries: Downtown, East Side, Hillyard, Manito, North Side, Shadle
Provides: Books and reference materials, computer automation, additional shelf space, more community
meeting space, land acquisition and construction costs.
Cost to average household: 63 cents per $1000 assessed value.
($2.63 per month, based on a $50,000 home)
Who can vote?: City of Spokane registered voters
When is election day?: September 18, 1990. Please VOTE YES!

If you have additional questions about Spokane's Public Library Bond Issue,
we encourage you to call the **Library Hotline**, staffed by citizen volunteers, at **747-5254**
beginning September 10.

Citizens for Libraries, Howard Mahan, Treasurer □ P.O. Box 251 / Spokane, WA 99210

FIGURE 10-13 Political Brochure: Vote YES, Fairfield Public Library. Provided Courtesy of Fairfield County Public Library, Fairfield, Iowa.

V O T E
YES

Fairfield
Public Library
September 21
City Referendum

Your vote for a new library building will mean:

- 21,900 sq ft of library space compared to the existing 8,500 sq ft
- 2,300 sq ft of children's area compared to 725 sq ft
- New community multi-purpose room seating 120 people
- Total seating of 125 compared to 52 seats today
- New information technologies such as CD ROM, computers, etc.
- Easier access for children, senior citizens and handicapped individuals

**We need your vote — It WILL make a difference
Vote YES on September 21**

V O T E
YES

Voter Information

Date: Tuesday, September 21, 1993
Time: 7:00 a.m. to 8:00 p.m.

Absentee ballots are now available at the Auditor's Office (472-2840) in the Jefferson County Courthouse.

Polling Places

1st Ward — Fairfield High School
　　　　　　Gymnasium Lobby
2nd Ward — American Legion Hall
3rd Ward — Nazarene Family Center
4th Ward — Court House
5th Ward — Pence School

"YES FOR NEW LIBRARY" COMMITTEE

Co-Chairmen
Myron Gookin
Willy Koppel
Brenda Narducci
Tom Thompson

Treasurer
Richard Thompson

Members
Earl Brown
Stew Gaumer
David Johnson
Tim Kuiken
Michael Mescon
Jackie Parkin
Bill Pollak
Lucile Taylor
Lillian Thada

Paid for by the "Yes for New Library" Committee – Myron Gookin, Co-Chairman

We need your vote — It WILL make a difference • Vote YES on September 21

FIGURE 10-13 *Continued*

BUILDING UPON A TRADITION OF LIBRARY LEADERSHIP

V O T E

O ver 5 years ago, the Library Board began reviewing usage and space needs. It became clear that Fairfield needed a much larger library. After much analysis, it was determined that remodeling our current library was structurally infeasible, as well as economically inefficient. Therefore, the Board recommended the construction of a new public library.

Since that time, the Library purchased a site for the new library at Main and Adams. In addition, over $1.1 million has been contributed/pledged by individuals, businesses, and other organizations toward construction of the new library.

We are now asking for your vote of confidence for a progressive future in Fairfield. We are asking you to vote YES on the following referendum question on September 21:

"Shall the City of Fairfield issue its bonds in an amount not exceeding the amount of $2,300,000 for the purpose of building and furnishing a new public library?"

The expected cost to taxpayers will be $1.19 per $1,000 of assessed property valuation. To be adopted, the proposition must receive 60% approval of those voting. Only registered voters within the City of Fairfield are eligible to vote.

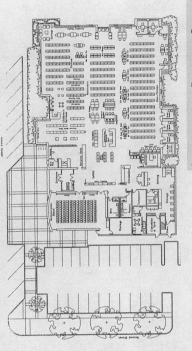

We're Looking to the Future

Your Library Board has spent several years developing a forward looking plan that will meet Fairfield's library needs for decades. Space is efficiently allocated to allow maximum flexibility as library needs and opportunities change. A high priority is given to our strong children's program.

Of great importance, our new library will be equipped to take advantage of new information technologies—CD ROM, Computers, Electronic Reference Access, and other technologies on the horizon. Fairfield will be ready to meet the needs of a community looking to compete in an information age.

The Multi-purpose Room will provide a priority that was lost long ago in our present library because of lack of convenient access. This room is designed to be a community crossroads—a place of many uses—meetings, forums, cultural displays, and programs.

In addition, there will be a Conference Room, Computer area, much improved reference area, and a pleasant and spacious periodical reading area that will be greatly used.

SERVICE	PROPOSED	EXISTING
Total Area	21,900 sq ft	8,500 sq ft
Collection Size	90,000	72,000
Newspaper Titles	20	7
Periodical Titles	305	160
Total Seating	125	52
Lounge Seating	13	4
Table Seating	32	34
Children's Seating	36	7
Study Room Seating	8	None
Conference Room	8	None
Media Carrels	5	None
Computers	3	1
Readers/Printers	3	
CD ROM	4	None
Index Counters	6	None
Children's Area	2,300 sq ft	725 sq ft
Public Meeting Room	120 seats	30 seats
Barrier Free	Yes	No
Circulation Desk	650 sq ft	50 sq ft
Information Desk	Yes	No
Parking	23 in lot	No
Security System	Yes	No
Automated Circulation/ Computerized Catalog	Yes	No
Public Access to Periodical Archives	Yes	No
Climate Control System	Yes	No

FIGURE 10-14   Political Brochure: Don't Close the Book on Our Children's Future. Provided Courtesy of Richland County Public Library, Columbia, South Carolina.

The future is now.

The joy of a library is that it knows no bounds. ■ It is open to everyone. ■ It benefits everyone. ■ It improves everyone. ■ And now, the time has come to make that happen in Richland County. The time to shape futures, and build dreams. The time to turn potential into reality. The time to advance as a county, grow as an economy, learn as a community. ■ On February 14, it can be ours. All of it. ■ On February 14, vote **YES** for the Library.

Don't close the book on our children's future.
ON FEB 14TH VOTE YES FOR THE LIBRARY

FIGURE 10-14 *Continued*

Don't close the book on our children's future.

The Richland County Public Library is stacked with more than just books. It's stacked with opportunity. ■ There's information. The Library gives business the opportunity to get what it needs, when it needs it, to ensure a better, more prosperous community. ■ There's leisure. The Library gives us the opportunity to relax, get wrapped up in a good book and generally improve who we are and the way we live.

■ But perhaps most of all, there's the future. The Library gives our kids the opportunity to share in a resource that can only enhance their hopes for a purposeful, confident, successful life. ■ On February 14, Richland County has a choice: Either open the door of opportunity to our children, or close the book on their future. ■ That's no choice. On February 14, vote **YES** for the Richland County Public Library.

Vote YES for the best.

The Richland County Public Library is the busiest in the state. In 1988 alone, it circulated more than 1.5 million pieces of material—enough books to fill 36 miles of bookshelves. More than 100,000 people use the Library every month. ■ But even though it is the busiest, it is also the poorest system in the Southeast. There is a shortage of books. Inadequate facilities. Insufficient resources. ■ All of which means that in an information society—where a child's hope for tomorrow is based on his knowledge and understanding today—if we don't vote to make the Library part of that education process, we are robbing our children of their future, and

their chance to be better. Moreover, the Library is simply not serving the sophisticated, often complex research demands of government, business and commerce. And that can be a major obstacle to efforts to attract new and expanding businesses to Richland County. ■ We have an obligation to this community, and to its children and grandchildren. Simply stated, we owe them the best, and a **YES** vote on February 14 will provide just that. The best possible Library for our children. The best possible information resources, so business can continue to grow and contribute to our prosperity and quality of life. And the best possible future for our kids.

Vote YES for a better future.

By voting **YES** on February 14, we'll be giving our kids and our businesses the kinds of benefits they need to grow and prosper. ■ A **YES** vote means new branches where we need them, and even better branches where we have them. ■ A **YES** vote means moving the Library to a new downtown location, perhaps the Post Office Building on Assembly Street. ■ A **YES**

vote means new books, enabling the Library to come up to minimum regional standards. ■ A **YES** vote means better informational systems, to enhance business and education in Richland County. ■ In other words, a **YES** vote on February 14 means better opportunities and a better future. For our children. For our community. For our economy. For everyone.

FIGURE 10-15 Political Brochure/Poster: Measure L is for Library, Oakland, California. Provided Courtesy of Neighbors for a Rockridge Library.

Measure L
Last on the ballot
First in importance
for your
neighborhood

We support a Rockridge Library.
We urge you to vote yes on L.

Site of planned Rockridge Library.
Neighbors for a Rockridge Library
(415) 658-4675

VOTE

YES ON L
NOVEMBER 6

YOUR
ROCKRIDGE LIBRARY
WILL HAVE

An increased collection of
material for adults and children.

A community meeting room.

Study space.

About 30 public parking spaces.

Measure L will create a special
assessment district to help fund our
library. Residential units will be
assessed a small sum,
no more than $25 per year.
You can make a difference!
A 2/3 Vote is required so your
vote is needed

Support your Library. Please put this sign in your window.

MEASURE

is for
LIBRARY

FIGURE 10-15   *Continued*

YES ON L
FOR A
ROCKRIDGE
LIBRARY

NEIGHBORS FOR A ROCKRIDGE LIBRARY
(A committee for Measure L
5837 College Avenue, Box 319
Oakland, CA 94618

Support your Library. Please put this sign in your window.

FIGURE 10-16 Political Brochure: Say YES to Library Bonds. Provided Courtesy of King County Library System, Seattle, Washington.

On election day you will have a rare opportunity to improve the educational development of your children, and their children, and all children in King County. Now and for many years to come.

You'll vote on a $67 million bond issue to make vital improvements in our library system. This is a much needed, no-frills proposition. About two-thirds of the money will be used to build new libraries and expand or refurbish older ones. One-third will go to buy books and other learning materials.

The library bonds are a must!

Since 1980, the number of items checked out of libraries has doubled, reaching a total of 8.4 million last year. Circulation is going up again this year. The parking lots are full. Lines at reference desks and check-out counters are much too long. And it's going to get worse. By the year 2000, just twelve years from now, our population is expected to increase by nearly 47%, from 820,000 to 1.2 million!

Say YES to wisdom.

We must fix leaky roofs and cramped quarters.

After over twenty years of heavy use, many older library buildings are deteriorating. Carpets are threadbare, heating and wiring are inefficient. We can't let them deteriorate any further. They must be refurbished and have their roofs and furnaces repaired or replaced.

We must have enough books and materials to go around.

To meet the ever-growing demand in all the communities around the county, we not only need many more books, we need much more.

We need to stock the shelves with more audio and video cassettes, reference titles, maps, charts, magazines, newspapers, compact discs, on-line computer data bases, films, filmstrips, records and other materials that enhance and encourage learning. If the bond issue passes, these library materials *will* be available to everyone.

Say YES to Library Bonds on September 20th!

Proposition No. 1 on the ballot.

We must say YES now. The longer we wait, the higher the cost.

Our last library bond issue took place over twenty years ago, in 1966. We built twenty libraries. We've paid the bonds in full. It's time to act again. We can't wait. The need continues to grow. We must act now and avoid even higher costs.

Say YES to learning.

We must meet the need for new libraries.

Many areas in the county are totally unserved, or drastically underserved, and in desperate need of library buildings and materials.

The plan calls for libraries to be built in Woodinville, Pine Lake, Carnation/Duvall, Shoreline, Upper Snoqualmie Valley, and two libraries each in East Kent and Federal Way.

Also planned are libraries in Algona/ Pacific, Juanita, Overlake/ Crossroads and Richmond Beach, plus a new service center for the district.

We must expand overcrowded libraries.

Libraries to be expanded are those in Bellevue, where major changes are planned, and in Burien, Maple Valley, Newport Way and Redmond.

Expansion is also planned for the Traveling Library Center, which serves retirement and nursing homes, community centers, and children's day care facilities.

Say YES to knowledge.

We must invest in our children's future. The cost is small, the dividends great.

A strong educational system requires good public libraries. Shelves filled with knowledge, understanding, wisdom. Places where learning never stops.

Your children can't vote. But you can. Say YES for their sake, and for the sake of their children.

FIGURE 10-16   *Continued*

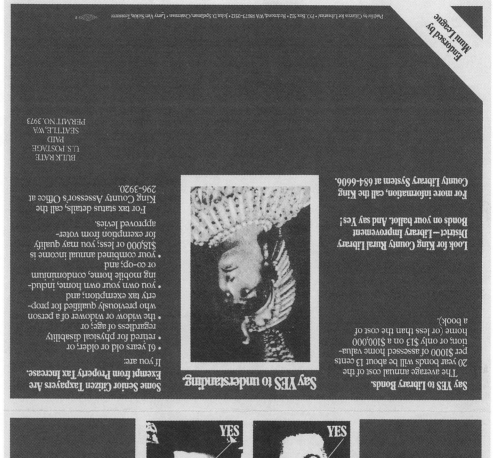

FIGURE 10-17   Letterhead: "The Library Bond." Provided Courtesy of Chesapeake
Public Library, Chesapeake, Virginia.

The Library Bond
Make books a priority in your life.

Dr. Alan P. Krasnoff, Chairman • Frank Gilmore, Treasurer
1101 Battlefield Boulevard North/Chesapeake, Virginia 23320/547-9266

Not paid for at public expense but by the Citizens for Better Libraries Committee, Frank Gilmore, Treasurer particular campaign activity such as $500 for a mailing of campaign literature in your neighborhood.

Cover Letters for Mailings

With many mailings, it is important to send a cover letter (on letterhead) which briefly explains the library issue and provides some form of specialized message for the target group.

Letters to Elected Officials, Civic Leaders, Etc.

Again, on letterhead campaign managers will often send letters to local elected officials and community organizations explaining the library issue and asking for support. These should be short and to the point. Letters of this nature should always be printed on letterhead and followed up with personal contact to make sure the letters have been received and to reinforce the point or request.

Specialized Letters to Support a Campaign Theme

Specialized letters to support a campaign theme may be developed. These letters can be written by children, senior citizens, businessmen, or any other segment of society. They can be used as campaign literature or as open letters. One particularly effective example of this approach was used in the Atlanta-Fulton County campaign for branch libraries where a letter written in a child's handwriting with a crayon was used to support the main campaign message of "Help keep the libraries from failing our children."[3] The emotional appeal of this letter (which was given to elementary school children to take home to their parents) was very effective.

Any and all letters should be signed by the individual sending them. Obviously photocopied form letters with stamped signatures should be avoided. Any letter should be short (one page if possible, but never longer than two pages), to the point (state what is being asked for, i.e., their vote, a contribution, or an endorsement), and should address the issues of high interest to the addressee. Additional information about the campaign can be enclosed, but remember it is essential to personalize letters. In addition to signing the letter, a personal greeting and inquiry about how the family is doing can mean a lot. Provide a telephone number where recipients can call to get more information and, if possible, follow up the letter with a telephone call to make certain the letter was received, as well as emphasize the importance of the correspondence. Remember to include volunteer and campaign contribution cards in almost every mailing.

POSTCARDS

Sometimes, if campaign funds are short, postcards can be used. They generally cost less to produce and mail and can be very effective in fundraising, volunteer coordination, campaign literature, or for simply reminding supporters to vote on election day. Including graphics like the campaign logo or pictures of the proposed facility can help with issue recognition. One of the major advantages to postcards is that there is no envelope to open which greatly increases the chances of the information actually being read by the addressee.

FIGURE 10-18   Postcard: VOTE YES! Provided Courtesy of Fort Vancouver Regional Library, Vancouver, Washington.

For More Information Call Your
Local Library

**Paid For By
Citizens for Better Libraries**

**Eugene Lehman, Treasurer
1611 N.W. 60th Street
Vancouver, WA 98663**

Bulk Rate
U.S. Postage
PAID
Permit No. 953
Vancouver, WA

V O T E   Y E S !

FIGURE 10-19   Postcard: "Don't Close the Book on Our Children's Future." Provided Courtesy of Richland Public Library, Columbia, South Carolina.

Don't close the book on our children's future.
ON FEB 14TH VOTE **YES** FOR THE LIBRARY

■ A good library means information resources for business, educational help for children, and a better life for all of us. On February 14th, vote YES to give Richland County a library that's one for the books!

P.O. Box 11843
Columbia, SC 29211-1843

Bulk Rate
U.S. Postage
P A I D
Columbia, S.C.
Permit #86

FIGURE 10-20   Postcard: YES on Measure L. Rockridge Library, Oakland, California. Provided Courtesy of Neighbors for a Rockridge Library.

Be Sure To Vote Tuesday, November 6

YES for a Rockridge Library!

YES on Measure

Last on the ballot...
First in importance for your neighborhood!

Call 658-4675 if you want information or
if you need help getting to the polls.

NEIGHBORS FOR A ROCKRIDGE LIBRARY
(A committee for Measure L)
5337 College Avenue   Box 519
Oakland, CA 94618

SLATE MAILERS

If the campaign budget is limited and the expense of a direct mailing for the library issue alone is prohibitive, slate mailers or "slate cards" may be used to communicate with the electorate. Slate cards are frequently used in partisan political campaigns where all of the candidates for the Democratic or Republican ticket are included in a brochure which is then mailed to targeted precincts. The library campaign can sometimes buy space on a slate mailer and reach many voters at a relatively nominal cost. A word of caution is in order. The cost of being included in these mailers varies greatly and can be highly dependent upon political connections with the sponsoring agency. This approach will only be effective for the library campaign if the target audience of the slate mailer matches the library's target groups. Further, be careful about the quality of the organization which is sponsoring the slate mailer; some are definitely more reputable than others.

FIGURE 10-21   Postcard: Your library is overdue! Provided Courtesy of
Willoughby–Eastlake Public Library, Willoughby, Ohio.

**24 Public Square
Willoughby, OH 44094**

Non-Profit Organization
U. S. Postage
PAID
Permit No. 273
Willoughby, OH 44094

*Your library
is overdue!*

**WILLOUGHBY-EASTLAKE
PUBLIC LIBRARY**

VOTE YES

Dear Library Patron,

VOTE FOR ISSUES #10 & #11 TO:

- **Enlarge Your Library Buildings**
- **Create Freedom Of Access To All Ages**
- **Provide More Books, Videos, Audio Cassettes, CD's**
- **Expand Services & Hours**
- **Improve Parking**

It will cost $16.41 per year for a $70,000
home and will be the first library property
tax in 27 years.

Please encourage your friends & neighbors
to vote yes.

PAID FOR BY CITIZENS FOR CONTINUING GOOD LIBRARIES
36500 Euclid Ave. 472B ■ Willoughby, OH 44094

CHARLES SNEE, TREASURER

FIGURE 10-22   Postcard: Yes. Yes. Yes. Yes. Libraries. King County Library System, Redmond, Washington. Provided Courtesy of the Kings County Library System.

Dear _____ ,
     I believe that well-supplied libraries are important to a healthy community and essential for our children's future.
     That's why I'm supporting the King County Library System Bond issue, Proposition 1, in this month's election.
     I hope you'll join me, and VOTE YES FOR LIBRARIES.

PLACE
POSTAGE
HERE

Printing Courtesy of Continental Printing Inc.
Paid for by Citizens for Libraries•P.O. Box 512•Redmond, WA 98073-0512
John D. Spellman, Chairman•Larry Van Sickle, Treasurer

DOOR HANGERS

Door hangers are a highly specialized form of campaign literature designed specifically to be hung on the doorknob of homes. They come in several sizes, but are usually relatively narrow (4"). On the top, the door hanger has a "hook" or a "hole" which can be used to affix the hanger to a door knob. Like a bookmark, the door hanger can be a very colorful way to

---

FIGURE 10-23   Door Hangers: Knock Softly....Chesapeake, Virginia (left—both sides), Save our libraries! Pasadena, California (right). Provided Courtesy of the Chesapeake and Pasadena Public Libraries.

Knock Softly
if you know what's good for you.

I HATE TO READ ALONE

JIM DAVIS

Our family's reading!

Illustration courtesy the American Library Association

On November 8, Chesapeake's citizens will be voting on a $10.65 million library bond referendum.

At present, the library system is below both state and national standards for space and the number of volumes which should be available for your use.

To remedy the situation, the funds from the bond referendum will be used for the expansion of the headquarters library, two new libraries for the Western Branch and Greenbrier areas, and the acquisition of land for a future library in the Deep Creek/Bowers Hill areas.

It also means bookmobile service can start to reach out to every area of the city where access to a library is a problem.

But none of these improvements is free.

If the bond is approved, the real estate tax rate will increase by 2.5 cents per $100 of assessed value, which translates to less than the cost of a hardback book.

Obviously, none of us wants to see our taxes raised, but look at it this way. . . voting for the library bond is our chance to set priorities ourselves.

To make certain that what we want is what we'll get.

But none of this will happen unless you vote, and why we need your help on election day.

Vote yes for the library bond.

Make books a priority in your life.

After all, who wants a mad cat in the house?

The Library Bond
Make books a priority in your life.

Paid for and Published by
Save Pasadena's Library
87 N. Raymond Ave.
Ste. 315
Pasadena, CA 91103

Polls Open From
7:00am - 8:00pm
TUESDAY, JUNE 22nd
For a ride, or
Information,
call:
793-8050

Save our libraries!
Vote YES
on Tuesday!

YOU VOTE HERE

5150139
Plaza Del Mar Ret.Htl
990 E. Del Mar Blvd.
Pasadena, CA 91106

URGENT REMINDER:

If you still have an absentee ballot, it's too late to mail it back. You must turn in your ballot on election day. **TAKE IT TO CITY HALL OR TO ANY BRANCH LIBRARY** (branches only, <u>NOT</u> Central).

Remember:
<u>Today</u> is election day!

provide information, encourage a "Yes" vote for the library issue, or simply remind people to vote. Door hangers are used by door-to-door canvassers when no one is home, or when canvassing is limited to literature distribution without much personal contact. This method is faster than personal contact, but has much less impact. In neighborhoods which are already highly likely to vote for the issue, door hangers put out early in the morning of election day are most effective in getting-out-the-vote—especially if they have the location of the polls printed on them along with the main campaign message.

CAMPAIGN PARAPHERNALIA

Along with campaign literature, most campaigns produce various forms of paraphernalia to help sell the library issue. The paraphernalia is often some form of gimmick which somehow relates to the campaign issue. However, a word of warning is in order—most of these items will have relatively little impact on actually helping to obtain "Yes" votes. Because of this, it is usually not wise to spend a great deal of time, energy, or money on campaign paraphernalia. If precious campaign funds are expended on paraphernalia, the most effective forms are buttons for campaign workers, posters, and yard signs.

BUTTONS

One of the most effective, but often overlooked methods of raising awareness for the library issue and getting name (or in this case "issue") recognition is the use of campaign buttons. They can be used in the early phase of the campaign in a neutral and informative manner which means they can be worn by staff as well as campaign supporters. Later they can be used in a more "pro" library way to encourage a "Yes" vote. Whenever they are used, the campaign logo or slogan should always be present. Why are buttons such a good campaign method? Mainly because they are worn by *people*. They foster personal contact, and personal contact is one of the most effective ways of acquiring support for a political issue.

Buttons go everywhere the campaign supporters go (provided they are worn religiously). They go to parties, sporting events, supermarkets, banks, gas stations, post offices, schools, movies, and even to the board rooms of major corporations. Buttons are an excellent ice-breakers. When a campaign worker notices someone looking at the button, they can say, "Oh, I see you noticed my button. Would you like to know more about our wonderful new library project?" Then the gentle art of political arm-twisting can begin. When buttons start showing up all over town and are worn by respected members of the community, the library issue cannot help but be noticed. Buttons can also be worn by volunteers going door-to-door to identify themselves with the library campaign.

STICKERS

Stickers are similar to buttons; they are less durable, but can be put on most anything. They also have the advantage of being much less expensive than buttons. While they can be worn on clothing (as long as the peel off, non-permanent kind are purchased), they are usually better placed on objects. The number of ways they can be used is limited only by the imagination of the campaign workers. For example, using them on the outside of the envelopes for campaign mailings is an effective way to reinforce the campaign logo to the target audience as well as

FIGURE 10-24   Buttons: "The Library Bond," Provided Courtesy of Chesapeake Public Library. "Libraries VOTE YES May 7," Provided Courtesy of Las Vegas–Clark County Library District. "VOTE YES LIBRARIES Nov. 6," Provided Courtesy of Greensboro Public Library, Greensboro, NC. "THE NEW LIBRARY Make It Fact Not Fiction," Provided Courtesy of Friends of the Atlanta–Fulton County Library. "Your Library THE BEST Bargain Around," Provided Courtesy of Upper Saddle River Public Library, Upper Saddle River, NJ.

FIGURE 10-25   Stickers: "Spokane Libraries . . . OVERDUE," Provided Courtesy of Spokane Public Library. "STICK WITH Libraries AUGUST 23," Provided Courtesy of Tulsa City–County Library System, Tulsa City, OK. "LIBRARIES 2001 VOTE September 16," Provided Courtesy of Pierce County Library District, Tacoma, WA. "Ask Me! LIBRARY LEVY Sept. 18, 1990, " Provided Courtesy of Fort Vancouver Regional Library. "Citizens of Montgomery County Libraries YES LIBRARY BOND," Provided Courtesy of Montgomery County Libraries, Conroe, TX.

convincing a lot of postal workers to vote for the library. Campaign workers can stick them on personal correspondence. Companies can put them on newsletters. Stickers can be stuck on bulletin boards, doors, windows, walls or anywhere they will stick and not cause ill will. They are generally unobtrusive, but they can become omnipresent like "Kilroy" was in the 40s and 50s.

REFRIGERATOR MAGNETS

One method which has been used by some campaigns is the refrigerator magnet. These are probably best used when handed out during door-to-door canvassing in order to ensure that they actually do end up on the refrigerator door. Refrigerator magnets don't have to be fancy. They can be as simple as a bookmark with some magnetic tape stuck on one side. It is a good idea to print the library's hours on the bookmark along with a "Vote Yes" reminder and the election date to help ensure that the resident will actually put it up on the refrigerator and refer to it in the future.

FIGURE 10-26   Refrigerator Magnet Containing Livermore Public Library Logo, Livermore, California. Provided Courtesy of the Livermore Public Library.

RIBBONS

Ribbons are another variation on buttons and stickers. The "blue" ribbon, awarded as a prize, has been around for many years and has been used in many ways. Ribbons can be pinned to a shirt or blouse and worn. They provide more room for information than do stickers and buttons. They also attract attention when they flop around in the wind. Ribbons utilizing the campaign's colors can be worn at special events and by campaign workers during door-to-door canvassing for identification. They can be given out as rewards to volunteers whose performance is exceptional. Or if bookmark supplies run short, they will serve this function as well.

BANNERS

Banners can be used to proclaim the library issue at special events like the kick-off event, or at luncheons, dinners, and receptions. They can be used to decorate the campaign headquarters or vehicles used during the campaign. Further, on election day they can be hung from prominent overpasses during the morning and evening rush hours or they can be hung from downtown buildings to remind people to vote for the library issue. They should be colorful and incorporate the campaign logo. Banners can come in various sizes, both small and large, depending upon the uses. Don't overlook this simple but useful method of proclaiming the campaign message. Remember, they should look professional and be pleasing to the eye.

BAGS

Bags of various kinds can often be used effectively during a campaign. Libraries can use the ever-popular library book bag to raise awareness by printing the campaign logo on it (as long as it's not obviously political). Small plastic bags can be used to stuff campaign literature in and be left as door hangers. Supermarkets, discount stores, department stores, and even fast food places can sometimes be convinced to print and distribute bags with the library logo and slogan. Again, these raise name and symbol recognition. The more the library's logo and name is reinforced, the more effective the campaign message will be at cutting through the distractions of other political advertising and getting voters' attention.

BALLOONS

Even though balloons are a simple technique, they can be used effectively at special events and particularly with children. One thousand balloons bouncing all over a mall and going home with children can be a surprisingly effective campaign communication technique. Balloons with the library logo on them can be used at library programs or as a "decoration" for tables at special campaign events. Again, repeated symbol recognition is the name of the game.

HATS & VISORS

Campaign hats have been around as long as politics. Again, they can use the campaign logo and colors to identify and attract attention to campaign supporters at special events, during door-to-door canvassing or while standing on street corners with campaign signs on election day. They don't need to be particularly sturdy, but a number of sizes should be acquired if they are going to be used. While library campaigns may not have enough funds to purchase hats, volunteers can make a reasonable facsimile out of construction and crepe paper for limited

FIGURE 10-27   Visor. Provided Courtesy of YES on Davis Library Expansion. A Committee for Measure B. Yolo County Library, Woodland California.

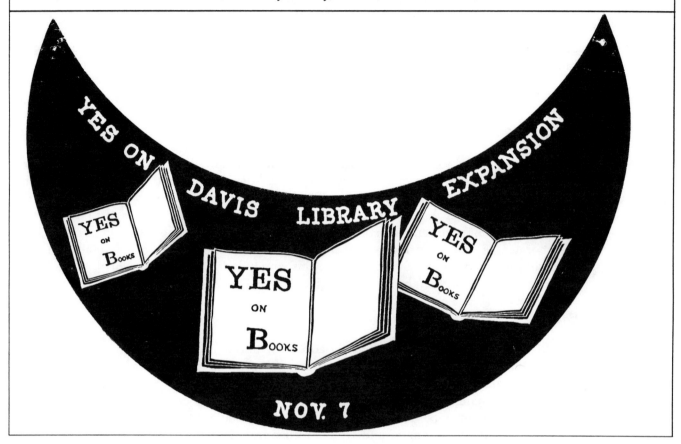

occasions. In the community of Davis, California, a simple paper visor was created and worn during the campaign.

T-SHIRTS

Some campaigns print T-shirts displaying the campaign's logo, colors, and slogan. T-shirts can be a good early campaign technique for raising awareness and funds. Rather than giving these shirts free to campaign workers, the campaign can get them to "buy into" the campaign by contributing $10 or more for a T-shirt. If the design is unique and attractive enough, it may be possible to sell the T-shirts to the general public at community events as well.

BILLBOARDS AND SIGNS

As many commercial firms have recognized, outdoor billboard advertising along freeways and major roadways is an effective way to reach a significant number of people. Obviously, unless funds are available to rent a large number of these signs, the drawback is that their visibility is limited to the locale in the community where they are put up. However, they may be able to be

FIGURE 10-28   T-shirt. Denver Public Library, Denver, Colorado. Provided Courtesy of the Denver Public Library.

used cost-effectively in certain targeted areas of town where the library issue is likely to be supported or where there is a high number of undecided voters. Because of the expense, library campaigns have used this approach infrequently unless the billboard space is donated. It certainly is possible to get billboard space donated for library issues especially if the sign is a public service announcement as opposed to political campaign advertising. This is not a major disadvantage, because the "soft sell" of PSAs can be very effective when placed on a prominent billboard right before an election.

A sign erected on the site for the proposed library can be a good way of communicating with the electorate. Many in the community may not be aware of where the site is, and this approach helps create awareness and information regarding the size of the project. The larger and more prominently displayed the sign is, the better. The lettering should be large enough to read while driving by the site. The sign should be fabricated out of materials which will withstand stormy weather, and it should be erected several months prior to the election for maximum impact.

The library campaign can fabricate additional large-sized signs out of 4 × 8 pieces of plywood and put them up at busy intersections. Signs on mass transit vehicles and bus stop benches will be noticed; however, they usually cost money. For free sign advertising on election day, try to get local churches, theaters, businesses or shopping malls to place supportive statements on their marquees, or if necessary, rent portable flashing signs and place "Vote 'Yes' for Libraries" messages at strategic locations in the community. Signs can be constructed for cartops or the back end of pick-up trucks which can then be driven around town on election day or used to deliver door-to-door canvassers. These mobile signs can be very effective in getting attention and creating enthusiasm particularly if combined with streamers and a sound projection system. Yard signs and posters can be effective as well and are discussed in detail in Chapter 13.

BUMPER STICKERS

Bumper stickers are yet another form of "outdoor advertising." These are like mobile signs which can be driven all over town by library patrons, Friends, and all campaign supporters. Again, bumper stickers are most effective during the last two weeks of the campaign, but they may also be used early in the campaign as an effective awareness raising technique. Bumper stickers can be distributed through mailings, special events, speaking engagements, or door-to-door canvassing. The campaign logo, colors, and slogan can be effectively displayed on a bumper sticker as well as "Vote 'Yes' for Libraries" statements. Bright "dayglow" colors are particularly useful since bumper stickers are "moving targets" and must attract the eye quickly before they are out of sight.

PORTABLE DISPLAYS & BOOTHS

Using portable displays or staffing booths at various community functions such as fairs, festivals, farmers markets, flea markets, auctions, parades, or any other kind of community activity that brings together a large number of people in one spot can be effective as well. A portable display can be designed so that it is attractive and provides information about the library issue. It can include renderings or floor plans of the building, graphics showing branch library locations in the community, fact sheets, or any combination of campaign information or literature. The display can be designed to be set up in two versions, informational or "political," so that it can be used in a number of ways. The display should also be easy to collapse and transport. For this reason, it can also be used in the library, at speaker bureau presentations, or at any other campaign function. While it can be set up and used as a stand alone, it is usually better to have volunteers standing nearby to answer questions or hand out leaflets. A good example of this approach was used in the King County, Washington, campaign as shown in Figure 10-30.

When the steering committee has determined all of the different forms of campaign literature and paraphernalia which will be utilized in the campaign, the next step is to utilize various campaign techniques to distribute that literature and paraphernalia. Getting the message out to

FIGURE 10-29   Bumper Stickers: "The Library Bond," Provided Courtesy of Chesapeake Public Library, Chesapeake, VA. "Yes Libraries!," Provided Courtesy of Tulsa City–County Library System, Tulsa City, OK. "Support THE Next Generation's LIBRARY," Provided Courtesy of the Library of Hattiesburg, Petal & Forrest County, Hattiesburg, MS. "VOTE LIBRARY JANUARY 15," Provided Courtesy of Rapides Parish Library, Hattiesburg, MS.

FIGURE 10-30   Poertable Display: "Our Library's Future." Provided Courtesy of Spokane Public Library, Spokane Washington.

the electorate is the name of the game, and all the campaign literature and paraphernalia in the world won't do any good unless it is effectively delivered to the electorate. The remaining chapters discuss several of the major ways that campaign literature can be delivered.

REFERENCES

1. Hall, Richard B. "The Votes Are In" *Library Journal* 115:11 (June 15, 1990), pp. 42–46.
2. Ibid.
3. Rickert, Susan. *Campaigning for Libraries.* Wheat Ridge, Colorado: Central Colorado Library System, 1988, p. 28.

11 NEWSLETTERS, DIRECT MAIL & LEAFLETING

It doesn't matter how pretty or well-written campaign literature is, if it doesn't get distributed effectively, it won't have any impact on the outcome of the campaign. Getting the message out through campaign literature and paraphernalia takes strategic planning, volunteers, resolve, and organization. Along with getting the information distributed, it is important to get it out on time. For example, GOTV postcards which arrive the day after the election simply waste campaign funds. Campaign planners should carefully consider all possible methods of promoting the campaign's literature and then implement those chosen methods in a timely manner.

NEWSLETTERS & MAGAZINES

An often overlooked method of distributing the campaign's message is through local newsletters. It is smart to get the campaign's message in as many publications as possible as often as possible. Overlap and repetition is good. Voters may not notice the message if they only see it once or twice, but by the seventh or eighth time, they notice and hopefully respond in the desired way. Newsletters and magazines of all forms are good avenues for the display of the campaign message. All kinds of agencies from private businesses and corporations to community organizations and clubs produce newsletters. Homeowners and neighborhood associations, PTAs, the Chamber of Commerce, museum, and art associations all have newsletters and can be avenues for the campaign's message.

If any of the above agencies might also be campaigning for their own issue, consider offering to publish information about their campaign in the library newsletter for a reciprocal article in their newsletter. Some of the best sources for good coverage are small regional or area magazines which report on community activities. In the campaign for the Rockridge Library (Oakland, CA), the use of a neighborhood newsletter published by a community planning council was extremely instrumental in communicating with the target audience of voters during a referendum to approve local funds for a branch library. It is often possible to get a feature article with front page coverage in these publications just before the election.

The Library or Friends newsletter should not be overlooked. Obviously the material will need to be informational, at least in the library newsletter, but this is an excellent way to inform library patrons of the upcoming election. It is a good idea to have both frequent articles about the project, and, just before the election, to have a "special edition" or insert which is dedicated solely to the library project and the referendum. Again, make sure that the articles in any newsletters are graphically appealing. Dull, dry text does not grab the interest of the reader as much as an article with an exciting rendering of the building or create an emotional connection like a picture of people standing in line for almost anything at the library waiting to get service and being delayed because of space or staff shortages. While none of these newsletters alone will likely have a major impact on the campaign, the overall cumulative effect of numerous articles could mean the difference between success and failure in a close race. Along with newsletters, another avenue for getting the campaign's message out is direct mailing.

DIRECT MAILINGS

The value of direct mail has been and will continue to be debated in many quarters for both political campaigns as well as for private fundraising purposes. The idea of communicating with the community by simply printing up a fact sheet or brochure to tell the library's story and mailing it out appears on the surface to be a simple and straight forward method of campaigning. However, there is more to consider than first meets the eye. Mailing one letter is easy, but mailing 5,000 or 50,000 can quickly become very time-consuming and costly. Further, there is disagreement over just how effective direct mail really is at not only informing the electorate, but also in persuading or motivating them to vote. There is mounting evidence that mailed campaign literature is often ignored and unceremoniously discarded because it is identified as "junk mail." This brings up the point that how the message is delivered may be as important, if not even more important, than what the message actually says. Campaign literature delivered through door-to-door canvassing or leafleting with personal contact has a great deal more impact on a potential voter than a piece of paper sent through the mail by some faceless campaign committee.

Even so, there may be times when making a campaign literature mailing is helpful, practical, and effective, but it takes planning. Once the decision to make a mailing is made, the next step is to determine the size of the mailing as well as who the mailing should be sent to. Mass mailings in which the campaign attempts to communicate with everyone in the local area are extremely costly and probably not worth the effort. However, if the steering committee feels that the "shotgun" approach is important in order to raise widespread awareness of the library issue, there are alternatives to mass mailings paid for by the library campaign. In smaller communities, one good approach to mass mailings is to talk utility companies, banks, or small business owners into sending out fact sheets or informational bookmarks with their monthly statements or advertisements. If a piece of campaign literature can't actually be inserted in the mailing, it may be possible to get the company to print a brief message about the library issue at the bottom of each statement. Further, it may be worthwhile to try to get an informational statement printed at the bottom of employee pay statements for large employers in the area as a reminder of the library issue.

Because most library campaigns can't afford to "blanket" the community with a mass mailing, they usually attempt to concentrate limited campaign resources on registered voters who are either already inclined toward the library issue or undecided. If campaign funds are short, it is necessary to expend funds on target groups which have the most to gain from the passage of the issue because these groups are most likely to turn out and support the issue at the polls. Given the expense of direct mail, it is essential to focus the campaign's "best shot" on as narrow a field as possible. For example, in a small community, it is much more cost-effective to make two or even three mailings to 1,000 people who are registered and likely to vote for the library issue (or at least persuadable), than one mass mailing to 3,000 people, some of whom may not even be registered to vote and a significant number who may not be disposed toward the library issue.

It is essential, then, to identify who should receive the mailings and obtain accurate mailing addresses as well as determine how the letters will be addressed and mailed. As mentioned, voter registration lists can be obtained from the election's office of the local jurisdiction, but these lists need to be cleaned up ("householded," etc.) and targeted individuals identified. Last minute mailings to supporters which have been identified by the telephone bank and/or door-to-door canvassers may be useful as a reminder to help get-out-the-vote (although a last minute telephone call is probably more effective). Once the campaign has identified the specific target groups it needs to mail to, the names and addresses must be placed on either envelopes or postcards.

Many feel that hand-written addresses are important to personalize mailings, while others feel that in this day and age, computer-generated mailing labels are the way to go as long as the content of the message being distributed is personalized. Computerized databases save a great deal of time and effort which would otherwise be spent by volunteers handwriting addresses on envelopes. When the database is set up, it can be quickly used for repeat mailings. If second or third mailings are anticipated for any target group, the computerized approach is probably the better way to go. Having campaign workers add personal comments to pieces going to individuals with whom they have some personal connection may provide the best of both worlds.

Modifying the message and directing it toward the interests of the target group is relatively easy with computer-assisted mailings. Any number of individualized cover letters can be written addressing the concerns of various groups or neighborhoods. Letters written to members of a homeowners group may highlight the small amount of tax increase per average home in their area compared to the benefits of good quality library service for their children. An economic argument can be used with a mailing to members of the Chamber of Commerce along with specific information on the new online and CD-ROM business reference tools that will be acquired with requested funds. Services to children can be emphasized in mailings to PTA members, neighborhoods with a high percentage of school age children living at home, teachers unions, or school administrators.

One way to save money is to mail at a bulk rate and presort the mailing by the carrier route. In order to understand what is necessary, contact the local post office and ask for information about bulk mailing. There are very specific rules which must be followed, but the savings are substantial. One of the downsides to bulk mail is problems with the timing of the delivery: "Whenever a campaign uses bulk rate, ask the Postal Service to 'red tag' your mailing as priority political mail, since otherwise it may sit around for a week or more."[1] It is important to determine early if mailings will be made by bulk mail or not, since it is easy to simply print the bulk mail permit insignia on flyers, envelopes, or postcards. Be sure to coordinate between the post office and the printer regarding the printing of mailers since there are significant cost savings involved if standard sized paper is used. By the way, it is smart to print the campaign logo, slogan, or some form of "zinger" on the outside of the mailer or envelope to help get the intended audience inside to read what is being sent. Zingers involving kids or money usually work the best.

Most library campaigns utilize volunteer help to produce mailings because it saves money, although for large campaigns it may be wise to consider using a "mail house." Some mail houses are set up to produce the flyer, attach labels from in-house prepared mailing lists, presort for carrier route, and deliver to the post office all as one turn-key operation. This can be a very helpful service if volunteers are short and money is not a problem. If campaign

FIGURE 11-1   GOTV Postcard: Provided Courtesy of Friends of the DeKalb Public Library, Decatur, Georgia.

To:

I'M A FRIEND
WON'T YOU BE A FRIEND
& BRING A FRIEND TO THE POLLS ?

Friends of the Library

planners decide to use a mail house, they should do so relatively early in the campaign and make sure to reserve time for their mailings with the mail house especially around busy general elections.

If planners decide not to use a mail house and do it themselves, one good way of getting a mailing out is to hold "mailing parties." The Dekalb Public Library (Decatur, Georgia) did this effectively with their campaign. It involves getting together a substantial number of volunteers and setting up an assembly line to prepare the mailing. This approach builds a sense of teamwork among volunteers. Then if funds are short for the mailing, and the mailing is not being made with a bulk mail permit, volunteers can be asked to take home a stack of envelopes or postcards and apply the stamps themselves thereby donating the postage for the mailing. This works well only if the volunteers are committed enough to actually follow through and make the mailing.

LEAFLETING

An alternative to mailing campaign literature is to deliver it by handing it out at any place people congregate. Mass transit stations, government buildings, factory gates, senior citizen centers, and festivals are all possible locations for leafleting, but some of the best choices are downtown commercial areas and shopping malls where there are a lot of people circulating at any given time. One of the reasons that leafleting can be effective is that it involves some personal contact. The leaflet, a handshake, and a few positive words of support about the issue can have a very positive impact on an individual. Usually the closer to election day leafleting is done, the more effective it will be. Unfortunately, one of the weaknesses of leafleting is that it is difficult to target individuals. Campaign volunteers who are handing out leaflets have no idea if the individuals they are contacting are registered voters or not, predisposed for or against the library issue or undecided. This decreases the value of leafleting, although in large campaigns it is possible to at least concentrate leafleting activities at specific shopping malls and mass transit stations which are located near or in neighborhoods known to have a high percentage of voters predisposed toward voting for the library issue. While leafleting can work, an organized door-to-door canvassing effort will probably be far more effective in the long run.

ALTERNATIVE METHODS OF DELIVERY OF CAMPAIGN LITERATURE

Along with more standard methods of campaign message delivery, there are a number of alternate "creative" methods which a few campaigns have used. One campaign talked a local pizza business into including its literature with every pizza delivery. Since Halloween is close to the November election day, there are inherent campaign opportunities. A recent library campaign had a youngster dress in a Halloween costume made to resemble the library poster and urged a "Yes" vote. In a Chesapeake, Virginia campaign Girl and Boy Scouts passed out campaign literature on Halloween night. They got candy, and the adults learned about the library. Delivery methods are limited only by planners' imagination. Frequently, the more unusual and outrageous the technique, the better (assuming it is in good taste) since it will draw more attention to the campaign issue. While creativity is important in campaigning, most campaigns use traditional methods simply because they have been proven over the years to work very well. One of these methods is the use of door-to-door canvassing.

REFERENCES

1. Jean Drodshaug Dugan et. al. *Campaigning to Win: A Workbook for Women in Politics.* Washington, D.C.: National Women's Political Caucus, 1993, p. viii-10.

12 DOOR-TO-DOOR CANVASSING, PERSONAL CONTACT & ENDORSEMENTS

DOOR-TO-DOOR CANVASSING

Targeted door-to-door canvassing takes a high degree of organization and commitment on the part of campaign planners, but may be the **SINGLE MOST EFFECTIVE CAMPAIGN ACTIVITY** for persuading undecided voters and for getting "Yes" voters to get out and vote. "Hitting the pavement" on weekends and evenings and talking, in many cases, with complete strangers, some of whom will not be sympathetic to the library issue, is not an easy job. Although this approach to campaigning is not for the faint-at-heart, it can be done in any campaign if planned properly. Door-to-door canvassing by volunteer block workers under the direction of a precinct captain is a time-consuming method, but it may make a significant difference in the outcome of an election. This is true in part because voter turnout is usually higher in areas where door-to-door campaigning takes place.

There are basically two forms of door-to-door campaigning. One method is to simply deliver campaign literature (the "drop") and the second is to deliver campaign literature *and* make personal contact. The first is the "hit and run" method which simply distributes campaign literature using legwork instead of envelopes and stamps. It involves covering as much ground as possible in a neighborhood with volunteers leaving campaign door hangers at as many addresses as possible. While this method gets more information to more households, it is generally not as effective as the second method because it lacks personal contact with the resident. Campaign planners may wish to use a GOTV door hanger for this first method in neighborhoods already highly committed to the library issue right before the election. This method is also better if some of the volunteers recruited for canvassing are not strongly committed or highly knowledgeable about the issue. Teens and college students often make good "runners" for the kind of extensive legwork required for this approach.

If the second approach is used, volunteers must be well-instructed in how to approach people, how to explain the library issue, and how to answer questions or refer the voter to others in the campaign with more in-depth knowledge. While dispensing literature, the campaign worker engages the resident in conversation and attempts to ascertain their position on the campaign issue. If the resident is undecided, the canvasser tries to convince them to vote "Yes" by utilizing any number of pretested strategies and arguments. It is wise to allow campaign volunteers to work in neighborhoods that are socioeconomically similar to their own neighborhoods. Not only will the campaign worker be more effective because they will likely know many of the people because of contact through schools, churches, or other activities, but the residents will also tend to be more receptive to canvassers that match their own background. This approach avoids the "outsider" syndrome and enhances the influence that the block walker will have on the resident because he or she will be accepted as "one of their own."

The effective allocation and organization of campaign workers is the key to success with this approach to campaigning. The logistics of door-to-door canvassing can take varying degrees of planning depending upon the size of the effort. Even in small communities, it may take a month or longer to organize canvassing activities. Because canvassing is usually done in the last month before the election, the entire process will probably take at least two months to plan and implement effectively. Volunteers should be organized into teams to cover specific areas or precincts. Each team should have a captain who leads and connects the team with the campaign leadership through a campaign committee. In large campaigns, a separate Door-to-Door Canvassing Committee should be established; in smaller communities the Campaign Literature Committee can handle this activity along with all mailings. Teams should meet well in advance of the main canvassing effort in order to get organized and plan the process so that it will go smoothly. If volunteers are inexperienced with door-to-door canvassing, it will be helpful to do some advance role playing. Further, although the pitch will soon be memorized, it may be helpful to develop a script like the one in Figure 12-1 to help team members get started with persuasive canvassing.

Prior to the start of canvassing, team members should meet to obtain written instructions, campaign literature, and paraphernalia, and maps, voter lists, refreshments, first aid kits for blisters, bug bites, and scrapes. Volunteer teams should be given a brief pep talk and their importance to the campaign should be stressed. Further, team members should be informed of the importance of completing their assignments for the day along with a comment about the necessity for accuracy in recording the sentiments of the residents for the subsequent get-out-the-vote effort. It is wise to provide coffee and donuts or some other form of easy-to-handle food for these "wake-up" sessions to help get the campaign workers started. However, it's usually best not to start actually walking until 9 a.m. or so, and canvassers should never be out after dark.

Decorating vehicles to be used during canvassing with campaign signs, colors, and paraphernalia is a good way to get additional mileage out of the campaign's presence in a neighborhood. Unusual or large vehicles like trucks, vans, and buses can be useful since they will transport more people and they attract more attention. Remember, campaign workers are in an area to be noticed and make an impression. There is no advantage to blending in; visibility is the key to any campaign activity. The more noticeable the campaign is in neighborhoods, the better.

In order to effectively canvass an area, it is essential to have a good street map of the precinct. These maps can be used to allocate block workers by dividing the area to be canvassed into segments which can be covered by a standard number of workers in each team. In dividing up these areas, it is important to consider not only the number of houses, but also the route that the campaign workers will follow. Avoid unnecessary backtracking. Sometimes seasoned political workers already have "mapped out" the community with very well-organized maps and routes for volunteers to use. Campaign planners should ask around to see if this information is already available before trying to create their own. Previous campaign leaders will know if this information exists or not. Another tip is that it is usually best to have canvassers work in teams. It's more fun, and the teammates will reinforce one another which will usually mean a higher number of houses visited per day and an increased likelihood of the job getting done on time. Precinct walking is hard work, and the more ways that it can be made bearable, the better.

FIGURE 12-1   Sample Canvassing Script

SAMPLE DOOR-TO-DOOR CANVASSING SCRIPT

GOOD DAY, MR/MRS _____*(NAME FROM REGISTRATION LIST)*_____

I'M _____*(VOLUNTEER'S NAME)*_____ AND I'M IN YOUR NEIGHBORHOOD TODAY ASKING FOR SUPPORT FOR THE LIBRARY ISSUE WHICH WILL BE ON THE _____*(DATE)*_____ BALLOT.

I WOULD LIKE TO GIVE YOU SOME INFORMATION ABOUT THE LIBRARY

(HAND OUT FACT SHEET, BROCHURE, BOOKMARK, ETC.)

BALLOT ISSUE (#) IS TO BUILD A NEW LIBRARY IN OUR TOWN.

THOSE OF US IN THE CAMPAIGN FEEL THAT THIS PROJECT IS BADLY NEEDED IN ORDER TO:

(BRIEF LIST OF REASONS)

MAY WE COUNT ON YOUR SUPPORT FOR THE LIBRARY PROJECT?

IF NO,   *(Write "N" _____)*

THANK YOU FOR YOUR TIME.
I'M SORRY YOU CAN'T SUPPORT THE ISSUE NOW,
MAYBE YOU CAN NEXT TIME.

(EXIT QUICKLY)

IF YES,   *(Write "Y" _____)*

WOULD YOU BE WILLING TO PUT UP A YARD SIGN, WEAR A BUTTON, ETC?

IF YES, (HAND OUT YARD SIGNS, ETC.)

COULD WE COUNT ON YOU TO GIVE A LITTLE TIME TO HELP WITH THE CAMPAIGN OR TO CONTRIBUTE TO THE CAMPAIGN?

(HAND OUT VOLUNTEER & CONTRIBUTION PLEDGE CARDS)

THANK YOU FOR YOUR SUPPORT. REMEMBER TO VOTE "YES" ON BALLOT (#) ON _____*(DATE OF ELECTION)*_____

GOOD DAY

FIGURE 12-1 *Continued*

IF UNDECIDED,

    MAY I EXPLAIN THE ADVANTAGES OF THE PROJECT?

    (PROVIDE AN OVERVIEW OF THE PROJECT & NEED)

    DO YOU HAVE ANY QUESTIONS?

    (TRY TO UNDERSTAND THEIR CONCERNS AND ATTEMPT TO ANSWER THEIR QUESTIONS)

    (IF UNABLE TO ANSWER A QUESTION, GIVE RESIDENT THE NAME AND NUMBER OF A DESIGNATED CAMPAIGN OFFICIAL WHO CAN RESPOND OR WRITE DOWN THE QUESTION AND PHONE NUMBER AND HAVE SOMEONE CALL THEM)

    DO YOU FEEL THAT YOU CAN SUPPORT THE ISSUE NOW?

    IF YES,   *(WRITE "Y" _____)*

        THANK YOU FOR YOUR SUPPORT. REMEMBER TO VOTE "YES" ON BALLOT (#) ON _____ *(DATE OF ELECTION)* _____

        GOOD DAY

    IF UNDECIDED,

        EVEN THOUGH UNDECIDED, WOULD YOU SAY YOU ARE LEANING FOR OR AGAINST THE ISSUE?

        (WRITE "U+", "U-" OR "U" _____)

        PLEASE CONTINUE TO THINK ABOUT THE ISSUE.

        IF YOU WOULD LIKE ANY MORE INFORMATION, PLEASE CALL _____ *(TELEPHONE #)* _____

        GOOD DAY.

    IF NO,   *(WRITE "N" _____)*

        I'M SORRY YOU CAN'T SUPPORT THE ISSUE NOW, MAYBE YOU CAN NEXT TIME.

        GOOD DAY.

        (EXIT QUICKLY)

Before a team goes out into the field, it must carefully plan where it will drop off "walkers" and where cars will be parked to pick them up for breaks and lunches. Each worker should have a specific assigned area with a map showing the area he or she must cover that day as well as support vehicle pickup points and times. Obviously, in order to plan this canvassing for the most intensive effort right before the election, it is necessary to pretest some areas to see how many houses an average campaign worker can cover in an hour's time. From this information, the number of houses which can be covered in a day can be calculated. This figure will vary from precinct to precinct because of variables such as the distance between houses, the amount of time spent at the door during each contact, the walker's efficiency, etc. The number of houses to be canvassed divided by the number of houses which can be covered per day will produce the number of days needed to complete the entire job. Based on the number of targeted houses, the Canvassing Committee can then calculate how many volunteers (and how many volunteer teams) will be needed to get the job done in the time available. Once this is done, precinct and block captains should be given specific assignments of the number of households to be contacted by a deadline and their progress should be carefully monitored through a reporting system of turning in completed voter registration lists at the end of each day.

Along with a map, canvassers should also be equipped with a list of registered voters for the immediate area being covered, since there is little point in wasting time on households that won't be voting on the issue. The voter registration lists will have to be organized by street name and then numerically by the house addresses (it is even more convenient if they are organized by odd and even sides of each street). Further, it is important to know the number of stops on each run in order to provide each walker with an adequate amount of campaign literature. It is very important for walkers not to run out of literature in the middle of a run, but there is also no sense in carrying a lot of extra material since canvassing is strenuous enough without extra weight and inconvenience. Careful planning can save a lot of time and pain in the field.

Each worker should be equipped with a presorted set of literature ranging from door hangers and fact sheets to brochures, bumper stickers, buttons, and yard signs. Rolling luggage carriers or some similar cart are also helpful; shoulder bags will work but, except for short trips, they get heavy. In order to make the door-to-door walking bearable, it is essential to wear good quality walking shoes and loose-fitting clothes. Although comfort is important, make sure that workers are attired in a respectful manner (no shorts or halter tops please!). Eye contact is also very important so it is better not to wear sunglasses (at least not at the door). Campaign workers should be identified in some manner, either by wearing campaign colors, a button, a hat, a chest banner, or ribbon.

Canvassers should always remember to be respectful when knocking on doors. They are intruding on the resident's privacy, and they must recognize that many people resent this form of campaigning. If animosity is experienced, the best response is to apologize and disengage as quickly as possible. Campaign volunteers must learn to cope with an occasional door slammed in their face—it goes with the job. Further, it is not beneficial to try and argue with a member of the opposition or a resident who is planning on voting "No" on the library issue. It is very unlikely that a "Yes" vote will be obtained. All that arguing will accomplish is wasted time, or worse, the confrontation may fire up the opposition.

Canvassing may be performed in phases at different times in the campaign calendar. In the early phase, along with distributing campaign literature, canvassers can collect valuable information about potential voters. Walkers should note the reaction of residents in houses visited on the voter registration list, although it is important that this be done so that residents can not see the activity (they wonder just what is being written down about them and it makes them feel uncomfortable). Voters can be categorized on the registered voters list as any of the following:

1. Positive,
2. Undecided, or
3. Negative.

Further, those that are undecided, may be categorized as "leaning towards," "leaning against," or "neutral." A simple coding system can be developed ("Y" for a positive or "Yes" voter; "N" for a negative or "No" voter; "U" for undecided, with U+ for leaning towards and U- for leaning against, etc.) and used by each canvasser to describe each individual contact.

Campaign coordinators can use this information in a number of ways. First, it provides a sense of how the issue is viewed in the neighborhood. Secondly, it provides a "short list" of those residences which will need a second "get-out-the-vote" visit, mailing, or telephone call. "Second calls" reinforce the campaign's interest in these individuals and makes them realize that their vote really does matter. It is best if all positive "Yes" voters receive a second contact during the final get-out-the-vote activities. Thirdly, supportive residents can be identified as potential donors or volunteers for the campaign. Those individuals identified as such can be contacted by campaign officials later and cultivated in whatever way possible to gain their assistance. Finally, if canvassing is to be extremely thorough, walkers should also make note of those houses where no one was at home so they can be revisited. If no one is home, the campaign worker can leave campaign literature like door hangers or plastic bags with literature packets stuffed inside. Canvassers should attach the campaign materials to doors as securely as possible so they don't blow away and litter the neighborhood.

LAST PHASES OF CANVASSING

Later phases of canvassing are the most hectic but the most effective. The closer to the election day, the more useful door-to-door canvassing is likely to be simply because the issue will be on the minds of the electorate. Further, only a brief gap between the point of contact by the campaign and election day ensures that the voter will remember the campaign message. If volunteers are limited for door-to-door canvassing, the most effective time is the last few days or last week right before the election. If canvassing efforts have been ongoing, this is the time to step-up the effort as part of the last minute GOTV effort. The GOTV script will be much shorter than the persuasive script. Since volunteers are contacting only "Yes" voters, the main point is to simply remind people to vote on election day and assist them any way possible to make certain that they do in fact go to the polls.

At this point the campaign "machine" should be in full swing and advancing on all fronts. The troops will be running as much on adrenaline and enthusiasm as on hot coffee and commitment. It is always an encouraging sign to have the campaign "generals" (steering committee) come to the battlefield in the waning hours of the campaign and participate directly in the effort by dispensing encouragement along with refreshments to get that "extra mile" out of each volunteer. It never hurts for these individuals to chip in and hotfoot it around the block a few times to really understand what the volunteers are experiencing in the "trenches."

PERSONAL CONTACT

There is nothing like the face-to-face contact that door-to-door canvassing provides in understanding a community. It is also true that personal contact, regardless of its form, is *the* best way to influence voters. People are frequently just plain impressed when volunteers are willing to take their own time to come out and support the library issue. Further, this personal delivery of the campaign's message by committed campaign workers makes an impression on residents which usually translates into a "Yes" vote at the polls. Because personal communication through face-to-face contact is the best mechanism for successfully reaching the undecided voter, it should be used extensively—especially in campaigns which are too close too call.

This approach can be practiced by all of the library supporters including the steering committee, library staff, Board of Trustees, Friends, campaign volunteers, and even committed patrons. *Referenda must be won one vote at a time.* They can be won at the coffee shop, the barber shop, in the bank, at the supermarket, and even over the back yard fence. Campaign supporters who realize the power of positive personal contact can become the most effective resource that any campaign has at its disposal. A campaign can flood the city with campaign literature, but if this information isn't followed up with personal contact, it will not have near the impact desired. When highly committed campaign supporters come in contact with potential voters, their enthusiasm rubs off on the voter. In a sense, the library supporter becomes a role model for the voter. If that individual is well-informed and excited about the library project, that message will generalize to the voter. Support for a project can literally become contagious and spread quickly throughout a community. Just as "word of mouth" is always the best advertising for any business, so it is with political campaigns. Strong, frequent, and effective personal communication of an issue in a community means that the voters will take ownership of the issue and support it at the polls.

CREATIVE PROMOTIONS

Promoting the library issue can be a lot of fun for supporters, especially if it's turned into a creative game. Just how many different ways can we find to influence people to vote for the measure? Supporters can compete with one another to tell the library's story in new and convincing ways. The more practice supporters have at making the "pitch," the better they will be. Getting the whole family involved is a good idea. There is nothing like seeing an entire family working to support a library issue to communicate that the library is truly an organization with "family values."

This approach can be accomplished in many ways. For example, in a campaign for the Rockridge (Oakland, California) Library, one campaign worker walked up and down the main commercial street talking with store owners to gain their support for the library issue and trying to get them to display a sign in their window illustrating that support. While this is not unusual, the campaign worker happened to be a mother who made these visits while pulling her young child behind her in the child's wagon. The sight of a child in a wagon filled with campaign signs along with their dedicated mother working for the library was an appeal most could not refuse. It simply cannot be said enough: the more personalized the library campaign is, particularly with an emotional, family-oriented theme, the better its chances for success.

ENDORSEMENTS

This approach to reaching voters through personal contact is what seeking endorsements is all about. Endorsements by influential community leaders are generally considered to be effective in influencing voters, especially if voters identify with and respect the endorsee. Endorsements by community leaders emphasize strong community-based public participation in the planning process and the campaign. Obtaining endorsements can also bring voters into the library's camp because they create the perception of a successful "bandwagon." Often, the earliest endorsements are the hardest to get. Each time an endorsement is obtained, it makes it easier to get the next one because the bandwagon provides visibility and credibility for the campaign. The campaign bandwagon can be promoted by having endorsees which are effective speakers address as many potentially sympathetic community groups as possible. Endorsees can be particularly helpful in making a big splash during the kick-off event for the campaign. Bring endorsees out early and repeatedly during the campaign.

Frequently library campaigns plan newspaper advertisements like a full-page ad listing their endorsees. Getting enough names to fill up a full page of a newspaper can be no small effort. One way to help with this is that when voters are contacted by campaign volunteers through whatever means, find out if they are willing to allow their names to be used in a newspaper ad. Names can be collected through any direct mailings, canvassing, or even telephone contact. In this manner, not only is a sizable list of names generated for the campaign, but voter commitment to the library issue is secured as well. In order to assist with the process of obtaining endorsements, it may be helpful to form an endorsements committee to coordinate the activity. This way the effort can be focused and the responsibility clearly defined and given to specific people insuring that the collection of endorsements doesn't "fall between the cracks."

Along with individuals, there are many groups which may be approached for endorsements. The League of Women Voters, the American Association of University Women, the PTA, and local school boards will frequently endorse educational and cultural issues like libraries. Homeowners associations and the Chamber of Commerce will often endorse library issues because libraries improve the quality of life in a community which generally enhances property values. In many states, governing agencies and their public officials can endorse the library issue as long as no public funds are used to promote their position. Endorsements by local public officials such as the mayor or chairman of the county commission lend support and credibility to most any issue unless the electorate is unhappy with those officials over some other matter.

The Chamber of Commerce & the Business Community

The Chamber's endorsement can be particularly important because they represent a very important segment of the community. The Chamber's endorsement frequently will influence business people because they feel that the Chamber would not endorse an issue that didn't make good business sense. The participation of the Chamber of Commerce and private businesses in general can be important in some campaigns. Its membership includes many influential members of the community. Convincing these individuals that an investment in the public library makes good business sense enhances the issue's chances of success. It can be particularly important to develop contacts here if start-up funds for the campaign are needed or if there is also going to be a private capital fundraising campaign effort to supplement the referendum campaign. In both of these cases, it is very helpful to identify those individuals in the business community who are also heavy users of the library. If this list is limited, these people can sometimes be tapped through their families if their spouses are library patrons. Another way the Chamber of Commerce can be helpful is in convincing its members to display a poster or yard sign at their place of business.

13 YARD SIGNS, SPEAKERS BUREAUS & SPECIAL EVENTS

POSTERS & YARD SIGNS

One relatively inexpensive, yet very effective method of promoting the library issue is printing and displaying posters and yard signs. Posters can be placed in the windows of residences and businesses, while yard signs can be placed in front yards and anywhere it is legal to place them. There are several variables in developing a cost-effective poster or yard sign. The first consideration is the graphic design of the sign, i.e., the content and format of the message. A campaign poster or yard sign should show the campaign logo and "colors." Posters and yard signs are usually silk-screened with just one or two colors. Pick colors that stand out from the background--bright contrasting colors are great. Display a very short message in as large a print size as possible so the poster or sign can be read from a distance. A short message might simply be *"Yes for Libraries on #12."* This reinforces the ballot number, the library issue, and the positive action needed from the voter. Yard signs are generally 11" × 14". It is good to make the sign or poster as distinctive and large as possible, but remember that custom cuts cost extra.

It is important to use material that will stand up to the locale's weather. If the campaign is being held in an area where it's not likely to rain or snow for a month prior to the election, the material may not be critical and the resulting cost savings may be captured. However, if inclement weather is likely when the signs are up, it is extremely important to make sure that the material can withstand this weather without colors running or fading or the signs themselves drooping or disintegrating. Numerous materials (cardboard, polyboard, plastic, etc.) are available at varying costs. Get cost quotations from several sources since costs can vary significantly from printer to printer as well as from one community to another. Some areas have sign makers that specialize in political signs—look on the back of other campaign signs to see who is producing most of them. These vendors usually provide the best and most cost-effective service available.

DISTRIBUTION OF POSTERS & YARD SIGNS

Putting up a poster or yard sign essentially endorses the library issue by saying *"I support this issue and you should too."* Yard signs and posters usually go up first in the yards and at the businesses of campaign volunteers, but the idea is to get as many voters to commit to the issue as possible and display their commitment prior to election day. It may be helpful to put up some posters and yard signs as much as one month prior to the election, especially if the campaign leadership needs to raise the recognition level of the library issue in the community; but as with most campaign efforts, yard signs and posters will be most effective in the last two weeks before the election.

FIGURE 13-1   Poster/Yard Sign: Grandfather and Granddaughter. Provided
                Courtesy of Tulsa City–County Library System, Tulsa City, Oklahoma.

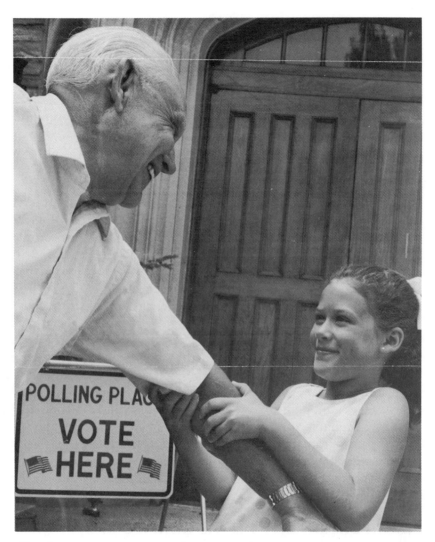

"C'mon Grandpa, please vote YES.
I love libraries."

VOTE   AUGUST   23

FIGURE 13-2   Yard Signs: Daniel I. Walters at a Campaign Rally with "OVERDUE" Signs. Provided Courtesy of Spokane Public Library, Spokane, Washington.

When you are putting up signs, make sure they are securely fastened. A few extra fasteners will ensure that the sign and the post are not separated by a strong wind or storm. Signs may be "posted" by attaching them to existing posts or to temporary stakes that can be easily removed by volunteers after the campaign is over. A yard sign usually consists of two signs stapled together and then stapled to a stake which can be driven into the ground. Keep this fact in mind when ordering yard signs because 2,000 signs will need to be printed to produce 1,000 yard signs. Some communities have codes regulating campaign signs which prohibit or control their placement. In many communities, campaign materials are routinely placed on utility poles and on stakes in right-of-ways, but it is wise to check with the local jurisdiction, utility company, or applicable business to avoid embarrassment, a fine, or having the signs methodically removed.

It doesn't take long to spot some of the best locations for campaign signs. Posters can be displayed anywhere people walk: around malls, on doors, bulletin boards, as well as in the windows of stores and business. In addition to placing yard signs in supporters' yards in targeted neighborhoods, it is helpful to place signs at all major intersections and along major arterial routes to and from workplaces and shopping centers in the community. Place them where the traffic is slow enough to be able to read them and where the driver will clearly see them "coming and going." In order to attract even more attention, it can also be helpful to have campaign workers standing at the major intersections on election day waving signs at motorists, making eye contact, and handing out campaign literature while vehicles are stopped at traffic lights. The best times for this activity on election day is between 6 a.m. and 9 a.m. and between 4 p.m. and the polls' closing.

POSTER & YARD SIGN COMMITTEE

Sometimes it is valuable, especially for larger campaigns, to set up a committee to create, construct, and place signs and posters. The committee chairperson should make sure to order the signs early enough in the campaign to make certain that they arrive well before they need to be distributed. The committee should have a "sign party" to put the signs together. Sometimes it helps to staple a colorful ribbon or streamer to a corner of the sign that can flutter in the breeze and help to attract attention to the sign. Once the signs are ready to go, they must be delivered and set up. The sign committee also has the responsibility of finding good locations to erect the signs.

Obviously, campaign volunteers, library staff, Friends, and patrons are good placement leads, but don't stop there. In addition to providing signs to door-to-door canvassers for distribution while they are making their rounds, it will be helpful to review voter lists from the telephone bank and contact "Yes" voters to see if they would be willing to display a sign. Campaign workers from previous educational or cultural campaigns often have lists of people who may be willing to display a sign. It is helpful to try to get small businesses, restaurants, and convenience stores to display signs since they will be viewed by many people. It is also a good idea to place yard signs as close to the polls as the law allows so that voters will see them as they drive to the polls on election day. A sea of library campaign signs can't help but make a last positive impression and may be just the nudge necessary to get an undecided voter to vote for the library issue.

Creative placement of signs can go a long way toward winning an election. It is also important to continue to monitor signs which have been put up to make sure that they are in good condition and haven't fallen over or been stolen especially if they were set up early. Yard signs and posters can both raise awareness of the library issue and get the "Vote Yes" message out into the community.

SPEAKERS BUREAUS

Another method of getting the library's campaign message out is to form a speakers bureau which will provide speakers for community organizations and events. In recent library campaigns, this technique was one of the more frequently used methods of pitching the library issue to the community.[1] This approach was deemed important because the memberships of community organizations like Kiwanis, Lions, Rotary, PTA, and homeowners associations are filled with influential people who are also voters. There is no more effective way to campaign than to expose these individuals to a professional quality presentation by a highly committed, articulate, and respected community leader. This approach emphasizes direct personal contact. Not only does the library have the opportunity to put its best foot forward, but there is also an opportunity for give-and-take during a question and answer period. These groups frequently look for speakers. Simply find out well in advance of the time desired who is responsible for scheduling speakers and request that the library be given a confirmed date.

Speakers should be carefully selected. Frequently, the speaker is more important than what is said. Before choosing a speaker, consider the makeup of the group before which the presentation will be made. Again, social peers are usually better received in this kind of setting. Endorsees frequently make good speakers, as do steering committee members and campaign

FIGURE 13-3   Yard Sign: Vote "For" Your Libary. Courtesy of Denver Public Library, Denver, Colorado.

volunteers from the ranks of the Friends group who happen to be good public speakers. It is wise to have the library director or a knowledgeable staff member assist with every presentation. This provides technical backup in case a question comes up that the speaker cannot answer and also provides as a double check by ensuring that no incorrect information is inadvertently provided.

Each speaker should be provided with either a predetermined script or a list of ideas and information about the library issue (fact sheets, question and answer sheets, etc.) for concise, well-thought-out presentations. While it is helpful to tailor presentations to the specific group, it is also important to deliver a consistent message. Conflicting information will only raise questions and hurt credibility. Frequently library directors are called upon to perform the role of the speaker, and this is fine if they are effective speakers, but the one drawback is that they are often perceived as having a vested interest in the matter. For this reason, it is usually better to have lay people make the presentations. Just as it is important to use graphics in campaign literature to help communicate the campaign's message, it is also helpful to use visual aids to help sell the library issue during presentations.

SLIDE/TAPE OR VIDEO TAPE PRESENTATIONS

To this end, it is often useful to have some audiovisual assistance for these presentations. A slide-tape presentation or a video tape can be produced which covers some of the main points and provides a graphic explanation of some of the problems with the existing structure. If overcrowding is a major problem, pictures of people standing in lines or books stacked on the floor and in window sills can make the point better than an hour of talk. If the building is literally falling apart, this can be documented most effectively through pictures. Many people in a community have no idea how bad the situation really is, but if confronted with crumbling foundations, falling ceiling plaster, and bookstacks drenched with rainwater, they can frequently be moved to vote for the measure. Remember, just because the problems are obvious to the library management doesn't mean that they are to the community at large. One of the main thrusts of any campaign is to communicate problems to the public. Often people have no idea how good a modern state-of-the-art library building can be. Showing pictures of an attractive, spacious, and well-lit library can be a shock when compared to the local "dungeon." Community pride can sometimes send people running to the polls to support the measure.

If presentations use audiovisual equipment and media, make certain that both the speaker and the staff support person can operate the equipment. It is helpful to schedule a "dry run" not only to test the equipment, but also to allow the presenter to rehearse. Along with polishing the actual delivery of the presentation, this will allow for the presentation to be timed. If it goes over the allotted time, the speaker knows that it must be cut back to only the essentials. It is important to leave time at the end of each presentation, not only for questions and answers, but also for distributing campaign literature and paraphernalia such as buttons and yard signs. Don't be afraid to ask for tangible support at these presentations. This is often a good opportunity to obtain volunteers, contributions, *and* votes.

SPEAKER'S BUREAU COMMITTEE

In small campaigns, the speakers bureau function can be performed by the steering committee, but if the campaign is large enough, the speaker's bureau may need to be elevated to the level of a separate campaign committee. Coordinating an effective speaker's bureau is no small effort. Not only do good speakers have to be identified, but dates for the engagements must also be acquired and scheduled. A calendar of presentations should be kept current. Scripts and information packets must be prepared, and AV presentations must be produced. Further, campaign literature, paraphernalia, and AV equipment must be gathered and readied for each presentation. It is usually better for the campaign to use its own equipment at each presentation rather than relying on available equipment which may or may not work. Finally, a coordinator must constantly follow-up with people to make sure that events are still on and that speakers will indeed show up. It looks very bad for a campaign if there is a room full of people and the promised speaker doesn't show up. Such an event could be the one thing about the library issue that sticks in the voter's mind when he or she steps into the voting booth.

BLOCK PARTIES, OPEN HOUSES, & COFFEE CLATCHES

An extension of the speakers bureau or possibly a function of the special events committee is the idea of providing speakers for in-home "block parties," "open houses," or "coffee clatches" which target specific neighborhoods. This can be time intensive, but is effective especially if a door-to-door canvassing effort cannot be mounted in the neighborhood. Again, this approach works well because it emphasizes personal contact. While the campaign has to hold many such gatherings to reach very many voters, they can be helpful in not only convincing people to vote for the issue, but also in recruiting volunteers and identifying potential donors. This approach works particularly well in older neighborhoods with established political networks. It is just a matter of tapping into these networks and the campaign message can be spread throughout the neighborhood with relatively few meetings.

One of the difficult aspects of this approach is recruiting hosts and hostesses to hold the activities in their homes. One way to do this is to start the function with committed campaign volunteers and spread it by use of the pyramid system. Beaudry and Schaeffer suggest starting with a coffee held by key supporters from targeted areas. Ask each guest to duplicate the event in his or her own neighborhood. To continue expanding the pyramid, the giver of each successive coffee should attempt to recruit at least two new people to hold coffees in their homes.[2] One person should be assigned to manage the pyramid and should be diligent about following-up with hosts and hostesses to make sure that they are prepared and that the process continues to grow. Again, bird dogging the process is the key to success, by making sure the parties are taking place, that speakers are showing up, that campaign literature is being distributed, and that volunteer and donor pledge cards are being collected and sent to appropriate campaign committee officials.

SPECIAL EVENTS

In addition to block parties, numerous other special events can be orchestrated by the campaign. In addition to the kick-off event, the campaign may wish to have rallies, media events, breakfasts, luncheons, dinners, receptions, or any kind of activity which attracts attention to the library campaign. These events can be fundraising efforts for the campaign or simply events to grab people's attention. Often these events must be coordinated with the speaker's bureau since speakers will normally be required. They are a good way to bring together people who are important to the campaign. Often these events feature special endorsees of prominence or celebrity guests who are supportive of libraries.

In a recent referendum campaign in Santa Cruz, California, a local bookstore sponsored an event for the Library's Friends group which combined a book promotion tour by Stephen King and the library campaign. This event was helpful because "2,000 people got the Measure L message and heard Stephen King tell them how important public libraries are."[3] Even though this particular campaign was unsuccessful because of an active opposition group, this kind of persuasive celebrity endorsement does have impact.

Special events like holding an "open house" at the library can be effective. They can demonstrate the library's need as well as underscore what the library could be if properly supported. Again, a good audiovisual presentation demonstrating new and improved ways of providing library service or showing recently constructed state-of-the-art public libraries can be very effective. Emphasize what people are missing either in facilities or services and thereby play on their community pride. Don't dwell on the negative; remember that people get excited about voting for something positive and creative.

Don't forget that special events can be created for campaign volunteers as well as for publicity. In Spokane, Washington, a campaign rally was held right before election day to help organize a leafleting activity. Further, it is usually desirable to organize a campaign victory party at the campaign headquarters. This helps to bring the campaign volunteers together for one last time at the end of the campaign and provides a forum for the steering committee to thank all who have worked on the campaign as well as an opportunity for the library management and supportive governmental officials to thank the members of the steering committee for their hard work. Thanking campaign workers is extremely important since they will continue to be the library's main voice for advocacy for many years to come if they are made to feel that their personal sacrifice was worth the effort and was appreciated.

SPECIAL EVENTS COMMITTEE

As with other campaign activities, it may become necessary to form a special events committee to handle the activities if they become significant in terms of time and are more than the steering committee or speakers bureau can handle. The goal is to make any special event, *the* event in town for the night or day and to obtain a good turnout and press coverage. For this reason, it is important to coordinate the special events calendar with other campaigns and community organizations to help minimize conflicts. Not only do special events planners need to be aware of the social activities calendar for the community as a whole, but they must have a good number of social contacts and be able to organize and promote the event adequately. Producing a successful special event takes skilled planning and coordination. The result can be a tremendous "push" for the campaign if successful, but the reverse is also true if the library campaign holds a big party and nobody bothers to come. This is why it is always critical to follow-up invitations with a telephone call from someone on the special events committee, preferably someone who knows the individual.

PUBLIC FORUMS

Another activity that is often considered a special event is the holding of a public forum. This is a highly specialized event because while the library supporters will certainly have an opportunity to make their pitch, the real purpose of these kinds of meetings is usually to gain input from the community. Forums usually help build consensus in the community in the early needs assessment and planning stages as well as early in the campaign when the steering committee is still assessing the strategy and wants input. Public forums held later in the campaign are generally less useful, except in special situations, mainly because they can give opposition groups an opportunity to criticize the library issue and publicly put the campaign supporters on the defensive. Unless campaign supporters are confident they can come out on top in this kind of situation, it is usually not in the best interest of the campaign to provide the opposition with a ready made platform from which they can sling mud at the campaign.

There are, however, occasions when public forums become necessary and even helpful in the later stages of campaigns. If there is a particularly controversial aspect to the library project which has gained a lot of attention in the press and which, based on the polls, is significantly hurting the campaign effort, it may be necessary to take the proverbial "bull by the horns" and address the issue in a public forum. This method of allowing the community to air their concerns and grievances and also provide the library supporters a chance to focus attention on their position can often clear the air on a matter and diffuse it prior to election day. These kinds of events are, at best, high-risk crap shoots because there is no way to control the situation and emotions can sometimes overrule logic and reason with the event backfiring and causing more damage to the campaign than if it were not held. Caution is obviously the watchword when it comes to forums in the later stages of a campaign.

An example of this kind of situation can be controversy over a site. The library management may have performed a professional quality site selection study and have all of the reasons for why a certain site was picked well-documented, but the opposition may take exception with one small negative aspect and blow it all out of proportion. If a public forum can be held and the issue hammered out so that the community can come to consensus on the issue, the approach will have been successful. But, if the activity turns into a shouting match between two camps and only serves to polarize the community, the effort will have failed and may well contribute directly to the demise of the library issue at the polls. Sometimes the best the library supporters can get if the issue is threatening to derail the campaign is a compromise with the opposition by promising to take another look at the matter after the referendum. The strategy here is to look magnanimous by extending the olive branch *"for the good of the library and the community."* If the library campaign has already built up a reasonable amount of credibility during the planning and campaign for the project, this approach may diffuse the situation long enough to get the ballot measure approved by the voters. After that is accomplished, the project planners can come back and take another hard look at the issue by including opponents in the process of analyzing the alternatives.

Hopefully, advanced project planning which builds consensus before the start of a campaign will avoid the need for a public forum late in the campaign and let the campaign concentrate on getting the message out instead of defending the current project proposal. There are a number of techniques which are considerably better for getting the campaign message out than public forums. One of these is telephone canvassing.

REFERENCES

1. Hall, Richard B. "The Votes Are In." *Library Journal* 115:11 (June 15, 1990), pp. 42–46.
2. Beaudry, Ann E. and Bob Schaeffer. *Winning Local and State Elections.* New York: The Free Press, Macmillian, 1986, p. 79.
3. Turner, Anne. "Notes From the Late Campaign." *California Libraries* 4:10 (November/December 1994), p. 12.

14 TELEPHONE BANKS & POLL GREETING

TELEPHONE BANKS

Another campaign method that is almost as effective as door-to-door campaigning is canvassing through the use of "telephone banks." Although the face-to-face personal contact of door-to-door canvassing is difficult to beat as a method to persuade the electorate to vote for the library issue, telephone banks are effective when volunteers are short or the campaign is being held in a primarily rural area where it is difficult to walk door-to-door. One advantage to telephone canvassing is that volunteers can usually contact more people per hour than block walkers can visit, so telephone banks are more efficient. Research seems to show that telephone contact is almost as effective at turning out the vote as door-to-door canvassing and that in some elections an intensive telephone bank may increase voter turnout by as much as 10 percent. Telephone banks are also easier to organize than door-to-door canvasses. However, it should be recognized that while telephone canvassing is more personal than a mailing, it is not as personal as someone standing on the doorstep of a prospective voter.

The use of telephone banks ranked just below the use of mailings in recently held library referenda.[1] Although this method is more difficult to organize than mailings, it does hold an advantage over mailings because it is interactive. Like mailings, telephone banks are most effective when directed toward targeted groups or neighborhoods. Calls made to specific target groups can be tailored just like mailings or door-to-door pitches. For example, if calls are being made to senior citizens, the arguments for the new library should emphasize aspects of the new library building which will be of interest to seniors—e.g., a large print book collection, a quiet reading area for them away from kids, or a new grandparents and books program, etc.

In addition to targeting information about prospective contacts, the actual telephone number for each individual must be obtained in order to perform a telephone canvass. In the same way that the direct mail committee must gather addresses for mailings, the telephone bank committee must gather telephone numbers and names for the targeted groups and individuals. Many membership lists for community organizations will include the telephone number of the member, but many do not. Voter registration lists frequently include telephone numbers; however, numbers are not usually required in order to register to vote and may be missing in many cases. Patron records generally do have telephone numbers, but these may not be able to be used unless the patron has given prior permission to do so in political campaigns. If names and addresses of target group individuals are present but telephone numbers are missing, it will be necessary for volunteers to sit down with telephone books or reverse directories and look up phone numbers. Voter registration lists are often alphabetical by street name and reverse telephone books list individuals by street addresses and provides their telephone number (unless unlisted).

If the target groups for mailings, door-to-door canvassing, and telephone contact are the same, it will be helpful for these respective committees to coordinate their efforts. For example, these committees can work together to build a computer database which lists targeted names, addresses, and telephone numbers. Further, as contact begins with any one committee the residents' response can be entered. If the telephone committee contacts an individual early in the polling, and they are decidedly negative about the library issue, this individual can be "crossed off the list" by deleting them from the database so that mailings are not sent, future telephone contact is not made, and door-to-door canvassers won't stop and waste their time. Further, just as with block walkers, telephone callers can identify "Yes" voters or undecided voters. These individuals can be coded so that separate lists of "Yes" and "Undecided" voters can be generated. These lists can be used in the last few days of the campaign by both the door-to-door canvassers and callers to concentrate and coordinate the GOTV effort.

STAGES OF TELEPHONE BANKING

The First Stage

Telephone banking can be performed in three stages—voter identification, persuasion, and GOTV—over the duration of the campaign. The first stage is an identification of the voter's preference regarding the issue, and this step should be started several months ahead of the election. This stage focuses primarily on identification of potentially favorable voters as well as those who are undecided about the issue. No background information is given about the issue and no attempt is made to persuade the voter to vote for the issue. This step establishes a baseline of support (or lack thereof) for the library issue by essentially polling registered voters. This stage should be performed early and periodically throughout the campaign. During this initial phase, callers should make registered voters aware of the upcoming election while they determine the level of support.

Further, callers should make note of which households express support for the library issue, which are undecided, or which express opposition. This kind of early information about how the community feels about the issue can help to establish an overall strategy as well as give the steering committee information about trends in specific precincts. Finally, during this phase, telephone bank calls can be used for fundraising and volunteer recruitment for the campaign. For those individuals who express a positive inclination toward the campaign, a donation of time or money can be requested by the caller and/or a pledge card mailed with another follow-up telephone call by someone on the finance committee. The sample script in Figure 14-1 could be used by telephone callers during the initial phase of a telephone bank.

The Second Stage

The second stage of telephone banking is persuasive in nature. Those individuals already identified as undecided should be called and encouraged to vote "Yes." Further, deeper penetration of the targeted areas will mean that it will be necessary to continue calling more individuals to determine if they are supportive or not and then try to persuade those who are sitting on the fence to vote for the library issue. Callers should identify "Yes" voters along with

---

FIGURE 14-1   Sample Voter Identification Phase Telephone Script

---

HELLO, MR/MRS. _____*(RESIDENT'S NAME)*_____

MY NAME IS _____*(NAME)*_____ AND I AM CALLING ABOUT THE UPCOMING
LIBRARY BALLOT ISSUE ON ____*(MONTH & DAY)*____. AS PART OF THE CAMPAIGN
COMMITTEE FOR THE NEW LIBRARY, I AM CALLING TODAY TO DETERMINE IF YOU
WERE AWARE THAT IT WOULD BE ON THE UPCOMING BALLOT?

　　　　(RECORD RESPONSE: YES _____ / NO _____)

IF AN ELECTION WERE HELD TODAY, WOULD YOU BE FAVORABLY DISPOSED
TOWARD THE LIBRARY PROJECT?

IF NEGATIVE, 　　　　*(WRITE "N" _____)*

　　　　WELL, THANK YOU FOR YOUR TIME.
　　　　I'M SORRY YOU CAN'T SUPPORT THE ISSUE.
　　　　GOOD DAY.

　　　　(DISENGAGE AS QUICKLY AS POSSIBLE)

IF UNDECIDED,

　　　　EVEN THOUGH UNDECIDED, WOULD YOU SAY YOU ARE LEANING FOR OR
　　　　AGAINST THE ISSUE?

　　　　　　　(WRITE "U+", "U-" OR "U" ____)

THANK YOU FOR YOUR TIME,

I HOPE YOU WILL CONTINUE TO CONSIDER THE ISSUE. WOULD YOU BE
INTERESTED IN A FACT SHEET ABOUT THE NEW PROJECT?

(RECORD RESPONSE, YES _____ / NO _____)

IF YES,

　　　　　　　MAY I VERIFY YOUR ADDRESS?
　　　　　　　THANK YOU FOR YOUR INTEREST,
　　　　　　　I WILL SEND THIS OUT RIGHT AWAY

FIGURE 14-1 *Continued*

IF NO,

> *(SUGGEST THEY VISIT THE LIBRARY TO SEE THE NEED FOR THEMSELVES)*
>
> THANK YOU FOR YOUR TIME.
>
> GOOD DAY.

IF POSITIVE,

> *(WRITE "Y" _____)*
>
> I'M GLAD TO HEAR YOU ARE A SUPPORTER. WE ARE WORKING HARD TO INFORM THE VOTERS OF THE ISSUE. WOULD YOU BE WILLING TO DONATE EITHER SOME TIME OR MONEY TO THE CAMPAIGN?

(WRITE DOWN RESPONSE)

YES, TIME   _____

> I'LL HAVE SOMEONE GET IN TOUCH WITH YOU.

YES, MONEY _____

> COULD WE COUNT ON YOU TO CONTRIBUTE $50?
> I WILL SEND YOU A CONTRIBUTION CARD.
> MAY I VERIFY YOUR ADDRESS?
>
> OR
>
> I'LL HAVE SOMEONE GET IN TOUCH WITH YOU.

REGARDLESS OF RESPONSE (DONATE OR NOT):

THANK YOU FOR YOUR TIME TODAY.

WE WOULD LIKE TO CONTINUE TO BE IN CONTACT TO PROVIDE YOU WITH ADDITIONAL INFORMATION AS THE CAMPAIGN PROGRESSES.

GOOD DAY.

---

undecided voters who seem to be leaning in a favorable direction on the issue. Undecided voters should receive special attention particularly if the campaign is close. Basic information about the library issue should be given, and the issue should be promoted without attempting to pressure the voter into a decision. Residents who resent being called at home or "No" voters should be disengaged quickly and they should be recorded so that they are not mistakenly called again. During this phase, telephone callers must have a good command of the basic information and issues of the campaign so that they do not create confusion in voters' minds. Along with a good orientation program under their belt, callers should be armed with a script, fact sheets, and a question and answer sheet. When a question is asked that the caller does not know the answer to, the caller should refer the call to an individual who is designated to handle difficult campaign questions. Figure 14-2 shows a typical script for the second phase.

The Final Stage

The final stage of the telephone campaign comes in the last week before the election, when the emphasis is on getting out the vote. In most campaigns, volunteer callers should contact only "Yes" voters. In campaigns which are very close, it may be important to contact undecided voters as well (particularly those "leaning for" the issue), but this takes more time and volunteers. If time is short, make certain that all "Yes" voters will be contacted first, and then allocate whatever time is available to the undecided voter list. Both "Yes" voters and undecided voters should be reminded to vote and asked to vote "Yes." This last GOTV stage will only be effective if the earlier two stages were performed correctly and "Yes" voters have been clearly identified. The registered voters lists must have been consistently and accurately marked in a standardized manner for the follow-up callers to know whom to call.

In addition to asking for their "Yes" vote, voters should be reminded of the date of the election as well as informed of the hours that the polls will be open. Further, voters should be reminded of where their individual polling place is located and asked if transportation or baby sitting services are necessary for them to get to the polls. To support this, telephone callers should have road maps for the precincts showing the locations of polling places and be able to give good directions. The GOTV effort can be enhanced by implementing a volunteer "taxi" and baby sitting service. This approach is particularly effective in communities with high numbers of senior citizens who don't drive or mothers without adequate child care. Neither service will likely be heavily used, but it is important to offer in close campaigns. Make certain to have responsible drivers and day-care providers available, since the campaign doesn't need to be marred by an unfortunate accident. Figure 14-3 presents a sample GOTV script.

TELEPHONE BANK COMMITTEE

Organizing a telephone bank can take a considerable amount of time depending upon the number of volunteers needed to reach the target audience. In many campaigns, an effective telephone bank will require a telephone bank committee. One of the primary duties of the telephone committee is to set up an orientation and training program for volunteers. Volunteers should be given an overview of the campaign along with a description of the role and importance of the telephone bank. Scripts will need to be prepared and provided to callers so that they can practice their delivery before actually starting the process. It may be helpful to have callers role play with one another and even record these sessions to allow the caller to hear themselves and make any necessary adjustments in the delivery. Further, sometimes it is helpful if callers start out by practicing on friends or relatives for the first few calls because this tends to build confidence. Finally, callers should be provided with all necessary materials, such as the list of people to be called and instructions on how to record the contacts.

FIGURE 14-2   Persuasive Phase Telephone Script

HELLO, MR/MRS. _____*(RESIDENT'S NAME)*_____

I'M _____*(NAME)*_____ AND I'M PART OF THE LIBRARY CAMPAIGN COMMITTEE TO SUPPORT THE NEW _____*(LIBRARY PROJECT NAME)*_____.

I'M CALLING TODAY ASKING FOR SUPPORT FOR THE LIBRARY ISSUE WHICH WILL BE ON THE BALLOT IN THE UPCOMING _____*(DATE)*_____ ELECTION. BALLOT ISSUE (#) IS TO BUILD A NEW LIBRARY IN OUR TOWN. THOSE OF US IN THE CAMPAIGN FEEL THAT THIS PROJECT IS BADLY NEEDED IN ORDER TO:

    (BRIEF LIST OF THE REASONS—LIMIT TO 2 OR 3)

MR./MRS. _____*(RESIDENT'S NAME)*_____, MAY WE COUNT ON YOUR SUPPORT OF THE LIBRARY PROJECT?

IF NO,   *(WRITE "N" _____)*

    THANK YOU FOR YOU TIME.

    I'M SORRY YOU CAN'T SUPPORT THE ISSUE AT THIS TIME.

    (DISENGAGE AS QUICKLY AS POSSIBLE)

IF YES,   *(WRITE "Y" _____)*

    THANK YOU FOR YOUR SUPPORT.

    WE ARE WORKING HARD TO INFORM THE VOTERS OF THE ISSUE. WOULD YOU BE WILLING TO DONATE EITHER SOME TIME OR MONEY TO THE CAMPAIGN?

    (WRITE DOWN RESPONSE)

    YES, TIME   _____

        I'LL HAVE SOMEONE GET IN TOUCH WITH YOU

    YES, MONEY   _____

        COULD WE COUNT ON YOU TO CONTRIBUTE $50?
        I WILL SEND YOU A CONTRIBUTION CARD.
        MAY I VERIFY YOUR ADDRESS?

FIGURE 14-2   *Continued*

OR

I'LL HAVE SOMEONE GET IN TOUCH WITH YOU

REGARDLESS OF RESPONSE (DONATE OR NOT):

THANK YOU FOR YOUR TIME TODAY.

WE WOULD LIKE TO CONTINUE TO BE IN CONTACT TO PROVIDE YOU WITH ADDITIONAL INFORMATION AS THE CAMPAIGN PROGRESSES.

REMEMBER TO VOTE "YES" ON BALLOT (#) ON _____*(DATE OF ELECTION)*_____ .

GOOD DAY.

IF UNDECIDED,

YOUR VOTE REALLY COUNTS IN THIS ELECTION, LET ME PROVIDE YOU WITH AN OVERVIEW OF THE PROJECT AND THE REASON IT'S NEEDED.

(IN-DEPTH LIST OF ARGUMENTS)

DO YOU HAVE ANY QUESTIONS?

(TRY TO UNDERSTAND THEIR CONCERNS AND ATTEMPT TO ANSWER THEIR QUESTIONS—USE FACT SHEETS)

(RESPOND WITH THE APPROPRIATE ARGUMENTS.)

(IF UNABLE TO ANSWER A QUESTION, TRANSFER CALL TO DESIGNATED OFFICIAL OR WRITE DOWN THE QUESTION AND PHONE NUMBER AND HAVE SOMEONE CALL THEM)

MR./MRS. _____*(RESIDENT'S NAME)*_____ , DO YOU FEEL THAT YOU CAN SUPPORT THE ISSUE NOW?

IF YES,   *(WRITE "Y" _____)*

THANK YOU FOR YOUR SUPPORT.

REMEMBER TO VOTE "YES" ON BALLOT (#) ON _____*(DATE OF ELECTION)*_____ .

GOOD DAY.

FIGURE 14-2 *Continued*

IF STILL UNDECIDED,

    EVEN THOUGH UNDECIDED, WOULD YOU SAY YOU ARE LEANING FOR OR AGAINST THE ISSUE?

    (WRITE "U+", "U-" OR "U" _____)

    THANK YOU FOR YOUR TIME, I HOPE YOU WILL CONTINUE TO CONSIDER THE ISSUE AND EVENTUALLY SUPPORT THE PROJECT SINCE IT IS SO BADLY NEEDED.

    WOULD YOU BE INTERESTED IN A FACT SHEET ABOUT THE NEW PROJECT?

    (RECORD RESPONSE: YES _____ / NO _____)

    IF YES,

        MAY I VERIFY YOUR ADDRESS?
        THANK YOU FOR YOUR INTEREST.
        I WILL SEND THIS OUT RIGHT AWAY

    IF NO,

        SUGGEST THEY VISIT THE LIBRARY TO SEE THE NEED FOR THEMSELVES.

        THANK YOU FOR YOUR TIME.

        GOOD DAY.

IF NO,   *(WRITE "N" _____)*

    THANK YOU FOR YOU TIME.

    I'M SORRY YOU CAN'T SUPPORT THE ISSUE, MAYBE YOU CAN NEXT TIME.

    GOOD DAY.

    (DISENGAGE AS QUICKLY AS POSSIBLE)

In addition to orienting volunteers to the campaign issues and instructing them on proper telephone bank techniques, volunteers must be scheduled so that an adequate number of callers are available when needed. The committee's chairperson should be responsible for having sign-up sheets available and for reminding each volunteer of their times. In addition, the committee will need to calculate how many volunteers will be needed, and for how long they

---

FIGURE 14-3   Sample GOTV Telephone Script

HELLO, MR/MRS. _____ *(RESIDENT'S NAME)* _____

I'M _____ *(NAME)* _____ AND I'M CALLING TODAY TO REMIND YOU TO VOTE "YES" FOR THE NEW _____ *(LIBRARY PROJECT NAME)* _____ ON *(DAY OF THE WEEK)*, *(DATE: MONTH & DAY)*.

WE REALLY NEED EVERYONE WHO IS FAVORABLE TO GO TO THE POLLS AND VOTE "YES" ON BALLOT NUMBER *(#)* FOR THE LIBRARY.

THE POLLS WILL BE OPEN FROM _____ *(A.M. TO P.M.)* _____ .

WHAT TIME WERE YOU EXPECTING TO VOTE?

DO YOU KNOW THAT YOUR POLLING PLACE IS? _____ *(PROVIDE LOCATION)* _____

DO YOU NEED ANY TRANSPORTATION OR BABY SITTING SERVICES IN ORDER TO GET TO THE POLLS?

IF NO,

> THANK YOU FOR YOUR SUPPORT.
>
> SEE YOU AT THE NEW LIBRARY!
>
> DON'T FORGET—VOTE "YES" ON _____ *(BALLOT #)* _____ !

IF YES,

> WHEN DO YOU NEED TRANSPORTATION OR BABY SITTING?
>
> *(WRITE DOWN TIME)*
>
> I WILL HAVE SOMEONE CALL YOU AND CONFIRM THE TIME AND YOUR ADDRESS.
>
> THANK YOU FOR YOUR SUPPORT.
>
> SEE YOU AT THE NEW LIBRARY!
>
> DON'T FORGET—VOTE "YES" ON _____ *(BALLOT #)* _____ !

---

will be needed based upon the number of telephones available at the telephone bank and the number of calls that must be made. At each step, it will be necessary to determine the number of calls which will need to be made based upon the telephone lists previously created. Further, it will be necessary to estimate the average length of each call based upon a reasonable sample of pretests. This information along with the number of telephones available will enable the committee to calculate how many volunteers are necessary and how many hours of telephoning will be necessary to accomplish the task. The more telephones and volunteers available, the fewer the number of days necessary to do the job.

This is one of the reasons why the telephone bank's location is important. Businesses with a large number of telephone lines like insurance agencies, banks, real estate offices, law offices, travel agencies, large corporations, etc. make good locations for telephone banks. They can frequently be talked into donating the use of their premises to support the library campaign. Most telephone banks will operate in the evenings and weekends when businesses are closed because the best time to contact people is between 7 p.m. and 9 p.m. in the evenings (never call after 9 p.m.) as well as during weekend afternoons. While calls can be made from the homes of volunteers (as was successfully done in the recent campaign in Oklahoma City, Oklahoma), most campaign professionals indicate that this is not desirable. It is usually better to have a specific location for volunteers to gather to make calls. This raises enthusiasm for the activity and usually gets better results because the telephone bank coordinator has better control over the process and is immediately available if a caller can't answer a voter's question.

Remember, telephone banking is dull and monotonous because it is a very repetitive process. The telephone committee chairperson should do everything possible to make the experience as pleasant and rewarding as possible, including providing refreshments and working to develop a sense of teamwork in the volunteers. "It is important to celebrate key milestones as the campaign reaches critical benchmarks. If you have identified 5,000 supportive voters, you should celebrate at every 1,000, for example."[2] Productivity can be increased through competitions to see who can make the most calls in an hour, or get the most undecided voters to say "Yes!" during one shift. Contests can be held to see who can maintain the most sincerity in their presentation, even though they are tired and just want to go home to their families. One of the greatest challenges with telephone banks is to keep the quality of the contact high regardless if it is the first call or the last one made during the campaign. The best way to insure this is to make sure that the volunteers are always thanked appropriately for their efforts.

Finally, the telephone work must be monitored constantly and data collected daily for database management which will be used to coordinate follow-up calls and mailings. If callers don't have a good clear speaking voice, are short tempered, or they are disruptive to other callers (thereby reducing productivity), they should be reassigned by the volunteer committee to other campaign activities. If they can't properly record responses, they will need to be retrained or reassigned, since it is essential to develop accurate data about voters. The telephone committee chairperson should be responsible for overseeing the transferring of this information and make certain that the files are kept up-to-date. One of the ways that this information can be used during the GOTV activities is to combine the telephone bank with a poll watching procedure.

POLL GREETING & WATCHING

Assuming it is legal (which it is not in all states), campaign workers or "greeters" can stand outside polling places (they must usually stand at least 100 feet from the doors) and make one last attempt to influence voters by handing them campaign literature and giving them a final pitch for the library. This can be quite effective because voters, having just driven through a gauntlet of yard signs on the way to the polling place, can then be personally greeted by an enthusiastic library campaign worker. In a close race, this last effort may be what's necessary to put the issue over the top, but be very careful to understand any legal restrictions.

In the early days of elections in this nation, poll watching was necessary in some areas to make sure that political corruption did not impact the outcome of elections. For the most part this problem has been eliminated, but several aspects of poll watching are useful for library campaigns. One of the main activities today is to have an individual checking the campaign's list of "Yes" voters which have been identified during door-to-door and telephone canvassing against the list of registered voters who have voted at the polling place that day. Many states require that a list of people who have voted at a polling place be posted there. Each individual who has already voted may be crossed off the campaign poll watcher's list.

The idea is to subsequently contact those who have not voted and try to convince them to get to the polls and vote. The lists can be checked around noon and then again late in the afternoon. Campaign workers should attempt to contact those who haven't yet voted either by telephone or by sending "runners" out to knock on their doors and remind them in person. This activity should be intensified through the dinner hour as the closing of the polls approaches. These last minute efforts may seem desperate, but campaign planners will certainly wish they had gone the extra mile if the issue loses by just a few votes.

REFERENCES

1. Hall, Richard B. "The Votes Are In." *Library Journal* 115:11 (June 15, 1990), pp. 42-46.
2. Allen, Cathy "The Alternative" in DeButts, Read "You Make the Call: Using Phones in your Voter-Contact Program." *Campaigns & Elections* 12:7 (April, 1992), p. 32.

15 SUMMARY & CONCLUSIONS

"Organizing a referendum campaign for a public library building is the most politically challenging enterprise that a library director will face in his or her career."

— *Dr. Herbert Goldhor*

Along with demonstrating that the chances of success are good for library referenda, this book also has attempted to serve as a primer on the political process of referenda campaigns. Many library directors and trustees are hesitant to enter into the "political fray" for fear of becoming tainted by politics; but frankly, it is becoming more and more necessary to do so if the public library as an institution is to prosper and, sometimes, even to survive. The world of politics, like any milieu, has its share of unscrupulous individuals, but it also can be an exhilarating experience which can return the reward of an adequately funded new library facility. As Dr. Goldhor's quote suggests, the process of building a new or improved public library is first, and foremost, a political process. Library referenda campaigns are won by exercising political power through the advocacy of library supporters to forge a community-wide consensus for the proposed library improvement.

The goal of any library referendum campaign is to convince the electorate that the new library building or expanded service is needed, desirable, and obtainable at a reasonable cost. The objective is to make people feel like the new facility, expanded hours, or new technology is something that they can't live without. The key to success is to find a way to present the library issue in a light which makes it compelling to as many people in the community as possible and then to get those people out to the polls to vote "Yes" for the issue. This is accomplished by doing the research necessary to understand what the major issues for the campaign are and then delivering the appropriate campaign message to the targeted voters who are likely to make the difference in the success of the election.

Public library supporters have the resources and ability to run referenda campaigns, but they must plan and organize effectively in order to be successful. Even when funds for a campaign are low and other resources such as time and professional expertise are limited, effective campaigns can be run on a shoestring if astute strategic planning is done ahead of time. There are, however, both potential pitfalls and opportunities. Nothing should be taken for granted in a campaign—the price of success is constant vigilance. No factor, no matter how small or seemingly unimportant, can be left to chance without running the risk of failure. To be successful, campaign planners should establish a well-researched and documented campaign plan and then stick to it.

Successful referenda campaigns do not just happen overnight; they require a great deal of planning. *It can't be emphasized enough: careful planning is critical to success in referenda campaigns,* and *it is not uncommon to spend as much time or more on planning as on actually campaigning.* In most cases, the issue is the result of many years of groundwork by many dedicated people. It's been said before, but it is worth saying again: plan, plan some more, and then plan again before starting out on the campaign trail. The campaign leadership must figure out exactly what its going to do and then lay it out in as straight forward and understandable a manner as possible by describing in detail any and all campaign techniques which will be used.

Although it is true that many of the same campaign methods will be used repeatedly in many campaigns, the reader must resist the temptation to believe that there is one tried-and-true approach or generic success formula that will work well in every campaign. There is no one "right" way to run every campaign. No one campaign strategy, or combination of campaign techniques, will work well in every case. Each community is different, and the library campaign steering committee must develop its own approach to a referendum based on the local situation. In order to be successful, each campaign must respond to the specific local conditions and effectively present and communicate the library issue to the electorate in a manner which best fits the particular individuals who are most likely to vote in that specific election.

Campaign planners must make a direct, personal connection between the library issue and the voter. There may be many different approaches to doing this, but the electorate must clearly see a direct personal benefit to themselves, their family, or their community if the library issue is to pass. Voters are often willing to support library issues at the polls only if they are very certain where the money is going and that it is going exclusively for libraries and cannot be siphoned off to other city or county budgets. In short, voters must be convinced that the funds raised by the ballot measure will go only to the library project, will improve their lives and their community, and that there is a clear need for the library project.

If the referendum is for a building project, the first step is to define the need. In order to do this, library planners must demonstrate not only the problems with the existing library building, but also offer a proposed solution which is based upon a thorough community needs assessment, facilities master plan, building program, preliminary architectural plans, and a project cost estimate. Once the proposed project has been specified, the next step is to determine where the funds will come from, which frequently leads library supporters to the conclusion that they must pursue a referendum campaign in order to raise enough money to finance the project. A major hurdle is to convince the elected officials of the funding agency to place the library issue on the ballot.

The next step in any campaign is to form a steering committee. It is important to have many of those who helped with the planning of the library project to be part of the campaign committee. This is necessary because they will not only have a better understanding of the background and development of the project, but *will also have a vested interest in the successful outcome of the project and thus the campaign.* These people will be some of the campaign's most dedicated and hardest workers. Personal contact with these highly committed campaign workers is one of the best ways to recruit more campaign volunteers and to influence the electorate to vote "Yes." The success of many campaigns can be attributed to this organized core of committed, influential individuals who form the basis of the steering committee.

For campaigns that can afford them, the next step is to hire a political consultant and a pollster. Both of these professionals will advise the campaign leadership throughout the entire campaign, but the first activity is usually to commission a voter opinion poll. The poll will test the viability of the library issue with the voters, determine maximum funding levels which will be supported by the electorate, uncover major issues and arguments, and identify specific target groups which will need special attention by the campaign. The poll, along with an analysis of previous election results and other research, will also form the basis of the overall campaign strategy and provide the main campaign message.

The campaign plan, which is the overall guiding document, is a synthesis of the poll, campaign strategy, calendar, budget, fundraising plan, and volunteer budget. It delineates any and all of the various campaign techniques which will be used to get the campaign's message out. Various forms of campaign literature and paraphernalia such as fact sheets, bookmarks, brochures, postcards, door hangers, slate mailers, buttons, and yard signs will assist in the delivery of the message. Voter contact will be coordinated through various campaign techniques such as direct mail, telephone and door-to-door canvassing, speaking engagements, distribution of yard signs, and the use of the media. Campaign planners should keep in mind that these various techniques are just campaign tools which may or may not be used based upon the overall campaign strategy of making sure that a majority of voters get out and vote for the library issue.

Timing and targeting are critical. Campaign planners must carefully time when the library issue should go before the electorate to ensure that it has its best opportunity of passing. Frequent repetition of the campaign's message to select target groups is a top priority. In order to expend precious campaign resources in the most efficient manner, the campaign leadership needs to focus on habitual voters and to a lesser extent on occasional voters. Potentially persuadable undecided voters as well as "Yes" voters should be targeted during the persuasive phase of the campaign. Subsequently identified "Yes" voters should be the primary target group during the GOTV phase of the campaign.

Library campaigns, like most low budget grassroots campaigns, rely heavily on volunteers to win the campaign one vote at a time primarily through one-on-one personal contact. This personal endorsement approach can frequently defeat any opposition as long as the campaign is selling something positive. However, library supporters should never underestimate the power of an organized opposition group. Keep in mind that the issue of increased taxation is often *the* main stumbling block for library campaigns.

A library referendum campaign is never a one time event held in isolation from the ongoing governance and financing of the operation of the library. A fringe benefit of the referendum process is that the community will generally be inclined to make certain that future operational budgets for the library are protected during economic downturns because their campaign involvement results in a high degree of commitment to the library. This is often true whether the campaign is successful or not. Even if the library capital issue doesn't pass, library supporters really haven't lost because they have made so many new friends.

Win or lose, in the long run a referendum campaign will probably be very beneficial to the library because of all of the publicity gained as well as all the new library supporters picked up during the campaign. Remember, that if the referendum fails the first time, there is always a chance to try again later. Further, the chances of success the second time around are usually higher because of the experience gained during the first campaign.

There is no shame in losing a well-thought-out and well-run campaign. It happens. However, it is much better for a community to try to pass a library referendum and fail than not to try at all and languish for years with an out-dated and ineffective library building or inadequate operating funds. Regardless of the quality of the planning and the effort on the part of many volunteers, any political campaign is a little like a roll of the dice, which is why the political arena is so fascinating. No matter how much you prepare, or what kind of "spin" you put on your strategy, sometimes you're lucky and win, and sometimes you're not and don't, *but you'll certainly never win if you don't play the game.*

When library supporters have been exposed to the political process inherent in campaigning, the library almost always comes out a winner. What could be more comforting to most library directors than having a politically savvy cadre of library supporters who are able to use the political process to the library's advantage? Once these advocates have had a taste of success at the polls, it is amazing how much more effective they are at convincing local elected officials to see things the "library way."

In closing, although the effort to pass a referendum is no small one, the library's chances for success are encouraging, and the results of success are very rewarding indeed. There's nothing like winning a hard fought campaign and gaining the means to finance a public library building, not to mention the respect of the elected officials of the jurisdiction and the community at large.

Libraries which undergo a ballot measure campaign usually improve not only their physical facility or expand their services, but also go forward into the future on a much more sound political and financial basis.

INDEX